Bla_K

ESSAYS & INTERVIEWS

M. NOURBESE PHILIP

BlanK

ESSAYS & INTERVIEWS

Book*hug 2017

Essais No. 3

Canada Council for the Arts   Conseil des Arts du Canada   Funded by the Government of Canada   Financé par le gouvernement du Canada    Canadä

ONTARIO ARTS COUNCIL
CONSEIL DES ARTS DE L'ONTARIO
an Ontario government agency
un organisme du gouvernement de l'Ontario

The production of this book was made possible through the generous assistance of the Canada Council for the Arts and the Ontario Arts Council. Book*hug also acknowledges the support of the Government of Canada through the Canada Book Fund and the Government of Ontario through the Ontario Book Publishing Tax Credit and the Ontario Book Fund.

Book*hug acknowledges the land on which it operates. For thousands of years it has been the traditional land of the Huron-Wendat, the Seneca, and, most recently, the Mississaugas of the Credit River. Today, this meeting place is still the home to many Indigenous people from across Turtle Island, and we are grateful to have the opportunity to work on this land.

Library and Archives Canada Cataloguing in Publication

Nourbese Philip, Marlene, author

Blank : essays and interviews / M. NourbeSe Philip. — Second edition.
(Essais ; no. 3)

Issued in print and electronic formats.
ISBN 978-1-77166-306-9 (softcover)
ISBN 978-1-77166-307-6 (HTML)
ISBN 978-1-77166-308-3 (PDF)
ISBN 978-1-77166-309-0 (Kindle)

I. Title. II. Series: Essais (Toronto, Ont.) ; no. 3

PS8581.H542B53 2017   C814'.54   C2017-902636-4
C2017-902637-2

cover image c/o NASA Image and Video Library
cover design and layout by Kate Hargreaves

…that's all them bastards have left us: words
—Derek Walcott

CONTENTS

ACKNOWLEDGEMENTS

Earlier versions of these essays were printed in several books and journals.

The Mercury Press published two of my previous essay collections. *Frontiers* (1992) included:

> The Disappearing Debate: Or, How the Discussion of Racism
>   Has Been Taken Over by the Censorship Issue
> Disturbing the Peace
> Echoes in a Stranger Land
> A Long-Memoried Woman
> Letter, January 1989: How Do You Explain?
> Letter, July 1990: Conversations across Borders
> Letter, June 1991: James Baldwin
> Letter, September 1990: Am I a Nigger? Incident at Congress
> Social Barbarism and the Spoils of Modernism
> Who's Listening? Artists, Audiences and Language

A Genealogy of Resistance and Other Essays (1997) included earlier versions of:

> Caribana: African Roots and Continuities
> Dis Place—The Space Between

"Six Million Dollars and Still Counting" was published in my book *Showing Grit: Showboating North of the 44th Parallel* (Poui Publications, 1993).

"Interview with an Empire" first appeared in *Assembling Alternatives: Reading Postmodern Poetries Transnationally* (Wesleyan UP, 2003).

"Dream Analysis" appeared online on *Visual Verse: An Anthology of Art and Words*.

The journal *Alt. Theatre: Cultural Diversity and the Stage* published "The Warm-and-Fuzzies; Or, How to Go to the Opera and Not Feel Guilty"

ASAP / Journal printed "Banana Republics of Poetry"

Rabble published "Peaceful Violence."

My thanks to these publications and their editors.

Thanks also to Jay MillAr and Hazel Millar at BookThug for publishing *Bla_K.*

SHOUT-OUTS AND THANK-YOUS

OUR SOCIETY IS ONE IN WHICH SOCIAL AMNESIA flourishes and memory is its casualty. In relation to the struggle against anti-Black racism in Toronto, many, many people not only talked the talk, but walked the walk, not necessarily in high-profile ways, but steadily and quietly in as many different ways as there are people. They all helped to humanize this city and country and contributed to us, African Canadians, feeling a greater sense of be/longing in a stranger land. Many are forgotten or not known. It often appears as if prior to this moment there was no struggle on the part of African Canadians. The fight today is only possible because of those who went before and who fought back against those forces that appear so much more brazen today in their attempts to reduce us once again to nothingness. Most importantly, I acknowledge and thank the First Nations of this beautiful land, strange to us, but which has provided us, orphaned by history, succour and a place to be/long.

Miigwetch.

With this in mind, I offer *Shout-Outs* to the individuals, allies and organizations who, over the last twenty-five years, have been a part of that struggle. I will no doubt omit many through ignorance or the limitations of my memory; for these omissions, I apologize. In no particular order they are:

Organizations: Black Education Project, Harriet Tubman Centre (this now-defunct organization was started by the YMCA on Robina Avenue in Toronto in 1973); Black Secretariat; Third World Books and Crafts; Tropicana; BADC; CIUT-FM; Caribana; Congress of Black Women; b current; Underground Railroad Restaurant; Pelican Players; Share; Contrast; Pride; Sister Vision Books; Coalition for the Truth About Africa (CFTA); A Different Booklist.

Individuals: Juanita Westmoreland Traore; Salome Bey and Howard Matthews; Gwen and Lenny Johnson; Owen Leach (Sankofa); Lennox Farrell; Cosmos; Rita Cox; Clem Marshall; Enid Lee; Diana Braithwaite; Ken Jeffers; Ayanna Black; Loris Elliott; Jeff Henry; Frances Henry; Alice Williams (Curve Lake Reserve); Charles and Hetty Roach; Sherona Hall; Cameron Bailey; Sistah Lois; Monifa; Itah Sadhu; Norman Otis Richmond; Mark Campbell; Diane Roberts; Vivine Scarlett; Grace Channer; Sandra Brewster; Alfred and Lorraine (neighbours); Louise (neighbour); Chloe Onari; Winston Smith; Dudley Laws; Afua Cooper; George Elliott Clarke; Rinaldo Walcott; Brenda Joy Lem; Robin Pacific; ahdri zhina mandiela; Rosemary Sadlier; Lillian Allen; Wendy Komiotis; Keren Brathwaite; Clifton Joseph; Dionne Brand; Krisantha Sri Bhaggiyadatta; Arnold Auguste; Herbert Boland; De Dub poets; Joyce Britton; Akua Benjamin—the list is long and by no means exhaustive.

Thank you to Julie Joosten and Paul Chamberlain.

And in all the languages of loss, thank you to the Ancestors.

Ase

JAMMIN' STILL

Whoever is uprooted himself uproots others. Whoever is rooted in himself doesn't uproot others.
—Simone Weil[1]

[T]he singing voice invariably revises the signing voice, it marks a point of exorbitant originality for African American cultures and expressivities....the singing voice, the originality, stands above all as a "disturbance" of New World configurations of value, a disturbance decried by the West from the earliest moments of contact with African and African diasporic cultures.
—Lindon Barrett[2]

The struggle against embedded journalism is not just being trapped in a green zone and how you break out of it, but how do you break out of a mental green zone that we're conditioned to embrace.
—Jeremy Scahill[3]

Social amnesia is society's repression of remembrance—society's own past. It is a psychic commodity of the commodity society.
—Russell Jacoby[4]

I write memory on the margins of history, in the shadow of empire and on the frontier of Silence; I write against the grain as an unembedded, disappeared poet and writer in Canada; I write from a place of multiple identities—Black, African-descended, female, immigrant (or interloper) and Caribbean—which often by their very nature generate hostilities within the body politic of a so-called multicultural nation. And what better place to write an introduction to this work than Tobago, the island of my birth, to which I've been making annual pilgrimages for the last thirty-five years. Some ten years of those visits were intended to bring my father, suffering from dementia and resident in Trinidad, on annual trips back to the island he called home, a place he loved dearly and which he wanted to see become independent of Trinidad.[5] As I walk past the spot where one of the houses I grew up in used to be, or drive past the Catholic school I went to as a child, where one of the nuns ran hurtling down the hill pursued by a bull, I often wonder what pulls me back here year after year—sometimes for as little as a week, at others for as long as eighteen months when my partner and I brought our young children to live and attend school here. This island has grounded my life in poetry and in writing; it often frustrates me, as it did my father and many others, leading him to move the entire family to Trinidad, where he felt the schooling was better, thus starting another train of exile and longing for belonging. And some mornings the ocean is at least three shades of blue; at other times grey and sullen, and always it is enough.

It was here, a little more than a quarter of a century ago, I wrote "Echoes in a Stranger Land," the introduction to my first collection of essays, *Frontiers: Essays and Writings on Racism and Culture*.[6] The title, *Frontiers*, was a play on one of its meanings, margin, whose connotation within social contexts often suggests a sense of being overlooked. The frontier, however, despite its historical links with colonial discourse, suggested to me a place where anything was possible. A place where one could, because one was far away from the usual systems of control, experiment and try out different ways of being, identities even, including writing as a different way of being in the world. Behind the frontier was the hinterland, and for me the connotation of that latter word was one of backwoods or backwater. As a Black writer, one has continually to strategize about how to use what is intended to incapacitate you to your own advantage.

"Echoes in a Stranger Land" grappled with issues and ideas of exile, home and belonging as they pertained to living in Canada, a former dominion and an unsettler state. At the time of writing, the Yonge Street riots, as they came to be known, were happening, sparked by the Rodney King tragedy in the U.S.[7] Now, some twenty-five years later, as I reflect on those issues, I gaze out at the still astonishingly blue ocean and once again I ask myself where I truly belong, wondering whether I have gained any greater insights over the past twenty-five years.

Labels remain, but I am now considerably older and embrace the idea that while indigenous to the world, I remain exiled, possibly permanently: since although African-descended, I'm not indigenous to that continent, nor am I indigenous to the Caribbean, given that my ancestors were brought into these spaces as enslaved labourers after the eradication of the Indigenous populations. And, being immigrant to Canada, I count myself among the "unbelonged" there. Despite these facts, I call at least two places "home"—Tobago, because it continues to stop my heart with its beauty and has over the years provided a place for me to ground myself and from which to write, and Canada, because my children were born there, and there is where I have done my life's work as a writer. Although I work always from the rock bed of the Caribbean, and in particular Tobago, the work I've done could only have been done in Canada. Although my entry to Canada was as a graduate student, I am among the immigrants this country has accepted. The usual destination of Caribbean immigrants, however, was not Canada but the United Kingdom, the Mother Country, and later the United States. My coming to Canada was breaking with a certain tradition. Had I, however, begun writing in the United Kingdom, epicentre of the former British Empire, or in the United States, epicentre of the current one, my path would have been a very different one as a writer. In the former case I would have had to engage with the long history and tradition of writing from the colonies, now the Commonwealth. Further, the weight of tradition in the U.K. is such that it would have been very difficult, if not impossible, to find a poetic language for what cannot be told yet must be told. And in a language that bore us no love and nurtured our non-being.[8] Writing from the U.S. would have meant an engagement with the long history of writing by African Americans, beginning with the enslaved poet Phyllis Wheatley. In Canada, it felt as if there was not a tradition that I could engage with—either in embrace or rejection.[9] I could count the Black writers on one hand when I began writing; it felt as if one were truly on the frontier. And lonely. What this loneliness meant was that one would either disappear in the nothingness or be forced to go deep to find the subterranean rivers of tradition that one could link oneself to.

The buzzword today is intersectionality—the nexus of the many ways in which we are and act in the world—we, each of us, are indeed a multitude. In the '70s and '80s, the remarkable thinker Walter Rodney helped to develop the idea of being politically Black, arguing that often the racist act and actor failed to discriminate in terms of his target—Pakistani, African, or Caribbean—the brute force of racism thus landed equally among peoples of colour. By the '90s, however, the broad-brush approach that allowed African Caribbean people, continental Africans and Asians to gather under the rubric of being Black in the political sense (particularly in the U.K.) had fragmented into the particularities of identities—Asian, South and East; Caribbean; continental African and other cultural markers of identity. In the twenty-five years, the list of markers has rightly expanded to include LGBTQ2, as well as the disabled. Riffing on the old and now outdated esoteric and philosophical discussions about the presence of angels, I'm sometimes tempted to ask how many identities can dance on the head of a pin.

"Back" then in Tabago a quarter of a century ago, I was reading George Lamming's *The Pleasures of Exile*, in which he writes: "The pleasure and the paradox of my own exile is that I belong to wherever I am."[10] Now I read *The Lights of Pointe-Noire* by Alain Mabanckou, the French Congolese writer who, on his first visit back to his home some twenty-five years later, observes: "I look for reasons to love this town, all smashed up though it is, and consumed by its anarchic growth. Like a long-lost lover, faithful as Ulysses' dog, it reaches out its long, shapeless arms to me, and day after day shows me how deep its wounds are, as though I could cauterise them with the wave of a magic wand."[11] Unlike Mabanckou's response to his home, Tobago gives me many reasons to love it, most related to its natural beauty, but the wounds that Mabanckou talks about, which are the wounds of colonialism, are present all the same, though at times better hidden. We cannot, try as we might, cauterize the wound of colonialism: it suppurates, bleeds sometimes, extrudes pus, sometimes appears healed but aches always. On some days, however, I gaze out at the ocean, count the shades of blue and am content, wounds and all.

Twenty-five years ago the Yonge Street riots would lead to a government-sanctioned investigation by Stephen Lewis, who would identify and name the deeply systemic roots of anti-Black racism in Ontario. It would be the latest in a string of official reports on the plight of African Canadians. Then-NDP premier Bob Rae, who had commissioned the report, accepted many of the report's findings, and under his governance Ontario saw the establishment of the Anti-Racism Secretariat.[12] Under the subsequent Mike Harris Conservative government, the Secretariat was promptly disbanded, and one of the government's first actions was to permit the use of hollow-point bullets by the police, despite the government publicly observing that the Black community would be unhappy about this. One of those bullets, shortly after their mandated use, would kill the unarmed First Nations man, Dudley George, in 1995, in what was known as the Ipperwash Crisis.[13] Black communities in Canada continue to be challenged by issues of police carding[14] of young Black men and women, unfulfilled expectations and aborted potential. Unwarranted killings of African Canadians by the police continue to plague the communities. In the passage of time, we've seen the opening, to great and vocal opposition, of an Africentric alternative primary school, which, while welcome, actually speaks to a failure of the mainstream educational system to provide a curriculum and pedagogical environment that meet the needs of young African Canadian children.

A subsequent attempt to start an Africentric high school at Oakwood Collegiate in the St. Clair/Oakwood area in 2011—the neighbourhood I have lived in for the last forty years—was greeted with great hostility by the neighbourhood, despite the fact that the school has traditionally had a large number of African Canadian students.[15] Yet another example of how African Canadians are made to feel unwelcome in this city.

A quarter of a century later has also seen the emergence of Black Lives Matter, the brainchild of queer and trans women from the United States, which has spawned offshoots in different cities in the U.S., Canada and overseas. A response to the wanton police shootings of African American men and women, BLM's name appeared to simply state a fact at the heart of which was actually a wish—that Black lives ought to matter in the face of utter disregard on the part of law enforcers, which offends and outrages members of the Black community.

It seems redundant that one has to state that Black lives matter; indeed, in a capitalist economy Black lives have *always* mattered, unfortunately, however, not for their intrinsic value but for their use value. The financial system we live with and in today has its roots in a system of speculative financing that was developed during the transatlantic trade in Africans, which, through a system of promissory notes, allowed for someone in Liverpool, for instance, to purchase an African in West Africa and have him or her transported to the Caribbean or the Americas for sale, and receive payment for that transaction in Liverpool.[16] Many European nations and Europeans made their fortunes on a trade at the heart of which was the purchase and sale of Africans. It is in this sense that I say that Black lives have always mattered, and it is this essential dehumanization of Black lives that generates the need for us to state today what should be redundant— that Black lives do matter. For their intrinsic worth. It has been remarkable, however, how the assertion of what should not really need to be stated, that Black lives matter, becomes an irritant for so many who insist that it is exclusionary or, in response, that all lives matter, or blue lives matter. As if the very statement that Black lives matter negates the value of other lives. Is it that, perhaps unconsciously, those who oppose the slogan understand that acceptance of, and acting on, the fact that Black lives do indeed matter would shift so much that we have taken for granted that they grow uncomfortable at the possibility of such a seismic change? For make no mistake, if Black lives truly mattered, or if Indigenous lives mattered, speaking to the two genocides at the heart of the unsettling of the Americas and the Caribbean, we would, indeed, be living in an altered universe.

In those twenty-five years the U.S. did the unexpected and twice elected a biracial African American man to be president and commander-in-chief, then turned on a dime and elected a wealthy, white businessman who appears cut from the cloth of the classic colonial governor and whose stated goal is to "make America great again."

Those of us who come from cultures that have been riven by colonialism understand its destructive impact: wherever they conquered and/or unsettled, colonial powers disregarded Indigenous and local traditions and practice, all of which would have been centuries if not millennia old, trampling them or forbidding them as they did the drum in Trinidad or the *mbira* (the musical instrument through which the Shona people of Zimbabwe speak to their Ancestors). People's languages and customary ways of running their lives, practising their religions, and governing themselves was of no consequence. Custom, tradition, mores, laws were all discounted and dismantled if they got in the way of the colonial project, and, more times than not, it was the colonial governor who administered these destructive practices. In his flagrant and wanton disregard of tradition; in his dismissal of long-accepted procedures and customs; in his wholesale abandonment of protocol and the established ways of governing, Trump hews closely to the role of the colonial governor.

There have been presidents who are Republican and who have governed from the right before, but what has unnerved and destabilized the populace, the world and many in the administration is not just the content of Trump's policies, troubling enough as they are, but his refusal to follow the accepted ways of governance. The comedic engagement with this process on the late-night talk shows provides a way of managing what is, in fact, the reinstitution of colonial governance. A small but powerful example: Secretary of State Rex Tillerson refusing to have the press corps accompany him on his most recent trip to Asia.

Among the complaints lodged against the colonial governor of Virginia in 1702 were the following: "He has taken upon himself the right to preside over the body and limit debate; he states the questions and overrules in an arbitrary and threatening manner; he threatens and abuses all who speak anything contrary to his opinions; he meets privately with members and uses all of the arts of cajoling and threatening for his own ends; his behaviour constitutes intolerable encroachments upon the liberties of both Houses."[17] All of which now appear utterly familiar. Colonized cultures and societies in Africa, Asia, the Americas and the Caribbean all found ways to resist, but none could withstand the colonial onslaught, and they essentially either collapsed or developed dysfunctional ways of accommodating colonialism. These are the wounds Mabanckou writes about; these are the wounds I witness in Trinidad and Tobago. These are the wounds the First Nations of this country live with. What is different this time is that for the first time we are actually witnessing what that process of colonial destabilization would have been like, the results of which are nation-states that today appear to have always been this way—poor, ravaged, war-torn. In the case of the U.S., we are witnessing a colonial threat to a democratic culture, and this is new, although not entirely unexpected given the colonial antecedents of the U.S. State.[18]

Consider, for a macabre moment, that Africa could not today support a slave trade. I insist we start from this difficult and possibly offensive place to better understand the enormity of what was done. To be able to sustain the removal of millions of healthy individuals over some five centuries requires that certain things be in place: that there be potable water; that there be the ability to grow crops to feed populations; that there be effective ways of managing sexuality so that the group continues replenish itself; that there be adequate systems providing for childbirth, so that infant and maternal mortality are kept at a minimal level; that there be effective ways of training and educating the younger generation in how to live and survive in their environments; that there be cultural systems that support people's human and spiritual needs for relationship with each other and with spiritual and religious forces. All these practices had to be in place to allow Africa to be the source of healthy people for a period of some five centuries. Today, as I write, there is now a famine (once again a repetition) in three African countries, Yemen, Northern Nigeria and South Sudan, where some four million people are at risk of death. So, I ask, what happened?

I don't pretend to have the definitive answer—the answers are many and myriad. Simone Weil, the French Jewish philosopher, offers one which I accept—that Europe, having unsettled and uprooted itself within its own boundaries, set out around the world to unsettle and uproot others, first through colonialism later wedded to capitalism, and later still to industrialization.[19] Some have lived this traumatic process, some have witnessed it, others have turned their eyes from it: the universal result has been peoples of colour being made stranger to and winnowed of their own lands, widowed of their cultures. Climate change, wars, famine, drought, floods—the list is endless, but it culminates in these times in our witnessing one of the largest mass movements of people fleeing those bereft lands for the mecca of Europe and the West as the cries mount from those places that they should go back to where they came from or stay where they are. *Never mind*, the West appears to assert through its historic indifference. *Never mind our wanderings over lands and seas to plant our flags in your countries and root out your languages and cultures to plant our own; never mind the depredations we have inflicted; never mind we have permanently uprooted you; stay where you are, in those very spaces that we, through our uprooting, have made inhospitable for you.*

What can we do but grieve.

What we are now witnessing in the U.S.—a split populace facing off against each other—is reminiscent of those historical examples of countries like India, where different ethnic groups traditionally shared common spaces, but under colonial rule are split between Hindu and Muslim. In the U.S., one half of the populace—including angry, white, disenfranchised voters having thrown their lot in with the Pied Piper of dissension—revels in a new legitimacy given to blatant racism, anti-Semitism and Islamophobia, delights in the banning and expulsion of immigrants and in walls erected between countries. The other half longs for that moral arc of justice that Martin Luther King spoke of. Both of these images are real aspects of the U.S. The upheaval in governance is the colonial onslaught writ large and taking place in a modern, developed and technologically advanced state— the most powerful in the world. It is a logical and predictable continuation of the colonial state now being run by a colonial governor. Indeed, states like Canada and the U.S. and the many other countries of the Americas and the Caribbean remain colonial states, most obviously in their relationship with their First Nations- and African-descended populations. Whether American democracy, unlike those earlier colonized cultures, is robust enough to resist and change this newest colonial attack is now the question that faces all of us. The consequences, as we are already witnessing, will impact us all, whether or not we live in the U.S.

In 1994, two years after the publication of *Frontiers* and four years after the release of Mandela, the system of apartheid in South Africa, begun in 1948, would come to an end. Many of us had spent the preceding years demonstrating against the regime's practices. Its Truth and Reconciliation Commission would become a model for other war-ravaged countries, such as Northern Ireland. I have often wondered how events may have been different if Truth and Reconciliation Commissions had been held in each and every Caribbean island as they came to independance and in the United States after the struggle for Civil Rights was successful. How might a public witnessing of "It"—that which still defies naming—have changed the views of those who saw themselves as losers—those invested in retaining systems that exploited Black and brown peoples—in a struggle that succeeded in bringing democracy to the U.S. and all those tiny Caribbean islands.

Colonialism has constituted a long and sustained attack against the First Nations of this country and their cultures: the establishment of the Truth and Reconciliation Commission into the Indian Residential Schools was, therefore, a significant, long-overdue and welcome event in the course of the intervening twenty-five years. Its findings seem finally to awaken many unsettler Canadians to the brutal and brutalizing effects of colonialism on the First Nations of this country. A very few years after my arrival in Canada, mercury contamination at the Asubpeeschoseewagong (Grassy Narrows) First Nation came to public attention. Some forty years later, in 2017, the river remains contaminated, as are the fish that live there. Residents drink bottled water as their tap water is also unfit for drinking. The health of the members of the reservation continues to be affected by the contamination. This remains a scandal of astonishing proportions, if only because of the length of time it has taken to not solve this problem, which has been normalized. This continuous mercury contamination remains a tangible and ongoing example of systemic racism. I am reminded of the water crisis in Flint, Michigan, in 2014 in which the town's water was contaminated by lead, affecting mainly lower-income and African American people.

What is clear is that in the last twenty-five years racism has remained an issue manifesting in old and new ways. The worldwide web is now a space where the most viciously racist comments can be made with little or no consequence. The new president of the United States has by his rhetoric opened the floodgates even further, beginning with his statements about

Mexicans being rapists and Muslims inherently terroristic, which has added fuel to an already-inflammatory and racially charged situation. Casting our eyes more closely home here in Canada, we appear to have our own Trump Lite in Kelly Leitch's[20] test for Canadian values.

My engagement with cultural issues through writing arises not simply because I'm a writer and poet who works in the cultural sector, but because African culture was a particular focus of attack by colonial powers. Über-missionary David Livingstone was of the belief that the most effective way to bring Christianity to Africans was first to destroy their culture, then introduce commerce, then religion. He understood that culture underpinned everything. Africans were prohibited from speaking their languages, practising their religions, playing their music. Even today something that should be commonplace—the grooming and styling of hair, a fundamental aspect of any culture—generates a raft of responses, from acceptance through prohibition and rejection on the part of non-Africans to great anxiety among Black women.[21] We've been told, as I was in high school in Trinidad, that we, Africans and African-descended people, unlike everyone else, had no culture or history, even as Europe, after having stolen the continent's peoples, not to mention its land and mineral deposits, appropriated and stole both its cultural artifacts and approaches to visual art that would lend new life to Western art. The erasure of the violent, exploitative relationship between colonizer and colonized has been woven into the ensuing relationships. And in all this, Europe remains as if untouched, ever innocent of its tremendous crimes against the peoples of Africa, Asia, Australasia and the Middle East.

The weight and influence of African music and dance continues unabated as our musical forms and styles are appropriated and taken up by different groups and peoples around the world. The sound of modernity is inextricably linked to the sound of jazz; hip hop is now an international, multi-billion-dollar industry influencing clothing and fashion around the world. Yet none of this redounds to African peoples being any more respected as they move through life. To the contrary, any claims on the part of African-descended people to be creative initiators of these musical forms and for appropriate acknowledgement are met, more times than not, with opposition and assertions about the universality of the music or, as in the case of hip hop, its multicultural origins. This reflects a disturbing parallel with the way in which the Black body and all that it produced, without and within—from crops to progeny—were the property of the slave owner, indeed anyone else but the enslaved herself. So too are the creative products of Black and African cultures seen to belong to anyone else but the creators themselves. More akin to the idea of the public domain rather than open-source and creative-commons approaches to digital technology: in the latter cases licences are required, in the former there is no protection provided for creative work. But imagine for a moment if record companies had to contribute one cent per album to a fund for every recording that utilized Black musical forms, and imagine if that fund were administered so that young people, the descendants of the *Maafa*, could utilize it for musical training, or education. Imagine. Then imagine again. This is but a small example of one of the ways economic reparations could happen for the crime the transatlantic trade in Africans constituted.[22] A crime which, although resulting in irreparable loss, still requires that justice be done.

In the wake of the latest Grammy Awards ceremony, Adele, having won Album of the Year, expressed bewilderment at what Beyoncé had to do to earn one. Become white, perhaps?, I thought. Adele's question is at best naive since she herself has stated that in her early years as a singer in England, she would buy discarded cassette recordings of Etta James and practise trying to sound like her. Artists find their inspiration wherever they will, and, I should add, I like Adele's sound, but what continues to escape too many is that the Black singing voice in the Americas comes out of a particular and tragic history. As Lindon Barrett argues in *Blackness and Value: Seeing Double*,[23] that voice and sound come out of a particular history of pain, trauma and a determination to make meaning of one's life no matter what; it is a sound lodged in a commitment to matter to and value one's self and one's community in the face of a culture that continues to assert that Black lives lack meaning and are irrelevant except and in so far as they are useful. The same can be said of the astonishingly innovative production, particularly in music and dance, that is found in all Afrosporic[24] communities in the Americas and the Caribbean. The only new instrument developed in the twentieth century has been pan, originally created in Trinidad by African-descended people out of cast-off steel drums, while musical and dance forms such as reggae, dance hall, zouk, rumba and calypso are now international.

One of Marxism's principles that I accept is that culture and its supporting system of production are inextricably linked. Afrosporic or diasporic African cultures and their ensuing arts have existed and continue to exist in exploitative and racist systems of production. Despite this, however, Black people have continued to create value for themselves and assign meaning to their lives through their music and art. Indeed, I would say, our singing and performing have been our healing, have been our medicine, as are all the forms of cultural expression Black cultures continue to generate, apparently effortlessly. And as we heal ourselves, if only temporarily, we have continued to heal and humanize the world with our gifts, with the genius of our people. This generosity has seldom if ever been reciprocated.

That necklace of small, coral and volcanic islands strung between the Atlantic Ocean and the Caribbean Sea, and referred to as the Antilles, the West Indies, the Caribbean, or simply the Islands, comprise an area that has traditionally punched above its weight intellectually, producing some of the foremost intellectuals of the twentieth century, whose writings continue to influence us. Frantz Fanon, Édouard Glissant, Aimé Césaire, Sylvia Wynter, C. L. R. James, Claudia Jones, and Marcus Garvey, to name a few: the list is an impressive one and I have not even mentioned the poets and novelists. The model I brought with me from the Caribbean, even though I had not grown up thinking that I would make a life in writing, was one where the writer had to be engaged with society. Was it because I witnessed a tiny island move from being a subject state to an independent one; was it because I listened to my parents talking long into the night about what independence would mean for them and their children; was it because I knew that had not certain changes happened, such as free secondary education, I would not be writing this today, my parents not being able to afford to pay for five children to be educated at the secondary level; was it because the all-girl high school I attended, despite being a model of colonial education, instilled in us a sense that we, young Black women, who didn't have a history, were the "salt of the earth" and the "cream of the crop," the all-white imagery notwithstanding? Perhaps it was all these things that led me to believe that I had to engage through my writing with events taking place around me. All the writers from the Caribbean whom I knew of did it—George Lamming, Kamau Brathwaite, Samuel Selvon—even V. S. Naipaul. They were public intellectuals long before the term became fashionable. I was not alone: writers like Lillian Allen, Dionne Brand and Clifton Joseph also engaged with these issues through their art and writing. The essays written over several years and collected in *Frontiers* were a tangible expression of my patterning myself on that tradition.

It came as something of a surprise, then, perhaps born of naïveté, when the pushback and hostility began, culminating when a group of artists including myself under the name Vision 21: Canadian Culture in the 21st Century[25] engaged in a demonstration against PEN Canada at their 1989 AGM held at Roy Thomson Hall. What we were doing was what Baldwin had described as the artist's job—to "disturb the peace."[26] We were all told to "fuck off" by June Callwood, then-incoming chair of PEN Canada, and the rest became history.

The firestorm that erupted in the media was swift and brutal, and the literary community was split over the issues of whether or not PEN had underrepresented writers of colour and whether or not there was racism in Callwood's dismissive attitude toward Vision 21. These events threw a long shadow, culminating in 1995 with a scurrilous and racist on-air diatribe against me by Michael Coren, a host of CFRB's 1010 radio station, in which the only truthful statement made was the year I came to Canada. In response to my being awarded the 1995 Toronto Arts Foundation Award for Writing, Coren accused me of doing nothing but "defecating" on Canada, calling June Callwood a racist, as well as taking Canadian taxpayers' money and "laughing all the way to the bank." (There was no money attached to the award.) I wore what looked like a "dirty tea towel on my head," he continued in his broadcast, wondering whether this was a form of "African costume." I brought an action for libel against Coren and CFRB in 1995, which was eventually settled seven years later. During that time, Mayor Barbara Hall, who chaired the Mayor's Committee on Race and Community Relations, called on Michael Coren and CFRB to apologize to the African Canadian community for his on-air statements. They have never done so.

Coren was not the darling of Toronto's writing and literary community, but there was no critique of him and his right-wing, racist statements. The Toronto Arts Foundation, for instance, never commented on Coren's statements about me in the wake of their award. Litigation is always wounding, even as the plaintiff, and the process was a difficult one, particularly in its aftermath; it took me several years to recover fully from the lawsuit and the fallout. What kept me on this side in more ways than one was poetry and, more specifically, working on *Zong!*, my last book of poetry.

I raise these matters not to rehash old controversies, but to demonstrate the links between our larger histories and our lived experiences, particularly as they relate to racism, and to demonstrate how these issues, particularly racism, return, albeit in different contexts. It makes itself visible, for instance, in the forty-year history of systemic environmental racism toward the Grassy Narrows First Nations. It makes itself visible in the media's embrace of Michael Coren as a reformed homophobe, but one who has not disavowed, as he has with his homophobia, his public racist and anti-feminist comments. As if his pro-gay stance now stands in for his position on issues of race and feminism.

I am mindful that to be disappeared in certain contexts is an event that usually results in death; it is a phrase that conjures a state of limbo for family members who, in contexts of political terror and instability, have lost contact with loved ones whose whereabouts remain unknown. Neither dead nor alive, they are disappeared. It is, however, the metaphor that best describes how I have felt as a writer in Canada for at least the last decade. Some of the reasons for my "disappearance" are undoubtedly rooted in the events described above, some no doubt are personal, and some are beyond my comprehension. The absence in Toronto and Canada of any critical reception of *Zong!*, published in 2008, provides a vivid illustration of the hollowing out of my presence as a writer in this country.[27]

Why Bla_K and why now?

Some readers may be inclined to read the title as Bla K; it is both—*BlanK* and *Bla_K*. Bla K, the colour of the ever-expanding universe whose apparent blankness belies the plenitude of black holes, stars—exploding and collapsing, planets, comets, nebulae, galaxies, red dwarves and red shifts, to name but a few of the bodies and events that comprise our universe; Bla K, the blackest version of which, known as Vantablack, was developed and licensed exclusively for use by the British sculptor Anish Kapoor in 2017 (does this mean that we can no longer be too Black?); Bla K, a word that we fled from, hiding in coloured, in light-, brown- or fair-skinned, in shabine[28] and brownin',[29] until we embraced it in all its power; Bla K, a word made to do the difficult work of holding a people together in a tension-filled multiplicity; Bla K, that place of mystery, strength and spirit within that often grounds me; and finally, Bla K, which, as many readers will rightly assume, riffs on the subject matter of this work—one Black woman's attempt over time and space to grapple with and understand through writing how and why the simple and profound fact of being remains insufficient in our world; how and why being continues to be contingent on so much—race, colour, gender, class, sexuality, ability, age; and how, through one's life work, to make a difference, however small for the better. On board the slave ship *Zong* being—being human—was simply not enough to save enslaved Africans from being thrown overboard. That was 1781. Today, in 2017, being human is still not enough to ensure survival or even equitable treatment.

Like the night sky whose blackness we often read as blank, but which is filled with unseen and yet unexplained activity, so too are the lives of Black people, which like the universe are complex, multivalent, and often not understood, seen as blanks or cyphers onto which others project their desires, suspicions, and at times ignorance. Blank is also the metaphor that best sums up the disappeared feeling I have lived with as a writer here in Canada. Blank and Bla K constitute the axis around which I rotate as a writer here in Canada.

The impetus for this collection originated with Dr. Nasrin Himada, who wished to see a reprint of the essay "Interview with an Empire," which she found particularly helpful in her work as a scholar.[30] This essay took the form of a self-interview and engaged with issues that remain troublingly relevant today some fifteen years after its publication. The continued relevance could be cause for despair: it means that racism remains as deep-seated and incorrigible as it was then, constantly mutating and changing to remain the same. I choose instead to use the continued relevance of essays like "Interview" as an opportunity to revisit certain issues and events I wrote about in *Frontiers* some twenty-five years ago in contexts which are very different, but which may further illuminate the reasons for the persistence of these pernicious issues.

Up until 1989, the areas of contestation for African Canadians had been primarily in areas of policing, the justice system, education, housing and health—areas that had direct bearing on the lives of African Canadians. The 1989 Royal Ontario Museum (ROM)exhibit *Into the Heart of Africa* marked the first time the African Canadian community in Toronto would, through a series of highly charged demonstrations, challenge the mandarins of high culture over an exhibit that was, we were told, intended to be ironic but whose impact was deeply racist. In 2016, the ROM, some twenty-seven years after the event, which resulted in African Canadians being arrested, issued an apology to the African Canadian community, in light of which the reprints "Social Barbarism and the Spoils of Modernism" and "Museum Could Have Avoided Culture Clash" become relevant once again. What I was arguing twenty-seven years ago in the latter piece—that the museum needed to understand the historical and contemporary needs of the Black community—is what eventually happened in 2016.

This particular engagement with the ROM would become the springboard for another cultural dispute that would galvanize the African Canadian community in Toronto in the early '90s: the production of *Show Boat* by Garth Drabinsky's production company, Livent.[31] Issues arose over the use of the n-word in the production, and demonstrations began against the production even as the earth was being turned for the construction of a new performance venue in North York. Every Saturday for an entire year, members of the African Canadian community demonstrated outside of what is now the Toronto Centre for the Arts[32] during the construction of the building. These two events in the early '90s marked a development in activism within the African Canadian community—its preparedness to engage with cultural issues. "Six Million Dollars and Still Counting," written after the show opened, was the last chapter in *Showing Grit: Showboating North of the 44th Parallel*, which I wrote to inform the Black community about the controversial history of the show.[33]

The Joseph Boyden affair recalls the issue of appropriation which split the literary community some twenty-five years ago, and I was struck by the absence of any reference to that earlier debate about appropriation in the discussions about the more contemporary issue. I have thus included "The Disappearing Debate: Or, How the Discussion of Racism Has Been Taken Over by the Censorship Issue."

"Disturbing the Peace" and "Peaceful Violence" both speak to an ongoing and now heightened need to take to the streets to protest and demonstrate a bodily solidarity as a form of resistance. The former essay recounts the events surrounding PEN Canada's 1989 AGM, mentioned above. There are resonances with the public outcry and at times racist response against BLM's stalling of the 2016 Pride march. "Peaceful Violence" bears witness to the June 26, 2010, public response to both the Harper government's harsh policies and its decision to host the G20 summit in Toronto, resulting in a virtual occupation of the downtown area by security forces.

Whenever one speaks out against racism, one has to be prepared for the insults and threats. "How Do You Explain?" and "Am I a Nigger?" describe my learning that the hard way. Twenty-five years ago, it was someone on the phone calling me "nigger." Today, the Internet allows this type of behaviour and worse to take place. Anonymity is the nutrient that fed it twenty-five years ago. It continues to feed it today.

"Who's Listening?" grapples with issues of audience, market and community. Working in a form that on the surface appears to have more in common with European formal traditions, I have wished over the years that the genre that chose me, poetry, had more overt references to the more vernacular traditions of the Caribbean. Still and all, I see the deep connections between these traditions. Here John-from-Sussex and Abiswa, two Ancestral mentors, meet for the first time over my shoulders.

"Conversations across Borders" are needed more than ever now as the right wing attempts to create and increase tensions between groups. Until my sister and brother are seen, heard and matter, the work for justice is incomplete best sums up this essay in which John-from-Sussex and Abiswa, two Ancestral mentors, face off yet again.

"CaribanA: African Roots and Continuities" engages with the street in another form—the carefully controlled and restricted performance by Black people of their annual Carnival rites in Toronto, formerly known as Caribana. It highlights the issues that Black people confront in negotiating the street and public spaces, particularly in light of the overpolicing of Black bodies moving through the white space that is Toronto, which stands in for the white spaces that the Americas have become. Maisie and Toto-ben, the protagonists of "Caribana," if an essay can be said to have protagonists, have been moving ever since they were locked in the holds of the slave ship, sometimes moving simply to remain still. And as Maisie occupies her body with wanton disregard for the laws of the fathers, so too she occupies the street with her sexuality as she "wines"[34] through the public space that is a white space, claiming it, if only temporarily, for the Black body. The female body. The Black female body.

"Dis Place—The Space Between" continues the exploration of and meditation on the problematic of the female body, in particular the Black, female body, in space and time in a patriarchal culture. It acquires renewed relevance in this moment of women fighting back against systems that license and permit predatory behaviour on the part of men.

"Letter to Baldwin" acknowledges my debt to the African American writer James Baldwin, who was responsible for my understanding that literature could be peopled with those like myself—Black and female. *I'm Not Your Negro*, the recently released film on Baldwin by Raoul Peck, is right on time in these troublous times; like *Bla_K*, its difficult work is to make itself irrelevant and essentially out of time.

In a society and culture that erases memory, or rather produces a form of social amnesia, "A Long-Memoried Woman" stakes a continuing claim for the revolutionary, oppositional and sustaining nature of memory.

I initially avoided writing about my 2015 experience in Morocco and was only able to do so when a colleague asked me to write about it for a publication. "Riding the Bus with Rosa in Morocco" is in some ways the fulcrum of *Bla_K*, an essay that brings many streams together—North Africa, which sets itself apart from sub-Saharan Africa as Arab rather than African; the precariousness of the Black woman's body in public spaces; the power of white privilege; resistance; the always-hovering potential disposability of the Black body; the appropriation and commercialization of Black cultural products; the profit motive; the Civil Rights Movement; the Sahara and camels.

"Ruminations" is a collection of shorter pieces, thoughts, emails and Facebook postings. "Letter to Haiti" was my *cri du coeur* for an island whose history had an indelible influence on my life as a thinker and writer. I continue to mourn Haiti's continued diss/placement in the eye of the hurricane—literally and metaphorically—and rejoice for every success, however small.

"Nasrin and NourbeSe" is an excerpted collage of my exchange with Nasrin Himada; it is in conversation with "Interview with an Empire" and "Echoes in a Stranger Land" as *Bla_K* is in conversation with Frontiers as each of these pieces, some written twenty-five years ago, others more recently, is in conversation with events today.

I now fully embrace my position as an unembedded writer in Canada—an adjective which best sums up my position and has resonances with those early thoughts about margins and frontiers. I come from the margins—born on a tiny island some 300 square kilometres, moved to another tiny island just over 1,000 square kilometres and landed on a vast land mass, Turtle Island, that now bears the name Canada. All colonial spaces. The trajectory has been a difficult, and at times, lonely one.

Many, many years ago when I left the practice of law, I came to the belief that although it was necessary for us African-descended peoples to enter the professions, it was our griots and griottes, our poets, writers, dancers, musicians and other artists, who would heal us of the great tragedy of our being enslaved and brought unwillingly to the Americas and the Caribbean. The issue that chose me was language, and I have spent my life as a poet and writer exploring what language means for someone like myself, condemned to work in a language that commits a rape in my mouth every time I speak.

I am sitting on a panel at Naropa University at the annual Summer Writing Program. The three panelists, myself included, are there to discuss a topic I cannot now remember. What I do remember is a younger Oglala Lakota poet taking a word, translating it into her mother tongue and then gently opening the word up to show us how and what it means in her culture and how it connects to the subject we were discussing. And I weep openly for the loss, the deep loss, I always feel when I visit Africa and hear and see how language bears culture and culture feeds language. It is a condition I will never know because English is not my mother tongue. It is my father tongue and one which meant me and my mother no good.[35] But it is my mother tongue and father tongue all wrapped together in some kind of ghastly embrace—or is it struggle? Or perhaps both?

I continue to be plagued by working with language that was fatally contaminated by its history of empire and colonialism, and having no language to turn to in order to hide or heal. I continue to be plagued by something as apparently simple as trying to find a word to describe what is commonly referred to as the Middle Passage, that expanse of ocean between there and here, then and now, before and after; between the west coast of Africa and the Americas and the Caribbean over which they, our Ancestors, travelled to never arrive. The Middle Passage, the latter word of which suggests narrowness, is in contradistinction to the vast and utterly fearsome expanse of nothingness of the ocean: that immensity of water over which Sahara dust travels to coat the lost sons and daughters of Africa in the Caribbean and the Americas; that sometimes calm and sometimes roiling water over which hurricanes travel after leaving the west coast of Africa to plague the Americas and the Caribbean. As if the Ancestors, having been uprooted and troubled, continue in their restlessness to trouble us, the still-so-newly arrived, the never-will-arrive in this new Old World. Quenching their thirst for us to remember and return, if only metaphorically, with the damp ocean air, only to release the pent-up liquid memory as rain and winds whistling around our ears, beating on the tin roofs a staccato call to come home, come home...we miss you. Always. The Middle Passage, which some South Asians call the *Kala Pani*, the Dark Water, which they crossed as indentured workers coming to the Caribbean after the emancipation of the enslaved.

After twenty-five years, I'm still hunting, trying to find the word or words to describe the Middle Passage, site of so much grief and trauma, final home to so many of us; searching through poetry to find the word that will best describe what happened to us, Africans, under the boot of history. Although there is no best in what happened to us. Was it trade? Kidnapping? Immigration, as some have suggested? Racial terrorism? Genocide? Ethnic cleansing? The Great Scattering? It? Some named it the *Maafa*,[36] a Kiswahili word meaning "terrible occurrence" or "great disaster"—that which is both an end and a beginning. Of sorts. Poetry becomes the tool that enables me in this difficult search and helps me to understand my own theorizing about the why, how and what I write.

Translation perhaps provides the best metaphor for what we, the descendants of the *Maafa*, do—translating what has happened, and is still happening, into words, music, movement, painting. Working with language, however, raises particular issues of translation. Is there a word in English, or other colonial languages, for that matter, for what happened to us? In an article on translation and the work of the late Malinke author Ahmadou Kourouma from Côte d'Ivoire, Dr. Haruna Jiyah Jacob asks whether it's possible to make French people understand the Malinke word *monnè* (*monnew*, plural), which "captures all the suffering and humiliations imposed on his people by colonialism," if there is no word in French for what happened to them.[37] Jacob asks whether the absence of certain terms in a language render translation impossible; I wonder whether the absence of certain words in a language make understanding an experience impossible. If those words do not exist, how do speakers of that language understand that for which no word exists, or what they cannot or refuse to perceive? Does this perhaps explain the need for the phrase Black Lives Matter? Because English and the languages in which colonialism happened do not have the words for what happened to us. And to them. Hence the confusion and outrage at the phrase Black Lives Matter. And if the experience cannot be understood, how then do the perpetrator countries understand what they did? And if it is not or cannot be named, does it even exist?

In conversation a few months ago with a colleague from Puerto Rico who is completing her dissertation on Édouard Glissant, the late Martiniquan writer, she raises a concern of his: the possibility of Caribbean people becoming autochthonous to the area. I am shocked at the question—as if someone has thrown cold water in my face. Is such an idea only conceivable, I ask, in an area like the Caribbean where the Indigenous people have essentially been erased? Perhaps, she concedes. In Canada such a question would be verboten, I continue. Later, I research the etymological origin of *autochthonous* and decide that one can never become autochthonous, since the very meaning of the word is that one is not a descendant of either a migrant or unsettler. But what if one were neither Indigenous, migrant nor unsettler? How can one ever spring from the soil or the earth of the stranger land, to go back to the original meaning of the word, if we are "...never autochthonous / still embarked upon...."[38] Can one ever be/long on what is essentially stolen land? Even if not stolen by you. And if there exists no word to describe one's state or condition in relation to where one lives, is one permanently erased? Perhaps, however, that nexus of conditions that appear to be negations—neither Indigenous, migrant nor unsettler—offer the potential of the state of Bla_K, from which this book takes its title, that belies an absence and instead contains a multitude, albeit unseen.

I love the physical land that is Canada, vis-à-vis the state celebrating its sesquicentennial as a colonial state, although the promotions don't say that. I am calmed by walking through the city's green ravines, startled by the vibrancy of fall and shocked into humility by cold, white winters, but remain convinced that loving this land is only possible because I love the island of my birth, Tobago, that continues to transfix me all these years later. Entering the idea of Canada or Turtle Island through the land rather than the state offers a possibility of being in a relationship of integrity and truth with the First Nations of this land, since they best know and understand it; it is, after all, theirs. As I wrote twenty-five years ago—we be/long here in these stranger lands, but "belonging" in its ordinary meaning implies a sense of fixity, which I don't feel. But perhaps in a world such as we live in, in which we have all been uprooted from ourselves, our homes and our cultures, even on and in our own lands, belonging must begin to embrace the idea of fluidity and movement.

What does it mean that we appear to face the same issues after twenty-five years of continuous struggle, BLMTO notwithstanding? Carl Jung's statement that what is not brought to consciousness comes to us as fate comes to mind. Perhaps as long as racism against Black folk—a practice that only occurs south of the border and not here, to hear some talk—is not brought to consciousness, in Canada at least, we are condemned to keep rehearsing its many practices. Is it that nothing has changed? Or is it, as I believe, that systems change to remain the same? The election of an African American president, for instance, did not significantly improve the lives of African Americans beyond the bump that they got from the fact that one very classy Black couple now inhabited the White House. Despite the change for better in some areas—the dislodging of apartheid, that brutal, aggressive and totalizing type of racism, supported by many Western countries, which is now consigned to history and memory—we seem, however, to be moving backward (or is it forward?) to a state of being that allows for greater permission to return to practices that are not only harmful to a wide spectrum of groups and people, but even to the very world in which we live. Murder, maroonage,[39] suicide, infanticide, the breaking of tools, and revolts are some of the ways the children of the *Maafa* in the Americas and the Caribbean have resisted being enslaved and the accompanying racism. While the methods may change over the years and even centuries, the resistance has never let up nor will it while the world continues to afflict us simply because of the colour of our skin. Like Totoben and Maisie, the protagonists of "CaribanA: African Roots and Continuities," we keep movin', jammin'…still.[40] Always. In the face of tremendous odds.

NOTES

1   Simone Weil, *The Need for Roots*, trans. Arthur Willis (New York: Routledge Classics, 2002), 48.

2   Lindon Barrett, *Blackness and Value: Seeing Double* (Cambridge: Cambridge University Press, 1999), 83.

3   Jeremy Scahill, *Dirty Wars*, 2013, Documentary.

4   Russell Jacoby, *Social Amnesia: A Critique of Contemporary Psychology* (New Brunswick, NJ: Transaction Publishers, 1997), 5.

5   Prior to 1889, when Tobago was made a ward of Trinidad, Tobago was a separate British colony.

6   M. NourbeSe Philip, *Frontiers: Essays and Writings in Racism and Culture* (Stratford, ON: The Mercury Press, 1992).

7   Rodney King was an African American man who, on March 3, 1991, was brutally assaulted and beaten by police officers in Los Angeles, California.

8   Please see M. NourbeSe Philip, *Zong!* (Middletown, CT: Wesleyan University Press, 2008), and M. NourbeSe Philip, *She Tries Her Tongue; Her Silence Softly Breaks* (Middletown, CT: Wesleyan University Press, 2015) for further discussion of these issues.

9   The scholar George Elliott Clarke has argued that there was a Black literary tradition of Black Nova Scotia. I am talking about a more overtly articulated literary tradition.

10   George Lamming, *The Pleasures of Exile* (Ann Arbor: University of Michigan Press, 1992), 50.

11   Alain Mabanckou, *The Lights of Pointe-Noire* (London: Serpent's Tail, 2015), 127.

12   The Anti-Racism Secretariat was established in 1995.

13   In 1995, the Stoney Point Ojibway occupied Ipperwash Provincial Park, which had been expropriated by the government during World War II, setting off a confrontation between the Ontario Provincial Police and the Ojibway residents of the area.

14   *Carding* is the term used to describe the controversial practice of the police stopping Black men and women and demanding to see identification for purposes of intelligence gathering.

15   An Africentric high school was eventually opened in Scarborough in 2012.

16   Ian Baucom develops this argument fully in his 2005 work *Specters of the Atlantic: Finance Capital, Slavery, and the Philosophy of History* (Durham: Duke University Press, 2005).

17   Thomas Ladenburg, "Government in England the Colonies," in *Digital History*, University of Houston, <http://www.digitalhistory.uh.edu/teachers/lesson_plans/pdfs/unit1.pdf>.

18   The colonial motif continues over into certain images we have been made comfortable with, primarily through Hollywood: the business mogul; the swashbuckler; the adventurer; the robber baron who, usually operating on the border of morality, law, and society, often on the "frontier," gets things done; in particular he secures land or resources for the colonial government. So what if a few skulls are cracked, a few "Indians" or "Negroes" killed? So what if the rivers are polluted? He gets the job done. We recognize this cultural image; it exists deep in our psyche.

19   Simone Weil, *The Need for Roots: Prelude towards a Declaration of Duties Towards Mankind* (London: Routledge, 2002). This work, like all of Weil's books, was published posthumously.

20   Kelly Leitch is one of the Conservative candidates in the upcoming leadership convention.

21   The good news is that there is a resurgence in pride in their hair and its styling among Black women worldwide.

22   In 2001 the UN-sponsored World Conference Against Racism (WCAR), August 30– September 7, passed the Durban Declaration and Program of Action, which among other recommendations declared the transatlantic trade in Africans… "a crime against humanity, and should always have been so."

23   Lindon Barrett, *Blackness and Value.*

24   *Afrosporic* is a neologism I have coined to describe the scattering of Africans around the world. It contains the roots of the place, Afro, and the idea of the spore which is scattered. It represents a continued drive on my part to develop words to speak to the experience of Afrosporic people losing their original languages.

25   Vision 21: Canadian Culture in the 21st Century was a small group of writers and artists from African, Asian and European backgrounds formed to raise issues of diversity and representation.

26   The essay "Disturbing the Peace" in *Bla_K* is a more thorough analysis of this issue.

27   The poet Barb Carey sent me a copy of a review she wrote for the *Toronto Star*. I have never been able to find a publication of that review.

28   *Shabine* is a French creole word used in the Caribbean to refer to a lighter-skinned Black person.

29   *Brownin'* is a Jamaican patwa (patois) word used to refer to a brown-skinned woman.

30   M. NourbeSe Philip, "Interview with an Empire," in *Assembling Alternatives: Reading*

Postmodern Poetries Transnationally, ed. Romana Huk (Middletown, CT: Wesleyan University Press, 2003), 195–206.

31 Livent was responsible for bringing a number of shows to Broadway after opening them in Toronto. In 2009, Drabinsky was convicted of fraud and forgery and sentenced to seven years.

32 When the venue opened in 1993, it was known as the North York Performing Arts Centre. It was then renamed as the Ford Centre for the Performing Arts.

33 M. NourbeSe Philip, *Showing Grit: Showboating North of the 44th Parallel* (Toronto: Poui Publications, 1993).

34 *Wining* is a popular Afro Caribbean dance movement in which the hips are circled and which is based on African fertility dances.

35 The poem "Discourse on the Logic of Language" explores these issues in my collection *She Tries Her Tongue; Her Silence Softly Breaks* (Charlottetown, PEI: Ragweed Press, 1998), and Toronto: The Women's Press, 1993, and currently reprinted by Wesleyan University Press, Middletown, CT, 2015).

36 *Maafa* is a Kiswahili term for a great disaster. It refers to the forced removal and enslavement of millions of Africans in the Americas, the Caribbean and, I would add, in Arab countries.

37 Haruna Jiyah Jacob, "African Writers as Practicing Translators: The Case of Ahmadou Koumoura," *Translation Journal* 6, No. 4, 2002, <http://translationjournal.com/journal/22kourouma.htm>.

38 Roberto Tejada, "Itinerary," *Poetry Foundation*, <https://www.poetryfoundation.org/poems-and-poets/poems/detail/53734>.

39 Maroonage is the practice by enslaved Africans of running away from slave owners to set up home and life elsewhere, more often than not in inaccessible areas such as mountains.

40 I refer here to the chorus of a 2017 calypso, "We Jammin' Still" sung in Trinidad by the calypsonian MX Prime. Jammin' in the title refers to dancing, and essentially the calypso asserts that Trinidadians will continue dancing even as they face the crises of an economic downturn in the economy and increased crime. Some have critiqued the song as being an ode to the party mentality of Trindadians, especially around the Carnival season. Others, among whom I count myself, see the song as talking about the ability to survive with joy through extreme hardship, akin to the biblical exhortation to "count it all joy" (James 1:2) when trouble afflicts you. Certainly the beauty that has come out of African life since enslaved Africans were brought to the Americas and the Caribbean attests to that.

ECHOES IN A STRANGER LAND

I have lost my place, or my place has deserted me. This may be the dilemma of the West Indian writer abroad: that he hungers for nourishment from a soil which he (as an ordinary citizen) could not at present endure. The pleasure and the paradox of my own exile is that I belong wherever I am. My role, it seems, has rather to do with time and change than with the geography of circumstances; and yet there is always an acre of ground in the New World which keeps growing echoes in my head.

—George Lamming[1]

They who have put out the people's eyes, reproach them of their blindness.

—John Milton[2]

The position from which I write this introduction is a hazardous and difficult one, if only because its fluidity does a disservice to the fixedness implicit in the word *position*. It is, however, appropriate that I should be writing this introduction in Tobago, since this is the first and remembered place of exile. Exile—which has come to be the signature and permanent mark of the modern age.

From one exile to another, island-hopping, first to Trinidad, "for an education," British and colonial, next to Jamaica, for a continuation at the tertiary level, and then to a more permanent exile in North America. Only to understand, finally, that exile had begun a long, long time before I left Tobago for Trinidad, a confused eight-year-old. The exile of which I speak is a much more lasting one than I had ever anticipated.

It coming right inside we house—this exile—along with "things for so" from America, pack up in a box that Tantee sending or a barrel that Cousin Pearl mailing, it coming smelling of "she gone a foreign," of strange and new, of anything that not us. And you playing with it, touching it, feeling it, putting it on—a new pair of shorts, a dress—"look what a pretty white dolly!"; it having a smell all it own—sharp, exciting, and smelling of America and it real real—this exile. Except we not knowing that is exile we smelling when excited for so, we pressing we noses against the new clothes; we not knowing that the literature and history, even the grammar we learning in school, is part of the contour map in we own geography of exile.

Back then the hidden curriculum wasn't hiding so much and we growing up knowing we leaving, that nothing around we having any value and that life only beginning when we walking up the gangplank to the big-for-so ocean liner, or up the stairs to the plane that taking we away to big country. We sucking the milk of exile at we mammy bubbies, we cutting we teeth on exile—exile in the very air we breathing.

Many-faceted and many-layered, this condition of exile is the legacy of colonialism and imperialism that first exiled Africans from their ethnicity and all its expressions—language, religion, education, music, patterns of family relations—into the pale and beyond, into the nether land of race. From this exile there would be no relief, no recourse, no return. In predicting that the twentieth century would be the century of race, Du Bois, the African American intellectual, was uncannily prescient.

In many respects, for Africans, exile from their ethnicity has not yet been repaired. In North America and to some degree in Canada, the re-forged links with that ethnicity appear to have grown stronger in recent years. Strangely enough, in the Caribbean, in these islands that are predominantly African, the links *appear* weaker, the flight from Africa manifesting itself in either a profound erasure and silencing or a submerging under a growing Americanism through the uncritical absorption of CNN news, *Santa Barbara, Knots Landing*, and *Dallas*. I say *appear* since the apparent absence is deceptive and is really a presence, albeit hidden.

Although presently "positioned" in the Caribbean (having been living here for the last ten months), I have for the last twenty-five years—almost—made Canada my *home*, another word of apparent fixity yet also subject to a dangerous fluidity.

It is May 1992, and Los Angeles burns in response to the verdict acquitting white police officers charged with assaulting an African American, Rodney King. It is May 1992, and in a night of riots, Toronto explodes. The word *finally* lurks there, somewhere at the back of my mind. Newspaper, television and radio reports about both events have provided the backdrop, both to the writing of this introduction and to my editing the essays collected here, which were written over the last eight years—two years short of a decade. The irony does not escape me as I read my own words cautioning against just this sort of eventuality, if Canadian society failed to grapple with racism. The irony *and* the pain.

It has been a disconcerting and disturbing experience to reread my own thoughts, opinions and conclusions on the racism permeating the institutions of Canada, including cultural ones, and to reflect on how little has changed over the years. It has, therefore, not been difficult to understand how the riots in Toronto could have happened. While the Rodney King verdict and consequent riots in Los Angeles may have been the catalyst, the ground had been well-worked in Toronto and Canada in preparation for this confrontation and outbreak of violence.

The currents of racism in Canadian society run deep, they run smooth, lulling white Canadians into a complacency that will see racism anywhere else but in Canada. Racism is as much the determining factor in the brutal and deadly confrontation between the police and African Canadians as it is in the traditional approach of arts councils and related institutions to African-based aesthetics and African Canadian artists. It still remains a difficult and sometimes impossible task to convince white Canadians of this, and often requires, as recently happened with the Stephen Lewis report, a white individual to validate what Blacks have identified for a long time.

Traditionally, however, culture has not been a significant arena of racial contestation. Education, employment, housing, and police relations have always, and for good reason, garnered most attention—political, academic, investigative, and personal. This is ironic, given that the European onslaught against Africans was as much against their culture as against their persons. The significance of the 1990 confrontation between the Royal Ontario Museum and the African Canadian community over the display *Into the Heart of Africa* lay in the fact that, for the first time, the issue of culture as a site of contestation attracted and galvanized wide-based attention. The dismissal by white Canadians, led by the media, of the complaints by African Canadians once again underscored the resistance of Canadian society to any acknowledgement or acceptance of racism.

Having said that, however, it is only fair to acknowledge that over the eight years during which I wrote the articles, essays, and letters now comprising *Frontiers*, arts councils and cultural institutions have made some changes. Many of these do not go far enough, being still at the stage of reports on what *ought* to be done. The Canada Council, the Ontario Arts

Council and the Toronto Arts Council all struck committees, ostensibly to consider how better they could serve their multiracial and multi-ethnic communities; many arts council panels are now much more representative of these communities. In their recognition that all is not well in the cultural body of Canada, these changes represent hairline fractures in the at-times-overwhelming and oppressive structures standing guard over "Canadian culture." This is the best possible interpretation of these developments; at worst, these responses may be seen as the system adapting and shifting, as systems always will, in order to remain essentially the same.

All of which brings me to the composite nature of the phrase *Canadian culture*. By culture I include all its expressions, including language, religion, and education—the many ways in which a people organizes its life and living that distinguish it from any other. The devastation that capitalism wrought on the culture of Africans brought to the Caribbean and the Americas, not to mention that of the Indigenous peoples, is illustrative of the significance, if not indispensability, of culture to human society. The intent of the onslaught against Africans was two-pronged: to achieve a cheap, unwaged source of labour *and* to destroy their cultural life. The latter was not an accidental by-product of the former, but integrally linked to it; an African workforce that had no cultural base or resource to rely on would be a more pliable, less rebellious one. David Livingstone understood this when he reasoned that he first had to destroy the customs and mores of continental Africans *before* he could bring commerce and then religion.[3]

There have been times when I have thought the unthinkable—that it is a less cruel act to kill a people, leaving their culture and respect for it intact, than to denude them of their culture and by various means deride and destroy it, leaving them to howl their pain and anger on down through the centuries. And isn't that partly what Los Angeles and Toronto, and before that Miami, and before that Watts, and before that the Haitian revolution and before that—have been all about? The howling of our pain and anger at the loss of our cultures.

[O]ur capacities for language, for thought, for communication, and culture— do not develop automatically in us, are not just biological functions, but are, equally, social and historical in origin…they are a gift—the most wonderful of gifts—from one generation to another. We see that Culture is as crucial as Nature.

—Oliver Sacks[4]

To strip a people of the gift of their culture is a double act of inhumanity—for both the victim *and* the perpetrator, who is also a victim. It becomes even more heinous for the perpetrators of this crime—Europeans and their descendants (in this case, white Americans and Canadians)—to condemn and blame the victims for their deculturation—their loss.

It is remarkable, in fact, to note how, after having had so much taken from them, having been given nothing, Africans in the New World have created so much that is new, exceptionally beautiful and indispensable to humanity: this is an astonishing act of survival and witness to the African genius. The Atlantic trade in Africans severed Africans in the Caribbean and the Americas from their cultural roots; the Atlantic now represents a synaptic break in the circuit of cultural continuities which run back and forth—the Yoruba drumbeats crossing to Trinidad, Jamaican reggae crossing "back" to Zimbabwe and South Africa, Nzinga to Harriet Tubman and Sojourner Truth back to Winnie, Malcolm to Biko and back, and on, and on.

Having lived for the last several months in a society also split along racial lines, this time African and Asian, and one which appears to thrive on racial brinkmanship, albeit verbal, once again the significance of culture and cultural continuity becomes apparent. Although Asian indentureship was, in very many respects, very similar to slavery, in one remarkable and significant aspect the experience of the African and Asian differed—in the permission the colonial government granted the latter to keep their languages, customs, rituals and culture, although white colonial society considered these at best exotic, at worst pagan, savage or primitive. Prohibition vis-à-vis permission—these diametrically opposed attitudes sum up the difference between how the colonial powers treated these two groups. In the one case the drum, the Orishas (gods)—Shango, Oshun, Yemoja and countless others—not to mention the tongue itself, would be outlawed; in the other, Hindi, Bhojpuri, the pundits, the *tassa* (drum) and even *ganja* (smoked by holy men) would be allowed. That African cultural practices have continued at all, in whatever fashion they have, is a testament to the vitality of African cultures and the will to survive.

The different treatment of these two cultures, African and Asian, has had a lasting effect on how these groups view themselves and their cultures—in one instance, to be cherished; in the other, to be ashamed of. Not only the effect on the peoples, but the difference in attitude to the two groups continues on down to the present time. It has its roots in a pernicious type of racism that ranked subject peoples, so that those whose cultures more closely approximated European culture, in having a written language and big stone buildings, were considered a cut or two above the non-literate savage living in the jungle—read African.

If there is one central point around which the essays and articles in this collection focus, it is the need on the part of what has traditionally been seen as Canadian culture, as represented by arts councils and organizations, to respect those cultures—African, Asian, and First Nations—that had long established circuits of culture, which Europeans interrupted, bringing with them their own cultures, with its central economic practice of capitalism. The absence of that respect—in many instances, the outright disrespect—makes itself felt all the way down from the boards of directors through the panels and staff to the individual artist.

I carry a Canadian passport: I, therefore, am Canadian. How am I Canadian, though, above and beyond the narrow legalistic definition of being the bearer of a Canadian passport; and does the racism of Canadian society present an absolute barrier to those of us who are differently coloured ever belonging? Because that is, in fact, what we are speaking about—how to belong—not only in the legal and civic sense of carrying a Canadian passport, but also in another sense of feeling at "home" and at ease. It is only in belonging that we will eventually become Canadian.

How do we lose the sense of being "othered," and how does Canada begin its m/othering of us who now live here, were born here, have given birth here—all under a darker sun? Being born elsewhere, having been fashioned in a different culture, some of us may always feel "othered," but then there are those—our children, nephews, nieces, grandchildren—born here, who are as Canadian as snow and ice, and yet, merely because of their darker skins, are made to feel "othered."

A long and passionate discussion with fellow African Caribbean Canadian poet Claire Harris (how many identities can dance on a maple leaf?), clarified some of the issues for me around belonging and becoming Canadian. Our discussion arose out of an article by Bharati Mukherjee about Salman Rushdie. In it, Mukherjee opined that, unlike in the case of the South Asians, Afro-Caribbean people in England could eventually become English because of similarity of language, religion and dress.

My friend agreed, and argued further that a similar distance and difference existed between a Northern and Southern European—a Swede and a Sicilian, for instance—as between the English and Afro-English or Afro-

Saxons. By extension, the same arguments can be applied to Canada—English Canada, at least, with all its institutional and cultural replicas of England. In a letter to her that was never mailed, I wrote:

We cannot, however, rely solely on dress, religion and language—even accepting that these are the same. And while they may be the same, we wear them all differently. While religion and language in the Caribbean bear the unmistakable stamp of Christianity and England, Africa has also left her indelible mark on these. This is not the place to go into detail on the African influences on religion, but suffice it to say that the practices of Spiritual Baptists, Rasta, and pocomania, to mention but three of the many aspects of religious worship of Caribbean people, all incorporate African beliefs and practices. Not to mention Orisha worship—worship of African deities—which has always been there but is rapidly growing among "Afrosporic" peoples. And wherever they have scattered, African Caribbean peoples have taken these forms of worship with them. In the heart of Toronto, I have seen Africa in the ceremony of worship in a tiny Spiritual Baptist Church. The Caribbean demotic, as well, is as much the linguistic descendant of Africa as of England. As Rex Nettleford has argued, Europe may have governed, but Africa ruled.[5]

The perceptions and attitudes of the dominant society, however, must also be taken into account in the dynamics of belonging and becoming. And there is nothing in either English or Canadian society that suggests that African people are particularly welcome by the host society. From the establishment—location and number—of immigration offices overseas, to the policing of Black people domestically, including their difficulty in obtaining adequate employment, housing and education, the evidence of the lack of welcome, if not open hostility, is there. From the point of view of white Canadian and English people, the distance between African peoples and themselves is infinite, not infinitesimal, as Mukherjee would have us believe, and they wish to keep it that way.

It matters not a jot that an African Canadian person may think herself very much integrated within Canadian society and a part of it—they may and do wear the same clothes, attend the same churches, go to the same schools, live in the same neighbourhoods—if the dominant society continues to see them—us—as alien, different and Other, they cannot truly belong to the society. It behooves us all to remember how much an integral part of German society Jews were prior to the rise of Nazism and Hitler. And, closer to home, those middle-class Blacks who moved to the suburbs, dressing and speaking like Canadians, driving the same cars Canadians did, discovered how much and how little they belonged when the police began shooting their young in the streets like dogs. Having a house in the suburbs like all good Canadians aspire to was no protection—not if your child was Black.

It is important that we not read a culture through the eyes of the middle class, whom I believe live the same the world over—from London to Toronto, to Port of Spain, to Bangkok—it matters not what country it is. They share the same aspirations, yearn after the same material comforts—their desire—historically—in the Caribbean was to become as white and European as possible. It hasn't changed much. It is those who occupied and occupy the lower rungs of the society who have been the caretakers of Africa as it exists in the New World today—from steel pan to calypso, to reggae, to *voudoun*, to *candomble*, to the very demotics that now exist.

On a lighter note, one only has to take a walk along Eglinton Avenue here in Toronto to see how we wear clothes differently—just the angle of a hat, perhaps, the slight crawl or sashay—to know that even in something as apparently superficial as dress, the continuities of style run deep.

To become unambivalently British or Canadian is to forget the history of empire that defined England, produced a Canada, and honed the beliefs and practices of white supremacy; it is to forget that our people and Europeans first met as equals—the latter being made welcome in Africa, as they were here in Canada—and that the latter would use their superior technology to attempt an obliteration of African peoples and their cultures. Not to remember those things; to forget that what we now *appear* to share—education, religion, dress, legal institutions—are really tombstones erected on the graves of African customs, culture and languages, is simply to collude in our own erasure, our own obliteration.

If the individual remains *in the knowing* of what her speaking English means, and what her worshipping an Anglo-Christian god means in terms of her people and what has happened to them—particularly given that the white supremacy and racism that fuelled colonialism and imperialism are still very much alive today—this knowledge must mediate her Englishness or Canadianness. While the divide may appear small, it runs deep.

I seem, however, to be arguing out of both sides of my mouth—on the one hand saying that Africans are not accepted by the dominant culture, but also suggesting that Africans not embrace unambivalently the dominant culture. What I am, in fact, saying is that the history of that lack of acceptance and rejection and hatred is *why* we cannot unambivalently embrace the dominant culture, and that the solution to racism and white supremacy is not through sameness, as Mukherjee's argument seems to suggest. I am also arguing for a subversive role for memory, that memory is more than nostalgia—it has a potentially kinetic quality and must impel us to action.

Should we African Canadians, therefore, turn in our passports, as some have suggested, since we have shown ourselves so ungrateful as to criticize our benefactors? We ought to leave, some have urged politely and not so politely—the theme of "nigger go home" is a persistent one. Those who think like this, however, will not see such a simplistic solution. Their worst nightmares have been and will continue to be confirmed. In the words of my only mother tongue, the Caribbean demotic, "We ent going nowhere. We here and is right here we staying." In Canada. In this world so new. To criticize, needle and demand; to work hard for; to give to; to love; to hate—for better or worse—till death do we part. And even after—in the African tradition of our ancestral role after death of advising and guiding our offspring—our descendants. African Canadians—Canadians.

For us Africans—the Americas and the Caribbean *were* a new world. An ocean—at times it appears an eternity—separates us from the land we came from—Africa. To reverse Blake's image of seeing an eternity in a grain of sand, at times the eternity of our separation appears a mere hop, skip and a jump away, particularly when we listen to our poets, our musicians, our artists and our griots, and witness that Africa has merely spored the New World with the genius of her sons and daughters.

The astonishing accomplishments of Africans who were freed in some instances not even 150 years ago—we are still some forty-six years short of the bicentennial of the earliest emancipation date, 1838—beggars the imagination.[6] And sometimes I believe the overwhelming impediments put in our way are a backhanded acknowledgement of our staggering potential. These obstacles are, in fact, partially an acknowledgement of fear on the part of the dominant white culture—the fear, *as they perceive it*, that, given half a chance, we will replace them in all fields.

However, the onslaught against Africans in this New World has not let up since the first African was brought here. At times, it appears that there is a loosening of the grip—the passing of Civil Rights legislation and the adoption of affirmative action policies in the U.S., and the adoption of human rights legislation in Canada—but, as in the last decade under Reagan, Bush, Thatcher and Mulroney, there has been more than enough reason to sit down by the rivers of Babylon and weep. Consider the plight of what is now called the Black underclass in the United States, or the African peoples of Azania; consider Haiti today—the first country in the Caribbean and the Americas to have a successful revolution led by the former African slave, Toussaint L'Ouverture; consider the shootings of Black youth and adults in Canada. Consider and consider, then consider some more.

For Africans in the Caribbean and the Americas, who in the words of the spiritual, have been trying to sing their songs in a strange land, be/longing *is* a problematic. Be/longing *anywhere*—the Caribbean, Canada, the United States, even Africa. The land, the place that was the New World was nothing but a source of anguish—how could they—we—begin to love the land, which is the first step in be/longing, when even the land was unfree? How could they—we—be/long to and in a land that was not theirs— ours—but some burgher's in Amsterdam, or London? How do you begin to be/long when everything around you conspires to keep you alien—the language, the customs, the spirituality? And yet they began—those early Africans—singing their songs in this land so new and so strange—songs that harked back to their earlier be/longing elsewhere, but in singing those songs they were making their first mark of be/longing to the land, the place—this world so new—the Caribbean and the Americas.

The only peoples who be(truly)long here—who be long here (I use *be* in the African American vernacular sense)—are the Indigenous peoples. Unlike all other peoples who came here, the African did not choose to come, but was forced to come as a consequence of one of the most cruel enterprises in history, the transatlantic trade in Africans.

Five hundred years ago, Columbus came sailing into the womb—cunt, if you will—that was the Caribbean, entering what was for the European a new world, sowing it with the poisoned seed of Europe to produce Old World mutations of genocide, devastation and racism. He did what Europe was going to do sooner or later—enc(o)unter the Caribbean and the Americas, and so began a 500-year experiment of testing their time-worn theories of white and racial supremacy in the laboratory of the Caribbean and the Americas, creating thereby the wound—the cut—that continues to suppurate. Womb and wound; cunt and cut—the paradigmatic axis around which the male European would move in the New World.

Five hundred years! Africans be long here now. Sometimes it appears we be too long here, but there *is* nowhere else to go. Not to Africa, not to England, not to Spain or France, but here in this world so new—the Caribbean, the Americas, including Canada—singing their songs in a stranger land—by the rivers of Babylon.

Sometimes it appears that we Africans in the New World have been weaned forever on the milk of otherness; we have been too long "othered" by those societies who traditionally have thought and currently think nothing of enriching themselves on our labour, then discarding us—the detritus of capitalism. I am reminded that there was a time when it was cheaper to get rid of an African slave who was no longer useful, and buy a new one, than to continue to provide for her. Could this have been the start of the "nigger go home" attitude? We need now, however, to be m/othered by those very societies and cultures which have destroyed our cultures, enriched themselves on our exploited labour, and who would now banish, if not destroy us. By Canada. But more important than that, Canada *needs* to m/other us. Her very salvation depends on m/othering all her peoples—those who be/long(ed) here when the first Europeans arrived—the First Nations peoples, as well as those, like the African, who unwittingly encountered History and became seminal in its development.

How best this m/othering will be carried out is the work of educators, parents, children, business people and politicians—the entire society. But it must *not* be left up to politicians. Further, it ought not to be and cannot be accomplished by obliterating the history of the First Nations, the African or the Asian, and Canada's role as an abuser. That is why it is so important to keep the slash—in *all* its negative connotations—in m/othering.

We must not forget. Neither the oppressor nor the victim—not Canada or the Indigenous person, the African or the Asian—we will not forget. As I wrote to my friend, to forget would be tantamount to engaging in massive and collective social amnesia. But since we each, individually and collectively, are equally entitled to share in this land, we had better find ways of encouraging ourselves and each other to sing our songs—in this land that, with the exception of the First Nations people, *is* a strange land for us all. (By behaving as if he was the only one who had a right to the land, the European even tried to make it strange for the Indigenous person.)

We all know the alternative; we witnessed it in May 1992, in Toronto. We will witness it again. And again. Unless all Canadians, particularly those who traditionally comprise the dominant groups—white Canadians—

understand how racism fatally affects the body politic. The choice is a stark one—between a society increasingly riddled with inequities—truly a stranger land—the haves ensconced behind burglar bars, the have-nots occupying the streets in increasing numbers, and between them both the police creating a buffer zone at best, or at worst performing the functions of an occupying army on behalf of the well-to-do, and a society which becomes a "home" where all Canadians be/long.

Whichever direction we take, it behooves us to remember that "our opponents are our co-creators, for they have something to give which we have not."[7]

This is the challenge facing all Canadians—African, Asian, European and Indigenous—finding out what we can offer to and accept from each other. It is the only way we will transform this place from a stranger place to one of true be/longing.

NOTES

1   George Lamming, *The Pleasures of Exile* (Ann Arbor: University of Michigan Press, 1992), 50.

2   John Milton, *Apology for Smectymnuus*, Section VIII, in *The Prose Works of John Milton*, Vol. III (London: George Bell and Sons, 1888), 153–154.

3   Tim Jeal, *David Livingstone* (London: Heinemann, 1973).

4   Oliver Sacks, *Seeing Voices: A Journey into the World of the Deaf* (Berkeley: University of California Press, 1989), xi.

5   Former Rhodes scholar, presently a professor at the University of the West Indies, and choreographer of the National Dance Troupe of Jamaica.

6   Although England abolished slavery in all her colonies in 1834 (the earliest date of emancipation for all slaveholding nations), Africans in English colonies had to continue under an apprenticeship period for another four years, until 1838.

7   Marion Milner, *Eternity's Sunrise: A Way of Keeping a Diary* (New York: Routledge, 2011), 90.

INTERVIEW WITH AN EMPIRE

Q: Why does a Black woman like yourself write the kind of poetry you do?

A: I'm not sure what you mean by "the kind of poetry you do."

Q: Your poetry has been described as "complex and abstract."[1] Do you care to comment on that?

A: No.

Q: Why?

A: Because the work is "complex and abstract." But so is jazz and that doesn't prevent anyone from listening to it, does it? A comment like that says more about the commentator than about the work.

Q: But doesn't being "complex and abstract" restrict your audience, and doesn't that bother you?

A: Your question reminds me of one of the most difficult readings I have ever done, which was to read after the Black British dub poet Linton Kwesi Johnson, whose work I greatly admire. I had been asked as a last-minute replacement to fill in for a Cuban poet who had not been able to obtain a visa to enter the United States. I arrived at the venue with very few minutes to spare and somewhat out of breath. LKJ, who was supposed to read second, offered to go first to allow me to catch my breath and collect myself. The audience loved him. His work is intended to be performed—he often works with a band; it is rhythmic, imbued with rhyme and carries an in-your-face political message.

My work, on the other hand, is page-bound and far more in the modernist tradition which abandoned rhyme and rhythm, if not metre, a long time ago. Furthermore the audience had really come to hear LKJ and his was going to be the quintessentially hard act to follow. I found myself reading my more politically obvious poems—earlier works, by and large—and avoiding those poems that challenged me as reader and them as audience.

Q: Were you envious of the audience response he got?

A: No. But I think it typifies one of the fundamental issues facing poets of African heritage who do not necessarily work within the context of performance.

Q: How so?

A: I believe some poets begin from a position where they take language as a given. Others, like myself, have a profound distrust of language. This may seem like an extremely odd position—it's like an artist distrusting colour, a sculptor distrusting stone, or a musician distrusting sound. With one difference. Neither the painter nor the sculptor nor the musician needs his medium to function on a daily basis. We all need words and language to function. We are told it is what makes us human. But in its day-to-day use this very language is very much devalued coinage. This is the same medium that is used to sell us goods we don't want and, through political half-truths and lies, to convince us that what we know to be the truth is not really the truth. In general one of the most insidious uses of language is to separate us from a sense of integrity and wholeness. Essentially what I'm saying is that the potential seductiveness of language is dangerous. I believe many of those poets who are described as language poets begin from this premise. But for me there is another layer of distrust—historical distrust, if you will. After all, this was a language that the European forced upon the African in the New World. So that the exploitative plantation machine could be more efficiently run. It was a language of commands, orders, punishments. This language—english in my case, but it applies to all the languages of those European countries involved in the colonialist project—was never intended or developed with me or my kind in mind. It spoke of my non-being. It encapsulated my chattel status. And irony of all ironies, it is the only language in which I can now function. And therein lies the conundrum—"english is my mother tongue," but it is also "my father tongue" (*She Tries her Tongue; Her Silence Softly Breaks*).[2] I begin from a position of extreme distrust of language and do not believe that english—or any European language, for that matter—can truly speak our truths without the language in question being put through some sort of transformative process. A decontaminating process is probably more accurate, since a language as deeply implicated in imperialism as english has been cannot but be contaminated by such a history and experience.

Q: How are you able to write, then, if you believe this to be the case?

A: With great difficulty. It is like having an abusive parent. You can't pretend you don't or didn't have the parent or the experience. First you have to find a way of healing—if that is at all possible—then a way of managing the memory of that experience. For me there is always a shadow around english and my use of english because this so-called mother tongue of mine is rooted in a very particular, brutal and traumatic history—that of the 400-year slave trade in which European peoples and nations kidnapped and traded African peoples to provide the labour force needed for the sugar and cotton plantations of the New World.

Even as I use the words *kidnap* and *trade*, they in no way begin to convey the horror of it all. The murders, the rapes, the physical mutilation, the destruction of families, villages, cultures, languages are all neatly packaged and managed in the expression *slave trade*. The exquisite challenge every writer faces is that language always stands in for the experience, the thought or feeling. The struggle is to reduce the gap between the experience and the expression of that experience. In my case, there is a double burden, if you will, because of the history of the language in relation to me and my history. Essentially, language represents a wound for me.

Q: Hasn't it healed by this time? After all, it has been over a century.

A: A mother never forgets the birth of her child. Ask any woman who has given birth, no matter what her age, and she'll be able to tell you what the birth of each of her children was like.

Q: I'm not sure I get your point.

A: There are certain experiences that defy the passage of time, is what I'm saying. The fact that the loss of a language didn't happen to me personally in no way means that I do not remember that loss. In fact, I remember it as if it happened yesterday.

Q: I'll have to take your word for it.

A: Yes, you will—in the same way we take a mother's word that she remembers the birth of her child. But to return to my earlier point: Because of this distrust that is lodged in the history of how I came to this part of the world, I handle language in a very self-conscious way—almost as a "foreign anguish" (*She Tries*). I hope in the way a painter approaches her paint, or a sculptor his marble. It is not me—it is outside of me—a foreign anguish. And yet it is me. As only language can be. The Heideggerian house of one's being, if you will. The only way I can then work with it is to fracture it, fragment it, dislocate it, doing with it what it did to me and my kind, before I can put it back together, hopefully better able to express some of my own small truths. And for me this is where form becomes so very important, because part of the transformative and decontaminating process is also to find the appropriate form for what I'm saying.

Q: What would you say then about poets who do not do this with their work—whose work is more accessible?

A: As in not being "complex and abstract"?

Q: If you wish.

A: Well, my role here is not to comment on their work—I believe that is more your function as critic. However, I would say that when a poet like LKJ uses a dub beat over his lyrics, I believe he is trying to accomplish the same thing I am trying to do when I fracture, fragment, then put language back together again—trying to decontaminate it, perhaps. Refashioning it so that it can carry what you want it to say: managing the brutal history that casts a long and deep shadow around the language. The cultural practice which has survived most intact among Africans in the New World is music and I believe it offers another layer to the meaning and speaks of that shadowing—the wound, if you will. One result of using music with words in that way, however, is that the work becomes far more capable of crossing over into non-African audiences. I doubt whether these audiences understand the context of the words any more with the music, but they are entertained at least. The challenge for critics like yourself is to understand the cultural specificity of works like my own without the aid of music.

Q: Do you have any readership within Black communities— Let me rephrase that. Is it only white people—critics and students who can appreciate your work?

A: Poets and writers like myself who question and challenge the very ability of the language itself to speak the truth of their memories and engage in what I call practices of dislocation find themselves on the horns of a dilemma. Their poetry can be described as being language-based and appears to share a great deal with those poets working within the European aesthetic of language poetry. The language-based nature of poetry such as my own starts from a very different place. That of the wasteland between the terror of language and the horror of silence. White or European audiences who do not understand the matrix of this poetry miss what the poetry is all about. They see it as postmodern.

On the other hand, there is a sense in which we have delegitimized ourselves to some degree in the eyes of our communities—who after all constitute our potential audience and market. Traditionally the Black poet has played a significant role in declaiming against the scourges that have plagued, and continue to plague, African people in the New World ever since their forced relocation. While wordplay is integral to certain African-based musical forms like calypso, by and large language is taken as a given.[3] A daffodil is a daffodil is a daffodil. Although for those of us studying english literature in the colonies it would have been far more accurate to say: "A daffodil is not a hibiscus, poinsettia, croton or flamboyant."

Q: I'm not sure I quite understand what you mean.

A: If there is one central image that sums up english literature studies in the Caribbean for me, it would be the daffodil. Every schoolchild had to engage with Wordsworth's daffodils at some time, although we had never seen them. And yet our very futures depended on being able to write about these bloody flowers.

Q: I see.

A: If I were to play around—riff on that image—I might turn out something like this:

> Is not a daffodil
> is
> and not
> is—

I'm far more interested in working with the structure of the language to destabilize the image of the daffodil.

It seems that the urgency of all the ills we have to rail against as New World Africans appears to militate against this sort of play. But given that the universe is always in play, what else is there to do but play? I suspect, however, that the memory of the horror and terror of loss of tongue lies so heavily on us that playing with language appears almost frivolous.

There is as yet no parallel between the way in which New World Africans have used their language of music in the New World to create complex new forms like jazz and our literary use of english. This may have all to do with the fact that because we need language for everyday communication, unlike music, there is a powerful urge to approximate the standard use of language. Playing music, and in particular African-based music, was never seen as a mark of being civilized. On the other hand, speaking and writing english, french or spanish, properly—in the manner that whites did—was, and continues to be, a marker of being civilized. It put some distance between you and your more downtrodden African brothers and sisters. The recent controversy over the use of ebonics proves that very little has changed around issues of language marking acceptability by the white society.

Far too many of us still take language for granted—assuming its transparency. It is too seldom treated as raw material, no different than stone—to be cut, shaped, moulded, twisted, broken and put back together again in a new way.

Q: Would you describe your work as postmodernist?

A: It is if you say it is.

Q: What do you mean by that?

A: Many years ago I had a constitutional law professor who taught his classes according to the Socratic method. He never asked a question, but parried every query from us timid first-year law students with "It is if you say it is." This phrase is the best response to those readers and critics who insist that *She Tries Her Tongue; Her Silence Softly Breaks* is a postmodernist work. It is if you say it is. Postmodernist, that is. But to see *She Tries* as only or primarily a postmodernist work is to miss most of what the work is about. Unless, that is, one understands the Caribbean as a postmodernist space long before the term became current. Which is not that far-fetched.

Q: Code-switching, bricolage, sampling, inventions—these are all significant markers of postmodernist work—

A: And of the Caribbean—but within a very different context. A context that is simultaneously African, European, Asian, creole and hybrid. However, I do understand that since the author, like history, is dead—my intentions as the humble author are dismissable.

Q: Not entirely—

A: My point is simply that while the work may look like a duck, walk like a duck and even talk like a duck, it is not a duck The deep structure of the work is of and from the African Caribbean. I believe what happens is that the multi-coded, multi-faceted nature of the work which plays with quotations, engages with polyvocality and works almost as a sort of hypertext is what leads the reader to assume its postmodernity. I am saying that it both is and is not postmodern. Simultaneously and disjunctively.

Modernism is understood to be a primarily Western, European phenomenon. This, despite the fact that what we now call the Third World, or more euphemistically the developing world, was an integral aspect of it—if only in providing the savage Other against which the West could preen its civilized self. As you well know, many of the ideas that influenced modernists like Picasso, Brancusi and company came from Africa and Oceania. And jazz, the creation of New World Africans, altered that most basic aspect of life itself—rhythm and timing. Yet when we think of modernism and its sibling and legatee postmodernism, we think primarily of European movements. Within that context, work like my own is not postmodernist. However, if we understand modernism and postmodernism to embrace more than Europe, if we understand the postmodern reality of the African Caribbean, then and only then I think is anything gained by interpreting the work as postmodernist.

Q: How would you have me interpret the Caribbean then?

A: To understand the Caribbean one needs to understand it and the entire New World as a site of massive interruptions. Of Aboriginal life, for the most part fatally. In the traumatic and violent wrenching from Africa that slavery entailed, African life would also be ruptured, also often fatally. Indentureship of the Asian represented another interruption. And while the European tried to maintain continuity in the face of the Other, there would be an interruption of another sort in that instance. The Caribbean is synonymous with rupture and break and hiatus and held breath. And death. And rebirth.

What I want you to do is hold the image of the woman's body—the Black woman's body—as central to all that is happening in the Caribbean. Because when we think of the Caribbean we have to think of cut—as in wound—and cunt into which Columbus, emissary of the Old World, would penetrate on behalf of his master. You could call it a surrogate fuck, or a fuck by proxy, because the raping and pillaging would truly begin in the english-speaking world with the robber barons like Hawkins and Drake and others of their ilk wreaking havoc on the virginal space in rabid search of redemption, utopia and riches—whatever the anglo version of the fabled el dorado was—while bringing death, disease and pestilence.

Q: That is a very gendered reading of the Caribbean, isn't it?

A: How else can it be read? Consider that Columbus sails under Spanish flags on behalf of a country led by a woman, Queen Isabella of Spain, and that Hawkins receives his first commission for the importing of slaves from Queen Elizabeth I.[4] Were these women men in drag, or were they merely powerful white women (how can you be merely powerful) using men to do their dastardly acts? There's a lot of work to be done looking at the role of these kinds of powerful women in the colonialist project.

Q: How do you represent this in your work? Or do you even try to represent it?

A: Given the fragmentation, the ruptures, the discontinuities, it seemed to me that to force a work like *She Tries* into a logical and linear way of reading—top to bottom, front to back—was to do the experience a second violence. The fragmented manner of representation was indeed a "truer" representation of the history. You can begin reading the work anywhere and within any poem—although certain poems, like "Discourse on the Logic of Language," lend themselves more to this than others. Begin anywhere. Doesn't this sum up the colonialist project in one respect?

Q: How so?

A: So many peoples—in my case African—were forced to begin anywhere—to pretend and behave as if there had been no before and would be no after. Begin anywhere—I began with wanting to subvert—to destroy the lyric voice. I felt it could not bear the weight of my history. All this was presumptuous perhaps, but that was how I felt. I also questioned the tradition of the solitary voice of the poet—often male, a white male, who embodied the wisdom of the society, and who spoke for, on behalf of and to *his* society or culture. In a voice of authority. Although he might be marginalized and he often was, his words were valued—he had a role to play even as outcast and had the authority to do so.

I would turn Eliot's objective correlative on its head—fog was supposed to be fog even in the Caribbean. And a little Black girl in the Caribbean was supposed to feel the same emotion as Prufrock.

Q: Did you succeed—in destroying the lyric voice?

A: I don't know. The certainties of youth appear to be just that now. I do know that what happened is that the work became impossible to read in the traditional sense—there were so many events happening on the page—not to mention the silences. In "Discourse," for instance—the poem that most typifies this challenge—there are four different voices clamouring to be heard on the combined facing pages.

It seems to me that the work engages with one of the most significant African musical techniques—that of call and response. I also think that it encapsulates an African worldview in which the ancestors become the call and we the response. In turn we humans call the ancestors into response, to act within our lives. It's like a snake doubling back on itself—eating its own tail. This call-and-response technique works both within poems and between poems. The contradiction in the centre refrain of "Discourse"—"English is my mother tongue / is my father tongue"—calls into response both the edicts against speaking in African tongues as well as the impulse to continuity of tongue, as in language, which the woman—in this case the Black woman—bears and expresses.

This does not—cannot—result in smoothly lyrical poetry. I saw the lyric voice as one of the tools used to further the ends of colonialism. And in upending the objective correlative, I would immerse the poem once again in the mess and morass of history—not remove it out of its context, as Eliot urged. History was not dead for me, as the postmodernists urge. I wanted a chance to rewrite it. According to *my* dictates—*my* memories. You may say this was presumptuous of me, but no more presumptuous than those who had written my history according to their dictates. And if the reader stumbled, stopped and started again, if s/he choked, and gagged on the words, then it was successful.

Q: I have some difficulty seeing how you equate success with—how do you put it?—the reader choking and gagging.

A: I once did a reading of "Discourse" with two other women. One was a Canadian of European background, the other was a First Nations woman. When we were done, the white woman said to me that she felt extremely uncomfortable reading the edicts forbidding Africans from speaking their languages. She understood, however, that the discomfort was an important lesson for her. The First Nations woman confessed to stumbling over the description of how the brain worked. This was also the section that spoke of the naming of certain parts of the brain after two nineteenth-century doctors who believed that Africans and other peoples of colour as well as women were inferior to white men. My answer to her was that as a First Nations woman, she was intended to stumble over those words. The parts of the brain that controlled speech—our speech—were not named with her in mind. We—as Black and First Nations women—were never intended to be in control of our own lives.

I want to take this metaphor about eating further. So much of the so-called developing world has been/is being consumed—literally—slipping into the great maw of the West and slipping down its throat to its stomach, there to be digested and transformed into some imitation of the original.[5] And bearing names like "world music" that separate the product from its source. In such a world, to be indigestible—to have the ability to make consumption difficult—is a quality to be valued.

Q: You've made reference on more than one occasion to history and memory. Would you care to talk about your history?

A: It's not only my history. It's also your history. Ours, if you will.

Q: Talk to me of our history then. And how it influences your writing.

A: How does one write about the rupture that is Africa and the Caribbean? One doesn't. First one has to acknowledge the silence, because what happens demands silence. As a form of respect. But as a writer and poet the impulse is always to words. The question is, do you—should you—turn the horror of a particular history into something beautiful, because of course it is that beauty which will make the work ultimately digestible. I confess to being disturbed by texts which attempt to deal in this way with aspects of slavery—fictional works, poetry, which are so "beautifully" written that the horror is also beautifully managed. For me the more seductive the language, the more I distrust it—with a centuries-old distrust. Of course this leads to issues of marketability and audience. Most people appear to want anodynes.

Q: Aren't you shooting yourself in the foot—you did say you wanted a wide readership for your work.

A: Every writer wants that. The question is, I suppose, how much you are willing to give up for such an audience and market. The challenge for me is to mark within the structure of the language itself that which I am speaking about, but which I can't really speak about.

Q: Why do you say you can't speak about it? I assume that it is your—what you say is our history here in the New World. You have been speaking about it in works like "Discourse."

A: Because "it" didn't happen in english. Or french or spanish. It happened in another language—that I am a stranger to. So how do I (w)rite/right that? What happened—indeed, is happening—happened within the spaces between words, between clotted clumps of words, between letters even.

Q: Are you saying that you find it difficult to write your history?

A: Yes, in the traditional sense of history. What helps is memory.

Q: You see them as being in contradiction.

A: Don't you? There are many, many memories, some complete, some not so complete. But there is also only one memory. A single memory. Of loss. Loss, loss, and more loss. The challenge for me is to write from that place of loss. Of nothing, if you will. To make poetry out of silence.

Q: I'm interested in how you read those poems that are speaking with more than one voice.

A: Over the years I had fallen into the habit of only reading certain poems—those that lent themselves most easily to the single voice. On one occasion a student asked me to read "Universal Grammar" (*She Tries*) for her. Without thinking about it I replied: "I will, if you read it with me." It was then that I came to the realization that I had, indeed, succeeded in what I had set out to do, although not in quite the way I had anticipated. I should confess at this point that most of the insights about *She Tries* have come to me after completion of the work—in this instance substantially after completion. As I have said before, I wanted to destroy the lyric voice. As a Black, female, colonized subject, what was the source of my authority, and was such authority necessary—indispensable perhaps?—to speech, public speech? To poetry? Being neither male nor white and without an observable or tangible source of authority, could I even speak? Or would I only speak a silence?

What I hadn't realized until "I will, if you read it with me" was that in shifting the lyric voice, in at least forcing it to share the page with other voices, with other histories—moving it from centre stage and page; in clearing a space—I had allowed for other voices to be heard. A multivocal, polyvocal discourse could now be heard. It was the chorus of the unheard, the not-heard, the barely whispered. This to me was closer to the discourse of women. To the call and response of African speech. I saw the text now as a jazz text. If you look at "Discourse," for instance, the centre refrain can be seen as the main musical theme and the linguistic events that are happening in english around this centre theme can be seen as riffs speaking into the silence around the "anguish that is English." Indeed, the entire work can also be seen to be working around the central theme that "Discourse" represents—the loss of language.

Q: I return to an earlier question—I assume you are writing about these issues—

A: I try not to write about issues when I write poetry.

Q: What are you trying to do then?

A: To get to the truth of certain experiences.

Q: The question remains—I assume that the audience you have in mind when you write is one which shares your context, but the issues—or rather your approach to them—appears—

A: You are back to the issue of "complex and abstract" aren't you? How do I bridge that gap? I confess that on completion of *She Tries* I became very aware that while the work was complete on the page, there was another completion that was needed—the completion of performance. I believe that one very crucial aspect of the Caribbean aesthetic is performance, so it is interesting that the work contains within its structure that potential. When the poems are performed, even within the classroom, each "reading" yields different information and new truths, as occurred in the reading with the First Nations woman and the European woman.

Q: The body appears to have played a large part in this work.

A: Yes, the body erupted into the text of *She Tries* in unexpected ways. There is a certain rightness to this, given how the African body was inserted into the New World. Given that the African body—"black ivory," "pieces of the Indies," as they were euphemistically called—was the sine qua non of the development of the New World. Those early Africans came with nothing but the body which would become the repository of everything they would need to survive. The Body Memory, if you will. For four hundred years those Black bodies would withstand the onslaught of empire. Those Black bodies are, in fact, the only thing standing between empire and a state of total annihilation. The erasure of memory in the face of history. Because to erase the body is to erase the memory.

Q: How is this work received in Canada?

A: I like to think of Canada as a space—the space that is Canada. What I should say right off the top is that works like *She Tries* and *Looking for Livingstone*[6] could only have been written in Canada.

Q: Why is that?

A: Had I lived in the U.S.A. the hegemonic weight of African American culture would have been so great that I would have had a great deal of difficulty—I doubt whether I would have been able to do it—speaking about the Caribbean—the wound that is the Caribbean. And had I lived in England, there would have been similar constraints of empire and its legacy—the Commonwealth. Only the space that is Canada allowed me the room I needed to work these ideas through. That space at times felt like a black hole in which everything was in danger of collapsing in and on itself. Both the U.S. and England have a long history of engaging with African culture in some way. Canada didn't, despite settlements in southern Ontario and the Maritimes that date back to the War of Independence. The deep cultural insecurity of Canada militates against the inclusion of African cultural practices except as they may fit under the rubric of multiculturalism. And the mantra of multiculturalism is repeated so often as to convince you of its talismanic properties. It is but a thin veneer which barely conceals a society as steeped in white supremacy as it is in hypocritical protestations to the contrary.

Having said that, however, the work is taught in some institutions and for that I am happy. As I said before, to erase the body is to erase the memory, and while this particular Black body is here in this white space called Canada, there is a memory.

CODA : The Potentiality of Space

I am particularly interested in my closing comments in the interview that explore the intersection of geography, race, memory, history and literature. The idea that what I call "the space that is Canada," albeit existing within a colonial paradigm, offered the potential for a certain kind of creativity and innovation that would have been more difficult, if not impossible, to achieve in other colonial or imperial spaces such as the U.S. or the U.K. I had earlier said in the interview—"what happened…is happening, happened within the spaces between words, between clotted clumps of words…" Is there perhaps a parallel between what is happening in a work like *Zong!* that works with breath and space, and about which I have said that the most important things happening in that poem are happening in the spaces between the words and word clusters. The space that is Canada is framed by a history of colonialism and racism against the First Nations, African-descended people, the Japanese, the Chinese and South Asians, to name some of the more egregious examples. It is provocative that such a framed space has allowed for works like *She Tries, Looking for Livingstone* and *Zong!* to be produced. This is less about the nature of the work or about Canada being a wonderful multicultural haven that we have been "lucky" enough to be let into. That so-called luck has been very expensive for Indigenous people; rather it is about the fact that the space that is Canada is the sine qua non of the work being produced, although it is not about Canada but rather about a larger history. Empire, colonialism, and racism work like the words on the page framing, or parenthesizing a space within which something life-fulfilling can take place. Like the mother in *She Tries*, blowing words—words of love, loss, history, and be/longing—into the space of her daughter's mouth.

NOTES

1   Rhonda Cobham, "Women of the Islands," *The Women's Review of Books*, Vol. VII, Nos. 10–11 (July 1990), 29.

2   M. NourbeSe Philip, *She Tries Her Tongue; Her Silence Softly Breaks* (Charlottetown, PEI: Ragweed Press, 1998 and The Women's Press, 1993, and currently reprinted by Wesleyan University Press, Middletown, CT, 2015).

3   Rastafarian language and speech contain many examples of unusual orthography and refashion words to reflect a certain worldview. For instance, instead of *oppressed*, they used *downpressed* and instead of *system*, they use *shitstem*. For work in this area, please see the work of Velma Pollard.

4   At the end of the sixteenth century Queen Elizabeth I and Ahmad al-Mansur, Sultan of Morocco, formed an alliance against King Philip II of Spain. The Sultan offered to assist the English in the Caribbean against the Spanish by sending troops to the area. Before plans for this expedition could be executed, Queen Elizabeth died in 1603. History might have been very different if Morocco had become one of the imperial powers of the Caribbean.

5   This idea of indigestibility is similar to Glissant's idea in *Poetics of Relation* in which he argues for a right to opacity.

6   M. NourbeSe Philip, *Looking for Livingstone: An Odyssey of Silence* (Stratford, ON: Mercury Press, 1991).

A LONG-MEMORIED WOMAN

In November, 1985, an amnesiac turned up in Italy; he believed himself Canadian, and evidence for his belief, the *Toronto Star* reported, lay in what he remembered—three names: Joe Clark, Brian Mulroney and Pierre Trudeau. Three men; three whites; three politicians. I remember laughing—not at the amnesiac—but at the detritus of his memory and at the savage workings of the unconscious. What if David (he believed this was his name), the amnesiac, had remembered three women—*any* three women would do—Jeanne Sauvé, Flora MacDonald or dear Mila Mulroney. Or what if he had remembered Louis Riel, or Mary Ann Shadd, the first African Canadian journalist in Ontario, or even the word *Haida*, or Grassy Narrows? Had I read too much into what this man remembered, and should any more significance be attached to the residue of memory, other than the possibility that he may have, shortly prior to losing his memory, read a newspaper article mentioning these three men?

I chose to see significance in what David remembered: it identified him and put him in context. I chose also to draw an analogy between the loss of his memory, what was left, and the attempted erasure of the memories of the Africans brought as slaves to the New World. In the latter case, what was left would also be of significance.

The policy of all slave-holding nations was to wipe clean the mind of the African slave; how else prevent rebellion, ensure passive workers and guarantee good Christians? The effect of this policy was the separation, wherever possible, of African slaves from others of the same linguistic groups. Slave-owners prohibited and punished the expression of African culture, language, music, religion, or dress, thereby denying any validity to the African worldview. Whatever remained of this process must, I believe, be inestimably precious and significant; as in the case of the amnesiac, it identifies and places in context the descendants of those first Africans in the New World. "They had," Katharine Dunham says of them, "an inborn intelligence to know if they kept up their tribal movements and rituals they would be saving themselves."[1]

In the course of writing a long poem recently, I listed some of the reasons why I consciously try to remember what did not happen to me personally, but which accounts for my being here today: to defy a culture that wishes to forget; to rewrite a history that at best forgot and omitted, at worst lied; to seek psychic reparations; to honour those who went before; to grieve for that which was irrevocably lost (language, religion, culture), and those for whom no one grieved; to avoid having to start over again (as so many oppressed groups have had to do); to "save ourselves." In making the list (by no means exhaustive), I found that even the mere determination to remember can, at times, be a revolutionary act—like the slave who refused to forget his or her rituals, or music, or whose body refused to forget the dance. All these acts of remembrance are, I believe, in the service of saving ourselves; as well, they replenish the scanty fund of memory we Africans in the West were left with, but which identified us, as indisputably as David's memory did.

Too many on both sides of the journey and the problem have forgotten the fifteen million that perished in the Middle Passage; too many are even more eager to forget the millions who continue to live marginalized lives because of that journey. (There is *The Cosby Show* after all.)[2] Far too many exhibit the social amnesia which, as Russell Jacoby argues in his work by the same name, results when the "vital relationship between mind and memory turns malignant; oblivion and novelty feed off each other and flourish."[3]

Some events, however, help to stimulate the memory: the revolution taking place within South Africa being just such an event. I can but only imagine the life of the Black South African in Soweto or Cross Roads, Jamaica, but I remember; I remember what I do not know and have never lived, whenever I read of the death of yet another Black in South Africa; and when I witness the obscene contortions of the white Western powers over the imposition of sanctions, and their fundamental refusal to act in any meaningful way, I remember; I remember that the slave trade only came to an end when it was no longer economically feasible for the slave-owning, slave-trading nations; I remember the Wilberforces and the many others who, like those who condemn South Africa today, saw the appalling immorality of the trade in Black humans, and I remember that their platforms only gained credence when those nations—France, England, Spain, the

United States—many of the same ones who today refuse to impose sanctions, saw that the continuance of the trade meant economic suicide.

I remember. And I believe that only when apartheid becomes too expensive for the West, will the latter become unequivocal in its condemnation and willingness to act. I remember and believe that most Africans of the New and Old Worlds—even those who think they have left the struggle a long way behind—remember. In remembering, I hope they see the continuum that stretches from the West across the Atlantic, across the centuries to South Africa, and those early Africans who came west—unwillingly. It is probably the greatest honour we pay the millions who died on that journey, as well as those who died on land, to remember.

Deep in my soul I remember; *je me souviens*; "i is a long-memoried woman."[4]

CODA: Memory Makes Matter
(written in the wake of Charlottesville, August 2017)

Make America Great Again!—the mantra of those who consider themselves Trump supporters. I call them MAGAites, a neologism that captures the Biblical fervour of their convictions of hate. At the heart of that phrase is a memory, which many, myself included, would say is a false memory, or perhaps in keeping with the times—a fake memory—the memory of the American dream, which for many around the world, and in America, has been a nightmare. That American dream has rested squarely on the destruction of the Indigenous people and the theft of their lands and on the enslavement, terror, racism and persecution of African-descended people.

The memories of the MAGAites is aided by historical evidence of how well white supremacy has worked for white-skinned peoples over Indigenous people, African Americans and other peoples of colour. Against that history, the memories of the victims and the done-to appear so frail at times. I myself have witnessed in the half-a-century I have been in Canada how easily the memories of our own struggles in this city go missing, so that the younger generation, enabled with Facebook and Twitter, believe themselves to be the initiators of a centuries-long struggle. Often in contestation with history, memory has a poetics that history lacks, appearing to reside in our bodies and not solely in the mind. Occupying a special place in our psyches, the weight of memories we accrue appears to impact us physically and some days I carry the weight of my own memories lightly; on other days, particularly when the passage of time seems not to have resulted in much progress, I feel their weight—personal, familial, social, political, historical, genetic and even of the body.

We may live in a highly literate, technocratic society, but we need our memory keepers more than ever. We are, indeed, our memories: as I write in my poem "Universal Grammar":[5] when the smallest cell remembers / how do you / how can you / when the smallest cell remembers / lose a language?"

NOTES

1   From the film *Divine Drumbeats: Katherine Dunham and her people*, in which Katherine Dunham, African American anthropologist and dancer, records her involvement with and study of Haitian dance and religion. Katherine Dunham, James Earl Jones, Norman Davis, Doris Bennett, Pearl Reynolds, Emilio Lastarria, Vanoye Aikens, et al., *Divine Drumbeats: Katherine Dunham and her people* (New York: WNET, 1980).

2   At the time this essay was written, *The Cosby Show*, which aired on NBC from September 20, 1984, until April 30, 1992, was a phenomenon and a first for African Americans. Unfortunately, Bill Cosby's sexually predatory behaviour has undercut all of his accomplishments.

3   Russell Jacoby, *Social AmnesiA: A Critique of Contemporary Psychology* (New Brunswick, NJ: Transaction Press, 1995), 151.

4   The chapter title and this final quotation are from the title and epigraph to the book *i is a long memoried woman* by English Caribbean poet Grace Nichols. Grace Nichols, *i is a long memoried woman* (London: Karnak House, 1983), 4.

5   Universal Grammar appears in *She Tries Her Tongue, Her Silence Softly Breaks*.

WHO'S LISTENING? ARTISTS, AUDIENCES & LANGUAGE

> If no one listens and cries
> is it still poetry
> if no one sings the note
> between the silence
> if the voice doesn't founder
> on the edge of the air
> is it still music
> if there is no one to hear
> is it love
> or does the sea always roar
> in the shell at the ear?[1]

Male, white, and Oxford-educated, he stands over my right shoulder; she is old, Black and wise and stands over my left shoulder—two archetypal figures symbolizing the two traditions that permeate my work. He—we shall call him John-from-Sussex—represents the white colonial tradition, the substance of any colonial education. Abiswa, as we shall call the other figure, represents the African Caribbean context which, as typical of any colonial education, was ignored. She is also representative of a certain collective race memory of the African.

Neither of these archetypes individually represents what I would call my ideal listener or audience. John-from-Sussex has always represented his standards as universal, but they all—with the exception of excellence which knows no race, class or gender—bore the trademark "Made in Britain." Abiswa, through an artificially imposed ignorance which I have tried to correct, I know too little of. To partake in her wisdom requires a different process from the one learnt from John-from-Sussex, demanding that one trust the body which, together with the mind, forms one intelligence. This was not what John-from-Sussex was about.

There has been a recent shift—since the completion of two manuscripts of poetry[2]—in my positioning of this audience of two: John-from-Sussex has become less substantial, more of an apparition; Abiswa has emerged even more clearly from the shadows. Bridging the split that these two archetypes represent is a difficult process: each represents what the other is not—each is, so to speak, the other's Other. A dialogue between the two is essential.

All of this may seem an unusual introduction to the issue of audience, but since I believe that each artist (*artist* here and throughout this piece is used inclusively to refer to all disciplines) has an ideal audience—made up of one or several individuals—lurking somewhere in her psyche, it seemed appropriate. These "ideal" audiences have some bearing on the real audience the artist and/or her work seeks or finds.

If we take the example given above, for instance, both John-from-Sussex and Abiswa have some rooting in a certain reality which faces me whenever I write—the need to make choices around language and place, both of which inevitably impact on audience. If I use John-from-Sussex's language, will Abiswa and her audience understand and vice versa? Which is the more important audience? Which do I value most and from what perspective? Will Abiswa even care to understand a piece such as this? One audience may have more economic clout than others, and one, certainly in my case, offers me a more profound emotional and psychic satisfaction. And some may ask: Why choose at all? Why the need to have to choose any audience?

Unless the writer creates only for herself, there comes a time when she must become aware, however vaguely, that there exists such an animal as an audience. It may only be an awareness that operates at a very basic level of trying to determine who will come out to a poetry reading, installation or display, or who will buy books, but it begins to make itself felt. And often the artist may only be aware of who her audience is not—often more predictable than who it is.

Audience is a complex and difficult issue for any artist, particularly in today's world, where any sense of continuity and community seems so difficult to develop. It becomes even more complex for the artist in exile—working in a country not her own, developing an audience among people who are essentially strangers to all the traditions and continuities that helped produce her. Scourges such as racism and sexism can also create a profound sense of alienation, resulting in what can best be described as psychic exile, even among those artists who are not in physical exile. The Canadian-born Black artist, artist of colour, or the white lesbian artist, for example, all face dilemmas over audience similar to that of the artist who has more recently—relatively speaking—arrived in this country.

It is as well to note that legal citizenship in no way affects the profound and persistent alienation within a society at best indifferent, if not hostile, to the artist's origins, her work, and her being. Many of us, no matter how old our citizenship, remain immigrants in a profoundly psychic sense. Some of us, recognizing this, choose to emphasize that alienation—it appearing a more positive position. This choice, however, results in all sorts of contradictions when it comes to funding and meeting funding requirements. Where the immigrant worker is required to have Canadian experience, the immigrant artist must show the Canadian component in her work to qualify for funding.

Even for those who have managed to adapt to Canada, there still remains the fact that much of their work will continue to draw on the imagery, rhythms, and emotional resources developed in their countries of origin. In conversation, this was how an Australian artist described the issue for her: "As an artist you use certain reference points which have a bearing in a different geographic location—unless the viewer knows what these reference points are, there is no comprehension beyond organization of the work in terms of shape, form and colour." A more blatant example of this problem lies in the different sense of colour that countries have. A Jamaican artist described to me how her colours became more muted and sombre when she painted here in Canada.

Which Canada do I speak of—the West or the East? Urban or rural Canada? These are important questions since most immigrants come to the large metropolitan areas, which is where many artists attempt to carve out a niche, however uncomfortable, for themselves. My experience is with the urban East—Toronto, to be more specific—and is that of a Black, female writer. I do not pretend to speak for all of Canada, and only the audience of this piece will be able to judge whether my experience may be easily transferable.

I cannot and do not intend to provide any definitive answers on the issue of audience for those in exile (by exile I mean not only those of us who have physically come to this country, but the many, many others who count themselves in exile for any number of reasons in this society). I don't think there are any definitive answers, and I am not even sure whether the questions I pose are the right ones for anyone else but myself. What I want to do, however, is raise the issues and questions, reveal the contradictions as they have affected me and others like myself, and see where, if anywhere, they take us. More than anything else, what follows is a meditation on the issues of audience.

RECEPTION, RESPONSE, COMPLETION

One of the most important impulses in all art is, I believe, the impulse to communicate; this in turn depends on reception and response for completion of the work in question. The late Raymond Williams, the Marxist critic, wrote as follows: "[I]n the case of art, where simple consumption is not in question, no work is in any full practical sense produced until it is also received."[3] How, then, is work from communities that appear marginal to the mainstream, with what Williams so aptly describes as their "emergent energies," completed—that is, received and responded to, both by audiences of the more dominant culture, as well as audiences that comprise the artist's natural community? A few examples will best highlight this dilemma.

The Rez Sisters.[4] I saw this play several months ago among a predominantly, if not completely, white audience. Everyone appeared to enjoy the play tremendously, yet I was uncomfortable. Uncomfortable because, although I was convinced that what I was watching was an authentic and successful attempt to portray one aspect of First Nations life on the reservation, I felt that the audience, which was, in fact, a settler audience, was being let off too easily. I felt that they could—I am sure they did—leave the theatre feeling that "reservation life wasn't so bad after all." Those who were feminist could comfort themselves with the remarkable strength of the women. I was equally convinced that an Indigenous audience would complete that play in a very different way—they could and would be able to contextualize much more completely the events that played themselves out on the stage. They would not leave the theatre as comfortably, or as comforted, as did the white audience.

So too with *The Colored Museum*,[5] which also played to full houses of predominantly white people. Here was a powerful, painful, and at times funny collage of Black American life over the centuries. There were many scenes that were "funny," which I laughed at, my laughter always tinged with the pain represented in those opening scenes on the slave plane—a pain that circumscribes my history. Why were *they*, the white audience, laughing, though? Were they laughing at the *same* things I was laughing at, and if their laughter lacked the same admixture of pain, was it laughter which, having been bought too cheaply, came too easily? Were they, therefore, laughing at me and not with me?

These are but two examples. There are several others that elaborate the same issue; they raise complex issues around marketing and audience. *The Colored Museum*, for instance, was never advertised in the Black newspapers, which is where many Black people get their information about activities of interest and relevance to them. Tarragon Theatre, however, did not need to advertise in the Black press to fill its house. Do they, indeed, have an onus to do so when they are staging Black works or works that relate specifically to a particular group in society? *The Rez Sisters* played first at the Native Canadian Centre of Toronto on Spadina, then returned for a run at a more mainstream theatre.

These examples raise issues applicable to all disciplines of art—even music, which appears to be the discipline that most easily crosses cultural barriers. The lyrics and music of the late Bob Marley were wrought and wrested out of the unrelenting poverty and grimness of the Trenchtown ghetto; he sang of better times for Black people, when "Babylon" would be no more. How many North Americans who "grooved" on his music cared to understand this or even cared?

It is a truism that we each complete a novel, play, poem or painting differently, depending on factors as diverse as age, gender, class, and culture. What concerns me is the ever-present danger that a white mainstream audience in Toronto is likely to come away from a play like *The Rez Sisters* or *The Colored Museum* with none of their stereotypes shaken or disturbed, which is not necessarily the fault of the playwright. He or she may have written the play in question with an Indigenous or Black audience in mind.

Can you ever have a valid completion of a work by an audience that is a stranger to the traditions that underpin the work? This question leads us back to that dichotomy between dominant and subdominant cultures—the old "mainstream versus margin" argument. The significance of this dichotomy lies in the fact that those of us who belong to those subdominant groups—women, Africans, peoples of the formerly colonized world—have been rigorously schooled in the traditions of the dominant cultures—European and patriarchal. This experience, along with the fact that we are constantly immersed in the dominant culture of the world—still patriarchal and now American—makes it much more possible for us to receive and respond to work from these cultures than it is or ever has been in the reverse. We are, at times, even better able to understand and respond more positively to works from the dominant culture than we do to work coming out of our own traditions—such is the pernicious effect of racism, sexism and colonialism. Could we, however, argue that education offers one solution to this problem? Possibly, but we would do well to remember that the education of colonized peoples—I include women in this group—has traditionally been closer to brainwashing than to education.

EXOTICA/NOSTALGIA

Those of us from hot, moist parts of the world (sex-positive cultures, as I have recently seen them described), who work in traditions originating in our countries of origin, face the ever-present danger that our work may be considered and categorized as "different" or "exotic." Not understanding the tradition and standards, the audience, including critics and reviewers, suspend the practice of criticism, replacing it with meaningless adjectives like "great" or "wonderful."

Another kind of reception and response is best illuminated by the following excerpt from a review of an anthology, *Other Voices: Writings by Blacks in Canada*, edited by Lorris Elliott:

European literature has benefited from Black writers such as Aesop, Pushkin and Dumas. American culture has incorporated the voices of Langston Hughes, Gwendolyn Brooks, Alice Walker, Marge Piercy, or Imamu Amiri Baraka (LeRoi Jones). But Canadian Blacks, like Canadian whites, still do not know if they are coming or going with their identity problems. *Other Voices: Writings by Blacks in Canada*, edited by Lorris Elliott, is a collection of poetry, prose, and drama without any direction beyond herd instinct.

The very word "other" in the title is a dim bulb in regard to visible minorities. It cues the reader (Black, white or other) to expect stereotypes. That is exactly what follows. "Nigger," "fight," "pain," "passion," "cause," "rage," "tears": the language falls predictably flat—though the suffering motivating the outpourings is very real. A few entries break though the barrier of boredom to move a heart and mind willing to open this anthology, which could have been an important book.[6]

Apart from revealing a profound ignorance—writers like Pushkin and Dumas did not write as Black men, but as Europeans, and to parallel their experiences with that of American Black writers serves neither experience well—the quotation reveals the latent racism always at work in Canada. By attempting to parallel the experience of Canadian whites and Blacks, the reviewer seeks to dissemble his racism: "Canadian Blacks, like Canadian whites, still don't know if they are coming or going with their identity problem." He exculpates, under the guise of "objective criticism," the white Canadian audience, including critics and reviewers like himself, for their massive failure to understand the history and traditions of racism that would give rise to the use of words like *nigger*, *fight*, and *pain*.

What is, however, even more instructive of the issues I raise in this section, is the imagery the reviewer approved of and selected to quote as examples of the better work appearing the anthology: from "Market in the Tropics," "Mangoes / Tamarinds / ...wild meat on hooks,"[7] and from "The Profile of Africa" which "expresses the sensuous beauty of blackness" [*sic*], "the beautiful, strong, exotic in profile / flowering lips / silhouette obsidian planes..."[8] These poems may very well have been the better ones (not having read them, I make no comment on them here), but it is, in my opinion, no accident that these are the poems and the imagery that the reviewer believes "save the volume from being another boohoo job." The sensuous beauty of Blackness—I could write volumes on this subject—is a far more appealing image for most whites than an angry Black man or woman. While I acknowledge that writing about one's anger and pain without appearing to descend into rhetoric, polemic, and cant is difficult, to dismiss the work of writers attempting to bring a long tradition of struggle against racism into literature as another "boohoo job" is racist in the extreme.

Ignorance and laziness. These are the qualities at the heart of both kinds of responses described above—the overeager response reserved for anything in the slightest bit different or appearing exotic, or dismissal. The welcome change in the picture comes from the attempts now being made by feminist critics, some of whom have finally begun to assess critically the works of women from other traditions.

The nostalgia factor presents another conundrum for the artist in exile—particularly those, like immigrants, in physical exile. The "natural" audience for such an artist is the audience from "back home." So starved is this audience for anything remotely evocative of "home," that it accepts uncritically whatever is reminiscent of it. This is what I mean by the nostalgia factor.

The need to maintain continuity and traditions is a powerful one with all groups; it is a need which is assuaged in the articulation of many mainstream art forms—the ballet, opera, Shakespearean drama. The more newly arrived (relatively speaking) are not the only ones who indulge in nostalgia.

There is, however, a danger for the artist—the danger of falling into complacency. In my case, for instance, coming from the Caribbean, where the use of demotic variants of English (dialect) is widespread, use of dialect is an immediate entry into the hearts and minds of a Caribbean audience. In such a context, the audience is less concerned with what the artist is doing with his or her discipline, provided the need to be reminded of "how it stay" back home is met. If the artist is content with this response, then a sort of stasis results which is fatal to any growth on her part. But audience response in this context is powerful, seductive *and* difficult to turn one's back on for the less tangible, less certain rewards of "growth" or "practising one's art seriously." I do not suggest that the last two goals are incompatible with a strong audience response—they should not be—but they often mean the audience has to do some work as well, and nostalgia appears far more compatible with entertainment rather than with art.

AUDIENCE AND LANGUAGE

The choice facing a writer from Eastern Europe or Italy or Latin America is a stark one: work in your mother tongue and—at least in Canada—be restricted to an audience sharing a similar linguistic heritage, or work in English with the potential of a much wider audience—minus your natural audience.

For the writer from the English or French Caribbean, the two official languages of Canada are also their languages. English is "theoretically" as much my mother tongue as it is for a writer from London, Ontario. But we know differently, and my experience with English encompasses a very different experience from that of the English-speaking Canadian. Like the writer from Eastern Europe, we too have a nation language (dialect) which is, however, a variant of English.

The choice of language for the Caribbean writer can, therefore, be as stark as that outlined in the first paragraph of this section. If you work entirely in nation language or the Caribbean demotic of English, you do, to a large degree, restrict your audience to those familiar enough with it; if you move to standard English, you lose much of that audience and, along with that loss, an understanding of many of the traditions, history and culture which contextualize your work.

Language has been and remains—as the South African example shows—a significant and essential part of the colonization process; the choice between Caribbean demotic and standard English becomes, therefore, more than choice of audience. It is a choice which often affects the choice of subject matter, the rhythms of thought patterns, and the tension within the work. It is also a choice resonant with historical and political realities *and* possibilities.

In writing correct sentences, ending words with "ing" instead of "in," making my verbs agree with their subjects, I am choosing a certain tradition—that of John-from-Sussex. My audience, for the most part, is going to be a white audience, and possibly an educated Black Caribbean audience. However, in order to keep faith with Abiswa, I must, within my writing self, constantly subvert the tradition of John-from-Sussex. This doesn't necessarily enlarge my audience to include the less formally educated speakers of nation language—on the contrary, it probably reduces that segment of the audience, since the work becomes more "difficult." It does, however, I hope, leave whatever audience there is less complacent and less comfortable with things as they appear to be.

COMMUNITY, AUDIENCE, MARKET

Raymond Williams writes that:

[O]ur way of seeing things is literally our way of living, the process of communication is in fact the process of community: the sharing of common meanings, and thence common activities and purposes; the offering, reception and comparison of new meanings, leading to the tensions and achievements of growth and change.[9]

Toronto is a city of many communities which individually meet the above description; these communities do not, however, make up a larger community—particularly in the arts where there is undeniably a dominant culture—"a central system of practices, meaning and values."[10]

The artist has always been sustained by community even if it was a community he or she rebelled against. Within traditional societies there was, and is, a constant dialogue between audience and artist. When, for instance, the African "commissioned" a piece of sculpture from a village sculptor (usually for spiritual reasons), he or she had a very clear idea as to what satisfied them and what was a good piece of sculpture: they exercised aesthetic judgments. So too in European cultures where the artist was in dialogue with the community in terms of its traditions, they shared or understood values, even if the understanding was but the first step to rejection.

Within the larger grouping of community, then, the artist may find her audience where she could find a "hearing" and with which she might be in some form of dialogue.

"Market" on the other hand suggests a role for art as a commodity, with all the trappings of that representation we have come to expect—manipulation of the market; selling the product—art—as investment and/or fashion.

There is a certain connectedness between these three apparently disparate groupings—audience, community, market—at the centre of which is the artist. Bringing them together raises certain contradictions. Is, for instance, audience synonymous with market? Can you have an audience but lack a market? To answer that last question: as a Black writer, I may have an audience for a novel about Black people—that audience being those Black people who are eager to read about themselves, as well as a growing number of whites who have begun to come to the understanding that other worlds apart from theirs exist. It is, however, clearly the opinion of publishers in Canada that there is no market for books about Black people: they believe that whites are not interested and that Blacks either do not, or are unable to, buy books. Therefore, there is no market for books about Black people. Despite the audience I may have, the perceived market forces, interpreted with a sizable dollop of racist arguments, supersede.

That a popular art form—dub poetry—has been able to widen the audience for its poetry is, I believe, because of the welding of the Black oral and musical traditions. The strongest African art form to survive outside Africa among its scattered peoples has been its music; it has been the most pervasive and persistent. In the case of the dub poets like Linton Kwesi Johnson, one of the first proponents of this style, the poetry was written in the Jamaican demotic—patois or creole—and underscored with reggae rhythms. Canadian dub poets, also using a demotic variant of English, have not restricted themselves to these rhythms, but use a variety of others. They are essentially protest poets working in the powerful oral and musical traditions of Abiswa.

The crossover mechanism between Black and white audiences in dub has been the music. Music serves the function of drawing those audiences who would rather be dead than caught at a high-art gathering—the poetry reading. And whether white audiences "get" the same message Blacks do from dub is not known. (In some instances, the language *must* present a barrier to complete understanding.)

That white audiences "get" something from dub is clear—one only has to look at the audiences that attend various events to know that, which may mean that the question is irrelevant. But not necessarily so, since the artist's audience does provide some challenge to the artist, if only in terms of expectations. That audiences often have a tendency to want only more of what pleased them before cannot be denied. The dub poet *may*, therefore, have to make decisions as to which traditions to emphasize—the one more familiar to Black audiences, or those with which white audiences are more comfortable. I have not discussed this particular issue with any dub poets, and it may all be irrelevant to them—as an observer and writer, however, the issues present a challenge.

To say that the average size of the traditional poetry audience is small—I have counted as many as ten bodies at some of mine—is an understatement. The audience for dub poetry has increased this average substantially, although it is still not a mass audience here in Canada—in that respect, rock and rap still reign supreme.

An artist with a market has little need for community. The reverse, however, is not as assured—the artist with both community and audience but no market will, undoubtedly, starve, unless someone supports her. The market, with its forces, can be a positive factor, provided it underpins the forces created by audience and community. The market becomes a negative force when it replaces or obliterates audience and community or, even more dangerously, determines "our way of seeing things" and replaces the "process of community: the sharing of common meanings, and thence common activities and purposes" with the process of commodification.

THE AUDIENCE ON THE MARGIN

As mentioned above, Toronto is a city of communities alongside the dominant Anglo-Saxon culture. Many of these communities share very little with each other except residence in the same city. Many would describe these communities as marginal to the dominant one. I have great difficulty with the concept of marginality as it is ordinarily articulated: it suggests a relationship with the dominant culture in which the marginal is considered inferior, and implies that the marginal wishes to lose its quality of marginality and be eventually absorbed by the more dominant culture.

Margin, however, has another meaning which I prefer to hold uppermost in my mind when I work as a member of two groups—Blacks and women—traditionally described as marginal. That meaning is "frontier." Surely this meaning is encapsulated in Stuart Hall's phrase, "emergent energies and experiences which stubbornly resist" the dominant culture.[11] The concept of frontier changes our perception of ourselves and the so-called mainstream. All of which is not to deny that there is a dominant culture, with a "central system of practices, meanings and values" (Williams). And this culture receives by far the lion's share of funding and government support. However, exploiting the other meaning of margin offers another perspective, one which challenges the old, lazy ways of thinking by which we have colluded in our own management. To twist the aphorism somewhat—marginality is in the eye of the beholder.

Many of these communities on the frontier are communities under stress. In the case of the Black community, for instance, there is always the issue of racism, as well as issues flowing from economic depression within the community. Artists with audiences within such communities often become spokespersons for the community—this is an activity very much in keeping with the role of the poet in African cultures where he (traditionally) was the voice of the community. In our more contemporary situation, the issues are many and complex: Should the artist take the audience as she finds it and reflect its views and demands, or is there an obligation on the artist's part to change the audience? Is the artist sharing with or challenging the audience, or both? And what of the Canadian audience—does the artist from the community on the margin/frontier have an obligation to teach such an audience that their practices may be negatively affecting other communities? Does culture change political realities any?

In South Africa, events have rendered many of these questions irrelevant; there, the African dramatist, poet, novelist, painter have all been drafted into the struggle—willingly or otherwise. Njabulo S. Ndebele, the South African writer, writes:

> The matter is simple: there is a difference between art that "sells" ideas to people, and art whose ideas are embraced by the people, because they have been made to understand them through the evocation of lived experiences in all its complexities. In the former case, the readers are anonymous buyers; in the latter they are equals in the quest for truth.[12]

These opinions offer one way of approaching the issues raised in the previous paragraph.

FEMINISM AND AUDIENCE

> Cut off from his natural audience Argueta has to imagine a public for himself, and is unsure how much he can take for granted at either the linguistic or the cultural level.
>
> The "pitfall" for the writer is that of becoming over-simple or over-didactic, as the writer strives to inform a foreign audience how things are in his country rather than being able to *share with them feelings about experiences that have a common base* [my emphasis].[13]

In many respects this quotation encapsulates the issues I have attempted to explore in this piece. I stress the last phrase both because it harked back to the opinions expressed by Williams and Ndebele, and because it provides me with an entry into the issue of feminism and audience.

There is much that I find to criticize in the articulation of Western liberal feminism: the movement has become racist and classist in its practices, although there have been some tiny tremors and even some cracks along fault lines. This is not to suggest that the movement is monolithic—quite the contrary; but its diversity and variety may be its weakness as well as its strength. It is, however, a movement which has the potential, often unrealized, to bridge some of those gaps—race and class, for example—isolating communities and audiences. It could, in some instances, promote that "common base" through which experiences might be shared.

The common base for women is a shared history of oppression in all its varieties and forms, as well as, I hope, a shared commitment to establishing communities organized along non-patriarchal, woman-centred, non-racist principles. While wishing to avoid reductionist arguments, as well as those body-centred theories which become at times tiresome, we must acknowledge that a basic common denominator of female experience—in all cultures and in all classes—has been the fact that our bodies have achieved a universal negative significance: bodies which have become palimpsests upon which men have inscribed and reinscribed their texts.

Feminism alone, however, is not the answer: we can hardly afford to jettison theories of class analysis. With modification and development in the face of change, they continue to offer indispensable insight into the arrangements of society; we need to continue to hone our arguments and analyses of the powerful workings of racism. While it is not *the* answer, feminism could make important and significant contributions to helping to resolve some of these issues—Black and white men, for instance, are certainly not talking to each other about race and class—or anything, for that matter.

Feminist communities are in many cases ad hoc, but there *is* a feminist audience and market. Thoughts of the recent Montreal Book Fair come to mind. It is a market which differs in some degree from the traditional mainstream market. It is not, in the words of Ndebele, a market selling ideas to the people but one trying to evoke the lived experiences of women. It is a market which is still plagued by racism and classism, but it is a market which has grown out of a need on the part of women to know about their selves, their histories and their futures; a need to communicate about feelings and experiences that have a *common* vis-à-vis the *same* base; as well as the need to find out about other women.

We are a long way from a true feminist community, and even further away from a true feminist culture—one that would not, as it has tended to do, emphasize one aspect (the white and middle class) of that culture, but a culture in which the word *feminist* is enlarged to include those groups which have, to date, been excluded. When that is accomplished—the establishment of a true feminist culture—we shall be a long way toward having audiences who are able to complete in more authentic ways the works of artists *whatever* their background.

Working in Canada as an Afrosporic writer, I am very aware of the absence of a tradition of Black writing as it exists in England or the U.S.

The great Canadian void either swallows you whole or you come out the other side the stronger for it. The Black writers here are, in fact, creating a tradition which will be different from both the English and American traditions of writing and literature by Black writers. Being the trailblazer for other writers to follow has been overwhelmingly difficult and daunting, for it has often appeared that there is nothing out there. Which was an accurate observation—for a long time there *was* nothing out there. As one dub poet described it, he felt responsible for everything—not only did he create the work, but he published *and* marketed it, while simultaneously developing an audience for it.

All artists working in the tradition of Abiswa have felt this burden— even those Black artists working more closely within the tradition of John- from-Sussex have felt it. But there are changes—the audience for newer genres like dub and hip hop are growing not only among Black people, but also among whites. These are two forms in which Abiswa's heritage can be most clearly seen and strongly felt. Subversion of the old order—which, in fact, was not order but chaos masquerading as order—and of the new, old order is alive and well in Abiswa's hands—in our art, writing and music. And there *is* an audience for it.

In keeping faith with Abiswa, we find that many from John-from- Sussexes' audiences are deserting in droves to seek the wisdom and vitality of the former. If revenge is what is called for, this may be the best revenge; it is also a way of reconciliation between these two traditions. It is the audi- ence which helps to mediate this process.

CODA: Listening to Abiswa and Growing Griots

Since this essay was published, there have been quite a few African Canadian writers who have been published by mainstream presses and have gone on to win high-prestige awards such as the Giller. All the arts councils have instituted changes to address the exclusion of Black artists, although I can- not comment on how successful these initiatives have been in practice. As immigration from the Caribbean declines, issues of writing in the vernac- ular or patwa also seem to recede as an issue. The children of earlier immi- grants from the Caribbean are now fluent in their demotics, be it French creole, Jamaican or Tobagonian patwa and standard Canadian English or French.

Winning prizes is always wonderful for the writer or artist; however the awards, no matter how well deserved, tend to hide the fact that in African Canadian communities the culture of writing and publishing is still very shallow. In other words, the prize winners are not the pinnacle, albeit for the moment, of a solid body of writers of different capacities and strengths that any writing tradition should have.

When I wrote this essay there existed two and possibly three publishers here in Toronto in the eighties—Williams-Wallace Press and Sister Vision Press. There was also the collective Domestic Bliss that published dub poetry. I was fortunate to have my first and second collections of poetry, *Thorns* and *Salmon Courage*, published by Williams-Wallace. The mandate of WWP was to publish the work of Caribbean Canadian writers. Today, in 2017, there exist no Black-owned publishers here in Toronto or even in Canada, as far as my research has revealed. In the last decade at least, publishing has become a risky business even for mainstream publishers, so it is not surprising that small publishers with niche markets have been at greater risk.

Further, the high-profile issue of appropriation has tended to hide a more insidious problem—the continuing, overwhelmingly white composition of the publishing industry, notwithstanding the increase in the number of African Canadian writers being published. What this means is that work by African Canadian writers is continually filtered through a Euro-Canadian cultural paradigm. I am thinking of editing, proofreading, distribution and all the other tasks that are a part of producing a book in which African Canadians play very little part, and more so now that there are no Black publishing houses. One of the most effective ways to combat the challenge of appropriation is to create conditions that allow writers from silenced communities to come to voice and build the infrastructures of the various artistic disciplines. Offering paid mentorships in white-owned publishing houses, for instance, would be one way to start to build skills within the community, or funding workshops for African Canadians interested in editing with organizations like the Editors' Association of Canada.

Had Williams-Wallace not published my first two books of poetry, I might not have continued to write, since I published those when I was still practising law. It was their publication that affirmed my then very tentative belief that I might have something to say that someone somewhere might want to listen to; it gave me the courage to turn my back on John-from-Sussex, listen to Abiswa and leave the practice of law. He still hovers but I'm still listening to her, some times better than at others.

NOTES

1   M. Nourbese Philip, "Anonymous," *Salmon Courage* (Toronto: Williams-Wallace Publishers, 1983), 3.

2   M. NourbeSe Philip, *She Tries Her Tongue; Her Silence Softly Breaks* (Charlottetown, PEI: Ragweed Press, 1998). *She Tries Her Tongue* was awarded the 1988 Casa de las Américas Prize for poetry and was recently reprinted by Wesleyan University Press. M. NourbeSe Philip, *She Tries Her Tongue; Her Silence Softly Breaks* (Middletown, C.T.: Wesleyan University Press, 2015). The second book is: M. NourbeSe Philip, *Looking for Livingstone* (Stratford, ON: The Mercury Press, 1991).

3   Raymond Williams, "Culture," in *Marx: The First 100 Years*, ed. David McLellan (London: Fontana, 1983), 48.

4   Tomson Highway, *The Rez Sisters* (Saskatoon: Fifth House Ltd., 1988).

5   George C. Wolfe, *The Colored Museum* (New York: Grove Press, 1987).

6   Ray Filip, *Books in Canada*, October, 1987.

7   Theresa Lewis, "Market in the Tropics," in *Other Voices: Writings by Blacks in Canada*, ed. Lorris Elliott (Toronto: Williams-Wallace Publishers, 1985), 107.

8   Maxine Tynes, "The Profile of Africa," in *Other Voices: Writings by Blacks in Canada*, 163.

9   Raymond Williams, *The Long Revolution* (Peterborough, ON: Broadview Press, 2001), 55.

10   Raymond Williams, "Base and Superstructure in Marxist Cultural Theory," in *Culture and Materialism: Selected Essays* (London: Verso, 2005), 38.

11   "Stuart Hall Remembers Raymond Williams," *New Statesman* 115, No. 2967 (Feb. 5, 1988), 21. Hall is drawing on Williams's concept of "emergent energies."

12   Njabulo S. Ndebele, "Turkish Tales and Some Thoughts on South African Literature," *Staffrider* 6, No. 1, (1984), 45.

13   Nick Caistor, "'Cuzcatlán, by Manlio Argueta," *New Statesman* 114, No. 2959 (Dec. 11, 1987), 33.

THE DISAPPEARING DEBATE: OR, HOW THE DISCUSSION OF RACISM HAS BEEN TAKEN OVER BY THE CENSORSHIP ISSUE

Argument by the white middle class, for the white middle class, about the white middle class. Such was the long-winded, rather tedious debate that took place in last winter's newsletters of the Writers' Union of Canada, relating to issues of censorship and the writer and voice.[1] This debate had been sparked by the rejection of three short stories by the Women's Press for an anthology of short fiction, *Imagining Women*, on the grounds that the writers in question, all white, had drawn on and used the voices of characters from cultures and races other than their own. The Press also took issue with the use, by one of the writers, of magic realism, a style pioneered in Latin America. According to the Press, these practices constituted racism. To buttress this position, the Press issued policy guidelines stating that it would "avoid publishing manuscripts in which the protagonist's experience in the world, by virtue of race or ethnicity, is substantially removed from that of the writer."

As often happens around issues such as these, the debate quickly assumed a dichotomous nature with the pro-censorship forces arrayed against the anti-censorship hordes. Racism was the issue that detonated the explosion at the Women's Press; to the exclusion of any other, censorship became the issue that has monopolized the media's attention. Censorship of white writers; censorship of the imagination; censorship by publishers. Censorship in all its myriad forms became, in fact, *the* privileged discourse.

The quantum leap from racism to censorship is neither random nor unexpected, since the issue of censorship is central to the dominant cultures of liberal democracies like Canada. In these cultures, censorship becomes a significant and talismanic cultural icon around which all debates about the "individual freedom of *man*" swirl. It is the cultural and political barometer which these societies use to measure their freedoms. Censorship is as important to the state intent on imposing it as it is to those who are equally committed to opposing it.

Since writers and artists are, by and large, the ones who express the cultural ideas of their age, their individual and collective roles are crucial to the process that assigns significance to ideas such as censorship. Western liberal democracies, in fact, usually grade their relative freedoms and those of other countries according to the freedoms allowed these self-appointed purveyors of cultural representation. In turn, the latter come to share, in no small way, in the rewards of the system.

Historically, racism has never been assigned a central place in the West. As an issue, it has remained remarkably absent from debates on the economy, society or polity; racism, in fact, has never been as privileged a discourse as censorship. In more recent years, however, we have seen the privileging of certain types of racism—such as anti-Semitism—over others: one can easily gauge the degree of privileging by the nature and frequency of media attention or by government activity on the matter. Racism against Africans, however, remains a relatively unimportant issue, except in those instances when the latter are perceived as potential or real disruptors of the social fabric. One very effective way of ensuring that this type of racism remains marginal to the dominant culture is to have another issue that is more privileged, such as censorship or freedom of speech. Two recent examples of the privileging of censorship and freedom of speech over issues of race arose from the public lecture at the University of Toronto in 1987 by Glenn Babb, the South African consul, and the much-publicized theories of racial superiority by University of Western Ontario professor Philippe Rushton.

In the latter case, despite public outcry and opposition from students, despite widespread reports of his shoddy scholarship, and despite his recommendations that governments act on his findings, Rushton has been allowed to keep his position at the university and to continue teaching. All in the name of freedom of speech.

Furthermore, on those occasions when racism against Blacks does assume a more public profile, as happened in the last few months in Toronto after the shooting of a Black adolescent, it usually occurs in an aberrational context. Racism is thereby reduced to the level of the personal and presented as a rare form of disease which, if treated appropriately—usually with a task force—will quickly disappear. There is a profound failure, if not a refusal, to understand how thoroughly racism informs all aspects of society.

At the heart of this attitude lies a paradox: the ideology and practice of racism has as old a tradition as that of the "rights of man." While John Locke argued for the freedom of man, he had no intellectual difficulty accepting that these freedoms could not and should not extend to African slaves. The ideological framework of Western democracies, erected upon the belief in freedom of the individual, is supported as much by this ideology (and its offshoots) as by that of racism. However, one discourse, censorship, becomes privileged; the other, racism, is silenced. To insist on its lesser status, thereby excluding it from the dominant forms and fora of discussion, becomes one of the most effective ways of perpetuating racism. To do so is, in fact, profoundly racist.

Woman as Other constitutes one of the building blocks of the patriarchy; Black as Other, one of the building blocks of white supremacist ideologies. The white, male author has never flinched from representing women or Blacks in his writing, misogynist and/or racist point of view and all. While many of the classified "great works of literature" have been novelistic studies of women by men—*Anna Karenina*, *Madame Bovary* and *Tess of the d'Urbervilles*, to name but three—and while there have always been significant literary sorties into "exotic" cultures by writers—Kipling, Conrad and Forster come to mind—a quick survey of English literature reveals that works written from the point of view of the Other, Black, female or even working class, have not comprised a major part of that literature. In that respect, contemporary literature differs not at all.

The vociferousness, therefore, of the defence of this right—to write from the point of view of the Other—as we have witnessed it recently, is clearly disproportionate to the actual exercise of that right. Is it merely that this right is all of a piece with the rights accruing to a writer living and writing in a liberal democracy? Or does the impulse for the unquestioning defence of this right lie elsewhere?

Sara Maitland, the English novelist, writes, "Whether men can do women's stories is another question, one that feminist literary discourse asks often; but it is certain that the oppressed develop insights about their oppressors to a greater degree than the other way about because they need them in order to survive."[2] In virtually every sphere of life, women have had to learn what men want and don't want; what turns them on and what doesn't. Black people, in the course of their individual and collective history of labour, have been privy to what no outsider ought to be in another's life. As cleaners, servants and domestics, Blacks have known when or whether the white master was or wasn't fucking his wife (or anyone else, for that matter). Black women have suckled their white charges and, in many instances, provided the latter with emotional nourishment that, through exploitative economic practices, they have been unable to provide their own children. Consider, for example, the many, many foreign nannies caring for the children of white Canadians, while their own children remain at home in the Caribbean or the Philippines. As in the case of women, which Maitland so well identifies, to ensure their survival, Blacks have had to know what angry white people look like, and how to recognize when the latter were happy and when not. And today the media, for the most part in flagrant contempt for all but the dominant culture, continue to teach Blacks how their erstwhile masters look as they go about their lives.

It borders on the trite and hackneyed to say that writers tend to draw on what they know best as raw material for their work. "Write what you know" is one of the most consistent pieces of advice given to young writers. One would, therefore, assume that when writers from traditionally oppressed groups begin to come to voice publicly, knowing almost as much about their oppressors as they do about their own lives, they would write about their oppressors—at least as much as they write about themselves. Blacks about whites; the working class about the middle and upper classes; women about men. They have good reason to do so: they have, by their labour, earned the vision of the insider.

The paradox, however, is that once an oppressed group is finally able to attain the means of making its voice heard—voicing its many silences— it is far less concerned in rendering audible the voice of its oppressors, and infinitely more interested in (and committed to) making public their own reality and their own lives. The explosion in feminist publishing, for instance, has resulted in women writing and publishing their own stories, *about* themselves and *for* themselves. Men have not been entirely absent from these works, but neither has there been a demonstrated eagerness to write from the point of view of men. And so too for Blacks. What Black writers have wanted to voice is not the voice and experiences of the white person, but the reality of Black people *from the point of view* of Black people. Given the ubiquitous nature of racism, whites or their systems of domination must perforce figure, to a lesser or greater degree, in these works: their point of view will, however, not be privileged.

This paradox ought to give us pause, if nothing else, to wonder why the *ability* to use the voice of the Other, as we have come to know it in literature and art, has for the most part realized itself in the oppressor using the voice of the oppressed, and not the other way around. It is an ability that is first engendered, then supported by the interlocking and exploitative practices of capitalism, racism and sexism. And, linked as it is to privilege of one sort or another—race, gender, or class, or all three—it is an ability which serves that privilege. It is, in fact, that very privilege that is the enabling factor in the transformation of what is essentially an exercise of power into a right. That right in turn becomes enshrined and privileged in the ideology servicing the society in general.

The "right" to use the voice of the Other has, however, been bought at great price—the silencing of the Other; it is, in fact, neatly posited on that very silence. It is also a right that exists without an accompanying obligation, and, as such, can only lead to abuse.

The ability to use the voice of the Other; the "right" to use the voice of the Other. In the trite words of the popular song about love and marriage, "You can't have one without the other." To those who would argue that in a democracy everyone has the right to write from any point of view, I would contend that for far too long certain groups have not had access to any of the resources which enable writing of *any* sort to take place, let alone writing from a particular point of view. Education, financial resources, belief in the validity of one's experiences and reality, whether working class, female or Black: these are all necessary to the production of writing. They are also essential factors in the expression of one's ability to write. The exploitative practices of capitalist economies have, in fact, deprived these groups of the ability to express themselves through writing and publishing. Without that ability, the right to write from *any* point of view is meaningless. It goes without saying that the ability to write without the right is equally meaningless.

All of this appears more than reason enough to prohibit white writers writing from the point of view of persons from other cultures or races. The emotion—anger at the injustices that flow from racism—is entirely understandable. However, despite the reckless exercise of privilege on the part of white writers, I believe such a proscription to be very flawed and entirely ill-advised. My reasons for this position are as follows: Firstly, such a rule or proscription is essentially unenforceable (unless, of course, one is the late Ayatollah) and for that reason should never be made. Secondly, prohibiting such activity alters not one iota of that invisible and sticky web of systemic or structural racism. If all the white writers interested in this type of writing were voluntarily to swear off writing from the point of view of persons from other races and/or cultures, it would not ensure that writers from those cultures or races would get published any more easily, or at all. For that to happen, changes have to be made at other levels and in other areas, such as publishing, reviewing, distribution, library acquisitions, and educational curricula. Thirdly, and, to my mind, most importantly, for those who unquestioningly clasp the rights of the individual writer most dearly to their breasts, such a proscription provides a ready-made issue to sink their anti-censorship teeth into. Such a proscription becomes, in fact, a giant red herring dragged across the brutally cut path of racism.

As the fallout from the Women's Press debacle so clearly showed, all available energy in the writing community went into discussing, arguing and debating whether white women writers, or white writers in general, ought or ought not to be using the voice of the Other. There was no discussion about how to enable more Black women to get into print, or how to help those small publishing houses committed to publishing work by Black authors, or any attention paid to the many tasks that must be undertaken to make the writing and publishing world truly non-racist.

Funding, publishing, distribution, critical reception—racism manifests itself in all these areas. For the Black writer, the problem is hydra-headed, its effect as multi-faceted as profound. If, as the late critic Raymond Williams argued, "no work is in any full practical sense produced until it is also received,"[3] then much of the writing by Black writers in Canada fails to be fully produced. "Burning books," the Russian poet Joseph Brodsky writes, is "after all…just a gesture; not publishing them is a falsification of time… precisely the goal of the system," intent on issuing "its own version of the future."[4] This "falsification of time" which results from the failure to publish writers is as characteristic of the dominant culture in Canada as in the Soviet Union. In both cases, the state's intention is to "issue its own version of the future." And the Canadian version will, if possible, omit the contributions of Blacks and other non-dominant groups.

It is not that the question of the individual privilege of the white writer is entirely unimportant. That privilege is heavily implicated in the ideology of racism, white supremacy and their practices. The weight of racism in the writing world, however, does not reside with the individual white writer, but in the network of institutions and organizations that reinforce each other in the articulation of systemic racism. The writer is but a cog in that system. It is, perhaps, typical of a liberal democracy that racism in the writing and publishing world would be reduced to the individual writer sitting before her word processor, with only the imagination for company.

The imagination is free! Long live the imagination! One could hear the cry echoing around Canada as the controversy concerning the writer and voice rippled out across the country. Many writers saw the suggestion that they merely consider their social and political responsibility in selecting subject matter as an attempt to control that great storehouse of the writer: the imagination. One writer argued publicly that when she sat at her desk, her imagination took over and she had no choice but to go with it. Are we to conclude, therefore, that there are no mediating actions between what the writer imagines and what eventually appears on the printed page? Are we, as writers, all engaged in some form of literary automatism? While acknowledging that surrealist writers have indulged in automatic writing, the product of their writing was not intended to be realist fiction. The mandate of surrealism, if writing can ever be said to have a mandate, was to challenge what had, until then, been the art traditions of the Western World.

The imagination, I maintain, is both free and unfree. Free in that it can wander wheresoever it wishes; unfree in that it is profoundly affected and shaped by the societies in which we live. Traditionally, the unfettered nature of the imagination has done very little to affect the essentially negative portrayal of women by men in the arts. By and large, this portrayal has conformed closely to patriarchal visions of women. It required, in fact, a feminist reform movement to ensure the more realistic and positive images of women with which we are becoming increasingly familiar.

To state the obvious, in a racist, sexist and classist society, the imagination, if left unexamined, can and does serve the ruling ideas of the time. Only when we understand how belief in the untrammelled nature of the imagination is a part of the dominant culture can we, as Elizam Escobar[5] suggests, begin to use the imagination as a weapon. The danger with writers carrying their unfettered imaginations into another culture—particularly one like the First Nations Canadian culture which theirs has oppressed and exploited—is that without careful thought, they are likely to perpetuate stereotypical and one-dimensional views of this culture.

Regarding the issue of whether a white writer should use a style pioneered in a Third World country, there is again the problem of unenforceability. There is, however, a more serious error in this approach. The assumption behind the proscription is that because the style in question—magic realism—was pioneered in Latin America, it must therefore be entirely a product of that part of the world. Yet much of Latin American culture, particularly that of the middle and upper classes, has traditionally drawn heavily on European culture; the main articulators and purveyors of this style within Latin America—white males, for the most part—are products of European learning and tradition. One could further argue that magic realism is as much an heir to European traditions of surrealism, for instance, as to the Latin American sensibility and mindscape. Does that make it a Third World or First World style? Would it be acceptable, then, to use a European style, but not a European style one step removed?

All of this is not to deny that magic realism, as we have come to know it, is inextricably bound up with Latin America and its unique realities. But the proscription and its underlying (and unarticulated) assumptions reveal how little understanding there truly is of the complex nature of these societies and their histories. Latin America plays the exotic, kinky Other to the straight, realist realities of the affluent West.

A proscription such as this, or the position of the Women's Press that they will only look at manuscripts where the protagonist's experience is one with that of the author, raises more questions than it answers. What does the latter policy mean for the Black writer using the novel form—a form developed by the white, European bourgeoisie? And does the Press's position mean automatic exclusion of a manuscript by a Black writer who, in order to explore racism, develops a white character? If we accept the argument that the oppressed know more about their oppressors than the latter do about them, and if we accept the fact that groups like Blacks or First Nations are, in the West, essentially living in a white world, how can we argue that a Black writer's experience is substantially removed from that of a white character? Surely, as the Kenyan writer Ngugi wa Thiong'o argues, the issue is what the Black writer does with the form, and not merely the origin of the form. But note here how the debate about these issues once again fails to address the issues and concerns of Black writers, how the controversy is continually presented in terms of issues for white writers—a trap the Press neither challenged nor managed to avoid itself.

This rather tiresomely limited approach, albeit rooted in a recognition of the appropriation of non-European cultures by Europeans and North Americans, takes us into very murky waters and distorts the issue: how to ensure that *all* writers in Canada have equal access to funding, publication, and to full reception. What Black writers can benefit from, in my opinion, is not proscription, such as we have to date, but equal access to *all* the resources this society has to offer.

If, however, the debate in the Writers' Union newsletter is evidence of where writers in Canada are in their thinking on racism in writing and publishing, then there is every reason to be pessimistic about the potential for change. With very few exceptions—all the more noteworthy and noticeable for their rarity—writers defended their rights and freedoms to use whatever voice they chose to use. I would have hoped that along with that defence would have been *some* acknowledgement of the racism endemic to this society, and to the literary arena. It would have been reassuring if the debate had revealed a wider acknowledgement and understanding of the Women's Press's attempt, flawed as it was, to do something about racism as publishers. The issue of racism, personal, systemic or cosmic has, however, been notably absent from this debate.

Some months later, in the spring of 1989, when presented with the issue, the Writers' Union failed to endorse the setting up of a task force to look into issues of racism in writing and publishing in Canada. This despite significant attempts by a female and feminist minority. The Union *did*, however, pass a motion condemning "the failure of the law of Canada to protect freedom of expression and to prevent far-reaching intrusions into the essential privacy of the writing process." If any proof were needed of my earlier arguments, this tawdry display of white, male privilege provided it; it also confirmed how little interest the Union had in even acknowledging the existence of racism.

The Writers' Union has, to my mind, entirely abdicated its position as an organization that claims to be concerned about the rights of all writers in this country. It is primarily concerned about the rights of white, male writers, and certainly not about Black writers. The Old Boys' Network of Writers would be a far more suitable appellation.

"All art," critic Terry Eagleton writes, "has its roots in social barbarism. Art survives by repressing the historical toil which went into its making, oblivious of its own sordid preconditions...we only know art because we can identify its opposite: labour."[6] There is an evident and appalling failure on the part of white writers to grasp the fact that, despite their relatively low incomes, as a group they are extremely privileged and powerful. There is an accompanying failure to understand how the silencing of the many enables the few to become the articulators and disseminators of knowledge and culture. This is the social barbarism to which Eagleton refers, and it continues today in the erasure of the presence of those who, by their labour and toil, still help to create art.

Furthermore, how can white writers insist on their right to use any voice they may choose, and not insist on the equally valid right of African or Indigenous writers to write and to have their work adequately received? How can white writers insist on this right without acknowledging that, on the extremely unlevel playing field that racism creates, the exercise of this right could, in all likelihood, mean that work by a white writer about First Nations, for instance, would be more readily received than similar work by an Indigenous writer? To insist on one's right in a political vacuum, as so many writers have, while remaining silent on the equal rights of other writers to be heard, is fundamentally undemocratic and unfair.

The corresponding obligation to the right of these writers to use any voice they may choose to, is first to understand the privilege that has generated the idea that free choice of voice is a right. Second, but more importantly, these writers ought to begin to work to expand the area of that right to include those who, in theory, also have a right to write from any point of view but who, through the practice of racism, have been unable to exercise that right, thereby making it meaningless. Ngugi writes that "the writer as a human being is, himself, a product of history, of time and place."[7] This is what many writers in Canada today have forgotten: that—to continue in the words of Ngugi—they "belong to a certain class" and they are "inevitably...participant(s) in the class struggles of (their) times." I would add to that, the race struggles of their times. These writers have refused even to acknowledge their privilege vis-à-vis their own white working class, let alone Blacks or First Nations.

Writers are no more or less racist, classist or sexist than other individuals. Neither are they any less sensitive to the issue of racism than the average Canadian—which is probably not saying much. Writers ought, however, to recognize and acknowledge that along with their privilege comes a social responsibility. Essentially, the individual writer will decide how to exercise that social responsibility. Writers may, of their own accord, decide not to use the voice of a group their culture has traditionally oppressed. Others may decide that their responsibility impels them to do something else, but they ought to be impelled to do *something*.

Writers coming from a culture that has a history of oppressing the one they wish to write about would do well to examine their motives. Is their interest a continuance of the tradition of oppression, if only in seeing these cultures as different or exotic, as Other? Does their interest come out of the belief that their own cultural material is exhausted,[8] and that just about anything having to do with Africans, Asians and First Nations is bound to garner more attention? Is it, perhaps, the outcome of guilt and a desire to make recompense? Such writers have to examine whether they can write without perpetuating stereotypes.

Many readers must be aware of the debacle the English feminist publishing house Virago faced when it found that one of its published titles—a collection of short stories about Asians in England—was, in fact, written pseudonymously by a white male—a Church of England minister. It is interesting to note that one of the readers of the manuscript prior to publication, an Asian woman, had drawn attention to the fact that all the girls in the collection of short stories were drawn very passively; the boys, on the other hand, were portrayed as being very aggressive. She actually questioned the authorship of the work, but her suspicions were overridden. We cannot conclude from this that writers from a particular culture would be above pandering to stereotypes about their own culture. For instance, the upper-class writer from any culture runs the risk of stereotyping the working class of that culture; however, the chance of stereotypes being portrayed is, in my opinion, far greater with a writer who is, essentially, a stranger to the culture as a whole.

White writers must ask themselves hard questions about these issues; they must understand how their privilege *as white people*, writing *about* another culture, rather than *out of* it, virtually guarantees that their work will, in a racist society, be received more readily than the work of writers coming from that very culture. Many of these questions are applicable to all writers: for instance, the Black middle-class writer writing about the Black working class; or the upper-class Asian writing about the Asian peasant. If, after these questions are asked—and I believe responsible writers must ask them if they wish to be responsible to themselves, their gifts and the larger community—writers still feel impelled to write that story or that novel, then let us hope they are able to "describe a situation so truthfully...that the reader can no longer evade it."[9] Margaret Laurence accomplished this ideal in her collection of short stories, *The Tomorrow-Tamer*,[10] the secret of her accomplishment lies, I believe, in the sense of humility—not traditionally the hallmark of the white person approaching an African, Asian or Indigenous culture—that writers need to bring to the culture to which they are strangers. Writers must be willing to learn; they must be open to having certainties shifted, perhaps permanently. They cannot enter as oppressors, or even as members of the dominant culture. That sense of humility is what has been sorely lacking in the deluge of justifications that have poured forth in support of the "right" of the white writer to use any voice.

While Canadian writers find it very easy to defend the rights of Chinese writers who have been silenced by the state, there is general apathy to the silencing of writers here in Canada through the workings of racism, both within the marketplace and through funding agencies. In an essay titled "The Writer and Responsibility," South African writer Nadine Gordimer argues that artistic freedom cannot exist without its wider context. She identifies two presences within the writer: creative self-absorption and conscionable awareness. The writer, she says, must resolve "whether these are locked in a death-struggle, or are really foetuses in a twinship of fecundity."[11] For some, artistic freedom appears to be alive and well in Canada; these writers, however, pay not the slightest heed to the fact that the wider context includes many who, because of racism, cannot fully exercise that artistic freedom. In Canada, that wider context is, in fact, very narrowly drawn around the artistic freedom of white writers.

As for the twin presences of creative self-absorption and conscionable awareness which Gordimer identifies, conscionable awareness on any issue but censorship has been disturbingly absent from the debate on the writer and voice. Creative self-absorption, or literary navel-gazing, is what rules the day in Canada.

CODA: Spot the Difference

In December 2016, APTN News broke a story questioning nationally and internationally acclaimed author Joseph Boyden's Indigenous heritage. In the face of great media attention, Boyden maintained silence for several weeks until an interview with Candy Palmater on CBC Radio.

Boyden and the Indigenous groups he understands himself to belong to will have to work out what his identity actually is: blood, it appears, is not the only way one can belong to an Indigenous nation. His celebrity status, his claims of Indigenous identity, and his ensuing silence ensured intense media attention. My initial question was whether Boyden's claim to be Indigenous was a response to the proscriptions against cultural appropriation in general and appropriation of voice in particular that some advocate—in other words, did Boyden feel that the only way he could write stories with Indigenous characters was to claim a blood relation and present as Indigenous? Was this perhaps a long-delayed outcome of the fierce debate about appropriation of voice that, after erupting at the Women's Press in Toronto in the late '80s, had gripped the Canadian literary community and the media? The issue would eventually split the Press.[12] My response to that debate was "The Disappearing Debate: Or, How the Discussion of Racism Has Been Taken Over by the Censorship Debate."

Identity is a vitally important issue among formerly colonized groups and peoples who have had their cultures erased. From oral history investigations to DNA testing, many of us who come from broken, fragmented and displaced cultures, like Afrosporic cultures in the Caribbean and the Americas, desire to know who we are and where we come from—where do the bones of our Ancestors' rest? Indigenous people who have been adopted out are also driven by similar desires to know their identities. It is, therefore, understandable that the debate relating to Boyden would flourish over how one belongs and who belongs to the various nations.[13]

What surprised me in the response to the Boyden matter in 2016 was the sole focus on issues of identity, almost to the exclusion of all others. There was no reference to that earlier debate that raged across Canada's literary community; indeed, there was no attempt to contextualize the discussions within the relatively recently lived history of the Canadian literary community itself, further cultivating even greater erasure around socially important issues, particularly those related to racism.

Without an historical context for the discussions surrounding the Boyden matter, like so many discussions today in our celebrity-focused culture, they remain primarily in the personal vein, which is a vital aspect of the neo-liberal culture we live in, where social amnesia is increasingly in ascendance. In more tangible ways, we observe this turning away from, or even physical erasure of, our past, in our haste to destroy the architectural legacy of our city, to erect yet another condominium tower. It is a practice that reveals little or no respect for, and (of even more concern) understanding of, the immense social and psychic value of that legacy, as we turn away even from our recent past to an uncertain future.

The past twenty-five years have seen the loss of an important community voice in the Ryerson radio station CKLN, which engaged more overtly with issues of this nature. The broadcast universe has also split into the various social media spheres, further diluting listenership. Being the official broadcaster of the country, the CBC broadcasts within a certain bandwidth in more ways than one, so it is probably naive to expect more in-depth exploration of the issues like the Boyden matter.

Here, then, are some of my questions regarding the Boyden matter, none of which were addressed in any of the discussions I read or listened to on the CBC: Would Boyden's work have been received and accepted in the way it has been if he had identified as white? He is quoted as saying: "The stories that I tell…the voices come to me…I have to tell the stories I am compelled to tell."[14] What would have been the response if a white author, male or female, expressed this view? Was Boyden more acceptable to a white readership as an Indigenous "informant" on First Nations life because culturally he was white, having grown up in that context, but he could simultaneously claim insider status, which gave him more "authenticity"? What, if anything, does this say about white society in which the white "informant" is, more times than not, more believable than the person from the represented culture, especially in matters relating to culture, race, and racism?

On August 5, 2017, the *Globe and Mail* published an extremely long article on Joseph Boyden in which the Dutch-Ojibway writer Rebeka Tabobondung is quoted as saying: "I think it comes down to asking yourself, 'Would you have read those books if it was someone who had next to no Indigenous ancestry?' […] I think a lot of people would not have." This is a question that raises many difficult and profound issues that range from quantum blood rules to why people read books from cultures other than their own. The former is for Indigenous people to decide, the latter gives me pause. I, myself, have not read Joseph Boyden and did wonder why, indeed, people had read him. In response to this question, my partner said he was interested in World War I and therefore wanted to read *Three Day Road*, set in that period. What follows are a few of the questions that surfaced in response to Tabobondung's comment: Was there a certain amount of duty, if not white guilt, at work in Boyden's readership? Was he being read only because he was Indigenous at a time when white Canadians wanted to show their commitment to reconciliation? Is his skill and competence as a writer even relevant? Should publishers ever publish work by writers who do not come from the cultures they write about? Should we only read books written by writers from their own cultures? What of academic publications, so many of which are based on studying the Other? Finally, given how white the publishing industry is in Canada, what effect does this have on the "authenticity" of any work by Indigenous, African, and other writers of colour?

Joseph Boyden is an extremely high-profile, prestigious writer here in Canada. He claimed to be Indigenous, which allowed many to consider and refer to him as a bridge between white Canada and Indigenous people— a symbol of reconciliation. Not surprisingly the APTN revelation did have a certain gotcha quality to it: I myself had been aware of earlier rumblings and questions about certain stereotypical representations of Indigenous people in his work. This begs the question about why editors of his work, undoubtedly white, had not caught these. Not surprisingly also, there is a sense of betrayal on the part of the powerful CanLit group and the mandarins and mediators of Canadian culture. Their embrace of indigeneity had proved to be misplaced. How else to explain the hatchet job so skilfully carried out by the *Globe and Mail* in the August 5 article mentioned above? Boyden thus becomes the focal point—the metaphorical eye of the perfect storm, if you will—of CanLit, identity politics, reconciliation, and appropriation. Appropriation because if Boyden is not Indigenous, is he then appropriating Indigenous culture? Yet appropriation has not been an issue in the discussions related to Boyden. Perhaps the unique facts around his position in Canada may explain the difference between the public response to the Boyden affair and the publication of another book by a white Canadian writer.

Karolyn Smardz Frost is a Governor General's Award winner for her historical work on the Underground Railroad, *I've Got a Home in Glory Land*. She is a historian and archaeologist who teaches at Acadia University. In January 2017, not long after the Boyden revelations had come to light, HarperCollins published her novel based on a true story, *Steal Away Home: One Woman's Epic Flight to Freedom—and Her Long Road Back to the South*.

The story is about an enslaved Black woman who flees to Canada during the time of slavery and then returns at the end of the Civil War.[15] Interestingly, there was no review of the book in the *Toronto Star*; instead, the newspaper stated that they "were kicking off February—Black History Month—with an excerpt" from the book.[16] I am not suggesting that *Steal*

Away Home is appropriative—I haven't read it, except for the excerpt in the *Star*, but it does strike me as odd that there has been no commentary on this in any of the reviews—there haven't been many—I have read. The closest we come to approaching the issue is to be found in the January 27, 2017, issue of *Maclean's*, in which critic and reviewer Donna Bailey Nurse questions whether Smardz Frost finds it awkward teaching a course at Acadia University on the African Canadian experience. Smardz Frost replies that if she teaches "properly" and writes "properly," nobody sees her face, or even sees her anymore. Perhaps that comment is an indication of belief in a post-racial society; some of us, however, never have that privilege. Another reviewer, Douglas J. Johnston, in the March 4, 2017, *Winnipeg Free Press*, critiqued the "nicey-nicey neutral language" which sees slaves becoming freedom seekers, for instance.

In many ways I am less concerned about Smardz Frost writing a novel about slavery, or claiming to be able to disappear if she writes "properly," than I am about the absence of any critical discussion about these issues. Is it because Black history is considered eminently appropriable? If we return to Tabobondung's suggestion that Boyden's readership was to some degree determined by the belief that he was at least part Indigenous, is this not an issue for Smardz Frost who, I might add, is not the first white Canadian author in recent times to fictionalize Black life?[17]

There are, however, insights that Boyden's and Smardz Frost's approaches offer, and perhaps there is more similarity than difference in both these authors' approaches than first meets the eye. As outsiders to the cultures they wanted to write about, they secured the covering of a certain validation or authenticity—he through claiming blood ties to the culture, she through expertise and historical knowledge of the culture. Both approaches illustrate in different ways a requirement I identified in "The Disappearing Debate" as crucial when an artist or writer from another culture, especially a dominant one, approaches another—the need to approach the culture with humility and not with a sense of entitlement. Another way of saying this is that perhaps the Outsider has to be moved to give to the culture in respectful ways. Leaving aside the issue of whether he was inventing his blood connection to the Indigenous community, from all that I've read, Boyden appears to have been someone who has given of his time and energy to certain First Nations groups; Smardz Frost, in her extensive research, has also made a contribution to the scholarship in an area of African Canadian and American history. I raise these arguments not as justifications, excuses or explanations: I continue to believe that in white supremacist societies, those from the dominant culture needs must tread carefully if they wish to enter the cultures of those who have been historically exploited. Cultural appropriation of Black culture is long-standing and very real. I raise the arguments merely to show the richness of the discussion that could have taken place; its absence says a lot about Canadian culture.

I do not accept the position that writers cannot or should not write about other cultures, genders, ages, abilities, sexual orientations, historical times, or universes, for that matter. As I argued in "The Disappearing Debate," I feel a more useful and fruitful approach is one where certain requirements should be considered by the writer as a part of preparation and research that most writers do when they embark on a project. Most importantly, it is vital that there be writers from the culture being written about who can critique the work in a more informed way from literary and cultural perspectives.

NOTES

1. In 1989, the Writers' Union ran a series of letters in its newsletter on the issues of cultural appropriation and the writer and voice.

2. Sara Maitland, "Triptych," in *A Book of Spells* (London: Michael Joseph, 1987), 117.

3. Raymond Williams, "Culture," in *Marx: The First 100 Years*, ed. David McLellan (London: Fontana, 1983), 48.

4. Joseph Brodsky, *Less than One* (New York: Farrar, Straus and Giroux, 1986), 293.

5. A Puerto Rican painter who is serving a sixty-eight-year sentence in state and federal prisons in the U.S. for seditious conspiracy arising out of his involvement in Puerto Rican liberation struggles.

6. "Terry Eagleton, Mark Fisher, Tony Dunn and Felix Culper Explore the Possible Relationships of Socialism, the State and the Arts," *New Statesman* 113 (March 20, 1987), 8.

7. Ngugi wa Thiong'o, "Kenyan Culture: The National Struggle for Survival," in *Writers in Politics: Essays* (London: Heinemann, 1981), 72.

8. This was the very reason Hal Niedzviecki, then-editor of *Write*, the Writers' Union of Canada (TWUC) publication, gave as reason for urging that non-Indigenous Canadians should appropriate Indigenous culture and their writing.

9. Nadine Gordimer requires of herself "the integrity Chekhov demanded: 'to describe a situation so truthfully…that the reader can no longer evade it.'" Nadine Gordimer, "The Essential Gesture," in *The Essential Gesture: Writing, Politics and Places*, ed. Stephen Clingman (New York: Knopf, 1988), 299.

10. Margaret Laurence, *The Tomorrow-Tamer* (London: MacMillian & Co., 1963).

11. Gordimer, *The Essential Gesture*, 300.

12. In 1991, for instance, TVO presented a discussion with those personally involved in

the Women's Press split, hosted by Daniel Richler.

13   In my very tiny island of birth, Tobago, for instance, as soon as one identifies oneself as being from the island, the question that usually immediately follows is what town or village your family comes from. I believe this helps people to "place" each other.

14   Tanya Talaga, *Toronto Star* (Jan. 15, 2017), A3.

15   *Toronto Star* (Jan. 28, 2017), E18.

16   Ibid.

17   *Rush Home Road,* by Lori Lansens, about a Black town in the Chatham area, was first published in 2002.

In the essay "The Disappearing Debate" I cautioned against white writers approaching other cultures from the position that their own European culture was exhausted and that other cultures were the source of some sort of missing vitality that they needed to revivify their own cultural practices. This is the very argument Hal Niedzviecki, editor of Write *magazine—the Writers' Union of Canada publication, made in his encouragement of writers to poach Indigenous stories. There was no vitality in Canadian writing, he argued, which was reason enough to take their stories and write about them. Niedzviecki titled his piece "Winning the Appropriation Prize." The proverbial firestorm erupted, accompanied by resignations and, even more disturbing, late-night tweeting by powerful cultural players offering financial donations to the said prize.*

RACE-BAITING AND THE WRITERS' UNION OF CANADA

Hal Niedzviecki has every right to express his opinion, as badly argued and uninformed as it is; after all, we do have protections regarding free speech short of hate speech. What I find inexcusable, however, and profoundly disrespectful is that the Writers' Union of Canada (TWUC) would publish an issue of *Write* dedicated to Indigenous writers—long overdue, I might add—and have the editorial introducing the work be a flippant and uninformed piece about appropriation.

I enter this debate for two reasons: some twenty-five years ago this very same issue erupted in Toronto and resulted in the then Women's Press splitting. The cross-country debate back then was equally fierce. My response to that was "The Disappearing Debate: Or, How the Discussion of Racism Has Been Taken Over by the Censorship Issue," a title that speaks for itself.

It's troubling to witness the return of these issues with apparently no greater understanding—truth and reconciliation notwithstanding. As a presently a paid-up member of TWUC, I feel implicated, albeit unwittingly, in this issue, and it is as such I enter this debate.

I want to draw readers' attention away from the issue of appropriation for a brief moment and ask them to focus on a smaller, less controversial issue—that of hospitality and protocols around how you welcome and treat a guest. It has many reverberations in the history of colonialism.

All cultures, traditional and modern, including Western cultures, have protocols about the guest and how the guest should be treated. Indeed, in early Christian times, Christians were expected to keep a bed, some bread and a candle for the unexpected guest. In African cultures, the appearance of a guest was often the occasion on which a large animal would be killed, so that the guest could be fed. (Invading colonizers used that practice to further exploit the people.) In the histories of the many, many cultures colonized by the European, you will find numerous instances in which the guest, the European, was taken in and treated well—even taught how to live on the land. As we know so well now, that generosity was often re-paid by conquest. My point being a very simple one—when a guest comes to your home, especially an invited guest, you honour them, you provide them the best. More to the point, you do not invite someone to your home or living space and then insult or disrespect them. What TWUC did was the equivalent of this, and I suspect that had those writers known what the editorial was going to be about, none of them would have submitted their work. What kind of culture, literary or otherwise, produces this kind of uncivilized behaviour? A culture whose very integuments are woven around everyday racism against peoples of colour.

TWUC, one of the gatekeepers of Canadian Literature culture in Canada, invited these writers to submit their work and then published an editorial that entirely disrespected the sea change that the publication of these writers represents. Why didn't TWUC invite an Indigenous guest editor, as often happens when magazines have themed issues, and of which there is a long history in the culture of Canadian literary magazines? Why did the oversight committee not catch this travesty before it was published? What has happened is tantamount to publishing an issue dedicated to women's issues or feminism and having an editorial, written by a man, making light of, or challenging the widespread sexual abuse of women, or domestic violence against women. Can we imagine the firestorm that would have erupted over such a glaring and brutal example of sexism and misogyny? Instead, what we have is a firestorm over appropriation, which was not raised by the invited writers, with two camps arrayed against each other.

I am suggesting here that the debate about appropriation simultaneously erases and supplants the racist act that the publication of the editorial represents; further, it illustrates how systemic racism functions and how we can all be baited to participate in a debate that hides even as it reveals.

Yes, the issue of appropriation is a very real one—I might add here that living in the present, globalized, commodified world, there are very few of us who do not indulge or partake in practices of other cultures—from yoga to mindfulness meditation to Buddhism, to karate and other Asian martial arts. Is any of this appropriation? If not, why not? Further, Black culture—especially musical culture—has always been and continues to be appropriated by all cultures, bar none—Elvis Presley, Adele, Lily Singh, A Tribe Called Red, the Beatles, the Rolling Stones—the list is long. There appears to be no understanding that Black music bears a name, has an address and a particular and tragic history. Indeed, to use a digital example, Black culture is approached as if it is a creative commons to which everyone ought to have access. And it is a zero-sum game because the widespread consumption of Black culture has not resulted in any greater respect for the original creators. Indeed, in an extractive capitalist world, the opposite has been the result. Indigenous peoples have their own arguments about how their cultures have been appropriated as, I suspect, do all colonized cultures and peoples.

Appropriation is a complex issue which often stems from a racist power structure which can do real harm to those who are racially, socially and politically marginalized. The debate over appropriation of voice, which this particular debate is all about, often lurches between those who are rightly concerned with the dangers of literary censorship on the one hand, and those who are concerned about very real damage that can be done by appropriative practices. There are those who argue that you cannot cage what is uncageable—the human imagination and inspiration, and that creativity and inspiration cannot be boxed in by identity politics. This is true, but it does not necessarily mean that one has a "right" to poach the cultures of others, particularly those whom your own culture had a hand in destroying. As I argued earlier in "The Disappearing Debate," a sense of humility is necessary when approaching another culture. Further, the imagination does not exist in a vacuum and is, more times than not, affected by one's social milieu. Just think of how many metaphors we use today that come from the digital world we live in.

In "The Disappearing Debate," however, I argued that the solution to appropriation of voice will not be found in prohibitions. The deeper structures of exclusion and marginalization have to be dismantled. We, those of us who have borne the historical, political and social brunt of white supremacist practices, are often suspicious of the practices that Western, humanist cultures hold sacrosanct, like freedom of speech. We know only too well how these beliefs have been used against us. However, as we watch the pillars of democracy, albeit a very imperfect one, being dismantled south of the border, it sharpens the appreciation of these practices and beliefs. Being against appropriation does not necessarily make one a supporter of censorship: there is a deeper wound that is being identified that perhaps a secular, Western state does not yet have the language to address. Being in support of the ability to imagine the lives of others who may be different from you does not necessarily make you racist.

What is important is that we realize that art does not exist in a vacuum, that writing, publication and success come out of many, many small decisions that can contribute to or hurt the coming to voice of the historically displaced, marginalized and erased. Writing and publishing are material acts in a material world, pace Madonna, and racism, sexism and all the other harmful practices impact negatively on those acts.

The pros and cons of appropriation are not the issue here, although many found Niedzviecki's opinions offensive. Indeed, his resignation was demanded because of what he wrote, and he complied with the demand. His arguments reveal an astonishing ignorance and can be easily demolished. I maintain, however, that having an opinion in support of appropriation, while offensive to many, is not necessarily racist, just as those who feel it should not happen are not necessarily in favour of censorship. At the risk of being repetitive, I return to the more fundamental issue of respect for the literary guests TWUC invited to publish in its magazine, *Write*. Why, for instance, wasn't the editorial about the literary history of Indigenous people in Canada, dating back to the poet, E. Pauline Johnson and before, so that we, the readers, could have a better idea of where these newer writers fit in? Why did the editor see fit to write an editorial about appropriation to introduce the Indigenous writers invited to submit work, when appropriation was not the theme of the issue?

The TWUC editorial was racist for the following reasons:

(a)   it made no attempt to place the work of the Indigenous writers in any literary context, and, by arguing for appropriation, revealed a dismissive and thoughtless attitude toward the writers, especially given that this was an issue dedicated to Indigenous writers who had been invited to submit work. (In other words, the editor couldn't be bothered to do any research on the literary history or context of Indigenous writers, and the issue of appropriation appears to be the primary association he makes with Indigenous writers);

(b)   the publication of a deliberately incendiary editorial, intended to inflame the feelings of Indigenous writers and incite debates between those on opposing sides of the issue, showed that the editor was completely indifferent to the writers, their history and culture, as well as the destructive, colonial history of Canada. (In other words, he used his editorial as bait—it could be said to be a form of literary race-baiting);

(c)   Indigenous writers were solicited to submit work on the understanding that their work would be treated respectfully and seriously. Instead the editorial was used to further debate on appropriation, which was not the theme of the issue. (In other words, the editor employed a literary bait-and-switch technique);

(d)   in his editorial, the editor privileged an issue that would ensure that white voices would be amplified, the result of which is that we now have a call for an appropriation prize. (In other words, he ensured that white people's voices would continue to be privileged in the ensuing debate.)

The discussion of appropriation is not the one we should be having as a consequence of TWUC publishing an issue of *Write* dedicated to Indigenous writers. By linking the issue of appropriation, as he did in his editorial, to the publication of work by invited Indigenous writers, Niedzviecki was being mischievous at best; at worst, unintentional or not, the editorial resulted in racism. Further, using this particular issue of *Write* as a platform to call for appropriative practices was tantamount to using the published submissions as a form of advertisement for the stories he was encouraging non-Indigenous writers to appropriate. It is an act deeply embedded in an extractive, capitalist culture—one that reduces all activity to use value.

Appropriation is an issue for all cultures dominated by white supremacist attitudes and practices, but speaking for my own culture, it's not an issue Black writers are overly preoccupied with. We engage with the full spectrum of life, including trying to piece together memories of cultures that have been pulverized by the onslaught of colonialism. We, like all writers, struggle with time management, grants, getting published and all the demands that writing exerts on one. Not to mention relationships and children. I suspect it is similar for Indigenous writers. Except when a red flag is waved in front of them, as it has been in this case. In this context, appropriation is an issue for white writers who object to those who rightly challenge systems of power and reveal how they also exist in art and artistic practices. White writers who feel this way know they can appropriate because they have the cultural power to do so; they also know that much in this culture supports them. As we see happening with contributions to the appropriation prize.

The issue of appropriation of voice is not new, and there is no excuse for this happening. Twenty-five years ago this was the very issue that split the Women's Press in Toronto and spawned intense debate across Canada. If there was any real interest in why it was an issue for those writing from formerly colonized cultures back then, we wouldn't have had the insulting editorial, nor would we have had the vague, confusing apology from the chair of TWUC regretting "the pain and offence caused..." and talking about *Write* magazine offering "a space for honest and challenging discussion" and being "sincerely encouraging to all voices." Expressing regret for "pain and offence" is not a true apology, nor was there anything "honest" or "challenging" about Niedzviecki's editorial, which has done nothing to encourage Indigenous and other writers of colour to submit work to mainstream publications.

We have all been played to some degree, because the debate about appropriation will be with us for the foreseeable future, which is not necessarily damaging. The more discussion and respectful exploration of the issues there are, the more we benefit. However, if we fail to drill down below the issue of appropriation in this case, we miss the deeper, systemic racism at work here.

Some twenty-five years ago I proposed that the Union set up a committee to look at racism in writing and publishing, which I was interested in being a part of. I did not receive a response to my letter and my proposal went nowhere. TWUC must be called out on the blatant racism of inviting

Indigenous writers to submit to an issue and then disrespecting those writers and their efforts. Anti-racism workshops are not enough. The Union should name the issue clearly—we are writers and words are our medium. It needs to name what happened as racism—the ROM's recent apology, some twenty-eight years later, for the anti-Black racism of the *Into the Heart of Africa* exhibit could be a model for the Union's action. Intention is not relevant, particularly as it relates to the functioning of organizations like TWUC long-steeped in colonial practices. No one may have intended to be racist, but the result is a racist one, and TWUC needs to apologize to the invited writers, the Indigenous communities and TWUC membership for this racism. Then it needs to meet with Indigenous writers and figure out where to go from there.

SOCIAL BARBARISM AND
THE SPOILS OF MODERNISM

The auditorium of the McLaughlin Planetarium was spacious and bright; I was there to learn about African art: a four-week series of lectures sponsored by the Royal Ontario Museum (ROM).[1]

Around me the room was full of people, all white with the exception of five—including myself—Blacks. I didn't miss the overwhelming irony of my being there to find out about something I should have been as familiar with as I am with the beliefs and practices of Christianity—and I don't mean African "art," since that is a Western construct, but African culture. And I was not familiar with African culture—at least not in the sense of being intimate with it.

The reason for my presence in that room was, I felt, deeply rooted in the very events and circumstances that had brought the pieces, now on display, courtesy of the ROM, to the West and CanadA: the same events that had brought the "primitive," the savage, the African—the Other—to the West in the form of "art" or aesthetics. The supreme irony in these events was that while the African aesthetic was being appropriated and manipulated to the West's own purposes; while African "art" was being extolled and praised—and at the same time being evacuated of any ritually appropriate meaning—the peoples of the continent from which these cultural objects originated were being oppressed, enslaved, and denied basic human rights.

It is pretty much received opinion now that the "art of tribal Africa was a major influence on Western art early this century and has remained so for decades."[2] For "major influence," I would substitute *indispensable debt*, for by the time the moderns came upon the idea of the "primitive," their artistic tradition had been depleted of much of its energy and vitality.

At the turn of the century European art had reached an impasse in its search for a new visual language sufficient to express the dynamics of the time. There was a growing discontent with the increased industrialization of European life. These two factors forced artists to look elsewhere for inspiration and spiritual solace—they turned to the ideas of primitivism and the exotic.[3]

This statement is, however, incomplete, for turning to the ideas of primitivism and the exotic would not have been possible for artists were it not for aggressive, expansionist, colonial policies of European powers. The two developments are inextricably linked—as linked as I was to those ROM pieces I had registered to learn about—and must be seen and understood together.

Layers of erasure is what we get instead. Beginning with the artists themselves. Many of these artists—Picasso included—who drew their inspiration from the work of Africa and Oceania were later to deny and rationalize the influence of this work on their own work. Picasso, for instance denied ever having seen any "primitive" art until *after* he had painted *Les Demoiselles d'Avignon* in 1907. There is evidence, however, that Picasso had seen examples of African sculpture in the studios of Matisse and Derain in 1906, and by 1907, had begun to build his own collection.

Constantin Brancusi initially extolled the qualities of African sculpture; later, he was to disassociate himself from its influence, cautioning not only against imitating Africans, but also describing African sculpture as charged with "demonic forces." He even went so far as to destroy a number of his early pieces because, he claimed, they were too African.

Another of the moderns—Jacques Lipchitz—both collector and artist, denied that African art influenced his sculpture, but did concede—magnanimously—that "we shook hands with Negro art, but this is not an influence—merely an encounter."[4] And what an encounter! Of an indispensable kind, I am tempted to say. To these three we can add Epstein, Archipenko, and others of the same period.

The trend toward erasure still continues, for in 1984, the MOMA[5] exhibition on modern and primitive art went to great lengths to assign responsibility for cubism to the West: in the development of cubism as curated, tribal art would play a minor role, with the identification of affinities rather than *causal* influences.

Why this denial of the African? Writing early in this century on the subject of African sculpture, Roger Fry unwittingly provides some clue. In his opening paragraph of an essay entitled "Negro Art," he writes:

> So deeply rooted in us is the notion that the Negro race is in some fundamental way not only inferior to others but almost subhuman, that it upsets our notion of fitness even to compare their creations with those of a people like the Greeks whom we regard as almost super human.[6]

He goes further than any critic I have read in articulating the impact of African art on the West: "Modern art owes more to Negroes than to any other tradition…the contribution of Africa to the spiritual inheritance may turn out to be of the greatest importance."[7] But the white supremacist approach he identifies in the opening paragraph explains much of the erasure.

"Primitive"—"primitivism." I have, so far, thrown these words around without defining them, not at all because I assume there is shared agreement on their meanings. These are words I am uncomfortable with, carrying as they do so much of the connotative imperialist baggage of the West. The dictionary meaning of *primitive* merely asserts the concept of being first, or early, which is at the etymological heart of the word. Today's connotations imply the savage, the illogical, the irrational, the dark side—all the West wished to project outwards on to others.

My sense is that if the primitive did not exist—as in the early peoples with non-industrialized, non-capitalist modes of production—the West would still have found it necessary to invent the concept of primitivism. There is a quantum leap from the early peoples and their cultures to the concept of primitivism, the underpinnings of which is colonialism. As Hal Foster argues in his essay "The 'Primitive' Unconscious,"[8] primitivism became a device to manage the primitive, which the West would have found too disruptive or transgressive.

What the West sought and got from Africa and Oceania was necessary, not only from the perspective of art and aesthetics, but also from the perspective of the psyche. Identify, describe, catalogue, annotate, appropriate—these words best sum up the West's relationship with Africa—the Other, against which are arrayed the forces of reason, rationality, logic and knowledge as possessable and certifiable. European powers would rationalize economic exploration of these areas by theories of racial and cultural superiority, equating the Other with all that was inferior.

With the "approach" of the West to these early cultures, with its appropriation of their aesthetics, with the development of "primitivism," went another sort of erasure—a double erasure, in fact: erasure of the *context* within which these objects existed, and erasure of the *circumstances* of their removal from the places where they belonged.

The African artist or sculptor from Africa or Oceania "carved in order to secure specific ends of ritual activity or to represent nature."[9] The Western view of these works was antithetical to this approach, the Western artist caring little for the ritual significance of these objects. The chance for Western art, Hal Foster argues, to "reclaim a ritual function," to "retain an ambivalence of the sacred object or gift and not be reduced to the equivalence of the commodity—was blocked."[10]

The second erasure, engendered by the concept of primitivism, was that of the barbarism, aggression, and exploitation that produced these spoils. The modernist experiment, successful as it was in art, was securely based on rape, pillage and murder, the common currency of colonial expeditions. The masks, effigies, totemic figures were all spoils of war, and nowhere is this fact ever articulated—least of all at the MOMA exhibition where the curators were interested in showing the *affinity* among the human races, and how primitivism as manifested by the modern artists is a result of this affinity. Simply put, primitivism is the result of theft.

> To value as art what is now a ruin; to locate what one lacks in what one has destroyed: more is at work here than compensation…a breakthrough in our art, indeed a regeneration of our culture, is based in part on the breakup and decay of other societies…the modernist discovery of the primitive is not only in part its oblivion but its death.[11]

I started this essay by locating it within a certain event—the ROM lectures on African art, which gave an honest account of the way in which many of the ROM pieces came into its possession. It was during those lectures I heard one of the truisms that form part of the canon on African art, and one which helps to foster another type of erasure—this time about Western art. It also reveals how useful African art and primitivism have become as countercultural alternatives to Western art practices.

African art is functional, inseparable from the social order, the argument goes, vis-à-vis the Western art tradition where art by designation is what we have come to understand art to mean. Integral to this approach is the belief that art exists here in the West over and above the social order—often *apart* from the social order. The commodity value assigned to art—*and* to the artist—makes it a part of the economy, but essentially it is a thing apart— alien, alienated and, at times, alienating.

It is, however, integral to the concept and understanding of art here in the West, that its connection to the social matrix—to labour, history and politics—not be seen, acknowledged or articulated. Which is where the African and Oceanic—the primitive—has served such a useful purpose, for with the primitive, the cultural connections between art and the social fabric—although irrevocably torn—could be clearly seen and held up as a significant difference from the Western tradition.

On the one hand, the cultural object forcibly torn out of its context, assigned artistic value and meaning, and reinterpreted as functional—an integral part of the social order; on the other, the cultural object still within its context, but with its connections to the social fabric hidden or obliterated. What are, in fact, flip sides of the same coin are presented as radical differences.

> All art has its roots in social barbarism, and an "emancipatory" work of art is thus in a sense self-contradictory…Art survives by repressing the historical toil which went into its making, oblivious of its own sordid preconditions; and part of the point of radical art is to lift that repression and help us remember. We only know art because we can represent its opposite—labour.[12]

Erasure—whether we're talking of African art or Western art. For the Western consumer of art—the reader of literature as much as the gallery devotee; for the poet as much as the novelist or visual artist—that connection between art and labour, art and history or politics, between art and barbarism, has been completely erased. The consumer must see art as, at worst, neutral, at best, transcendental—existing over and above, standing over from any of the more crass aspects of our lives. For the practitioner, art is often the manifestation of the everlasting, overworked ego, dehistoricized and existing in a vacuum.

And what of political art? It often states the obvious; becomes overly didactic in preaching to the converted; and merely serves to induce that most transitory of emotions in the liberal breast—guilt. Each person, I assume, has her own method for grappling with the utter and banal irrelevancy of art and the artist: Eagleton talks of being "popular and experimental... undermining realist [ruling class] ways of seeing"; Foster, of resisting the "commodification of culture" and constructing counter-representations. Each artist and person—if so concerned—has to find her way of resisting the erasure and amnesia—the resulting irrelevance—of art today in the West; of blowing wide open the myths and hidden assumptions—the knowledge that continues to foster the practice of forgetting.

Since I work with the written word, I see this process most clearly when I consider how *literature* came to the Caribbean societies. The novel, poetry, Shakespeare—all came as cultural appendages to the Empire, expressing "universal" values—the limpid objectivity of Eliot, which meant that the little Black girl in the Caribbean should be able to feel exactly what he was feeling when he wrote about cats, fog and Prufrock. And surely, that same child, whose childhood boundaries were constant sunshine, black skins and mangoes, could understand about Wordsworth's field of daffodils. Why the hell didn't she?

All this talk of universal values and objectivity was, of course, just so much rubbish—a carefully designed ideology to hide the fact that these art forms were very much a part of middle- and upper-class English life. Their export was an important aspect of empire—as important as, and probably more damaging than, colonial administrative practices.

That epitome of bourgeois art forms, the novel, whose origins, authorship and consumption lay in a class which rose to economic success and affluence on the backs of the white working class in England and the Black labouring classes in the Empire, somehow had shed all its more crass connections by the time it came south. But, as Kenyan writer Ngugi wa Thiong'o has argued, "perhaps the crucial question is not that of the racial, national, and class origins of the novel, but that of its development and the uses to which it is continually being put."[13]

Unless the artist understands that capitalist society has not only commodified the "work of art," but has also erased the barbarism which both underpins and allows the "work of art" to exist; unless the artist understands that this erasure is one of the linchpins of capitalist society which, in its own way in the West, makes art and the making of it functional, we can never begin to make the art that will challenge the hidden assumptions that support the system.

The prognosis appears bleak for artists here in the West: the split between art and labour, between art and historical underpinnings, gape ever more widely. We may take some small hope from the integrative aspects of African creative works, as well as from the tradition in the West expressed by artists like Blake and William Morris, who saw in art an example of non-alienated labour, and perhaps more importantly, from the work of the many feminist artists who seek and create—admittedly often piecemeal—that integrative and thereby revolutionary context for their work.

I have come full circle, returning (like the objective Eliot) to where I started—the ROM, but coming from left field: why doesn't the ROM have a permanent African collection on display? Much as I abhor the history behind collections such as these, it is a grave and significant omission. It is not that the ROM doesn't have the artifacts—it does—but they're all in boxes in the basement. The ROM should either return them to the nations, tribes and countries from which they were pilfered, give them to Africans here in Toronto or Canada, or display them. Right? But that's a whole other ball game, isn't it.

CODA: La Même Chose

It is now received opinion that it was contact with Africa and Oceania and the approaches to the plastic arts in those areas that revitalized European art, leading to the birth of modernism. It is uncanny how history repeats itself, for in 2017 this is the very reason Hal Niedzviecki, editor of Write, the Writers' Union of Canada magazine, uses to justify his urging of writers to go out and appropriate Indigenous stories and culture. This is the repeating trope, the vampiric nature of colonialism, or is it that repetition itself is the trope? That repetition itself can contain anything. If this is the case, how do we ensure that what gets repeated is always life affirming?

NOTES

1   The lecturer of this series was Jeanne Cannizzo, who subsequently guest-curated the ROM exhibit *Into the Heart of Africa*, which opened in November, 1989.

2   Christopher Hume, "Black art: Simmering vitality," *Toronto Star* (April 12, 1987).

3   Daniel Mato, "Gauguin to Moore: Primitivism in Modern Sculpture," *Artmagazine*, Nov./Dec./Jan. 1981–82, 12.

4   George Heard Hamilton, *Painting and Sculpture in Europe, 1880-1940* (New Haven: Yale University Press, 1993), 276.

5   *"Primitivism" in 20th Century Art: Affinity of the Tribal and the Modern*, Museum of Modern Art, New York (Sept. 27, 1984–Jan. 15, 1985).

6   Roger Fry, *Last Lectures* (London: Cambridge University Press, 1939), 75.

7   *Ibid.*, 84.

8   Hal Foster, *Recodings: Art, Spectacle, Cultural Politics* (Port Townsend, WA: Bay Press, 1985), 181.

9   Mato, "Gaugin," 12.

10   Foster, *Recodings*, 181.

11   *Ibid.*

12   Terry Eagleton, "How Do We Feed the Pagodas?" *New Statesman* (Mar 20, 1987), 8.

13   Ngugi wa Thiong'o, *Decolonizing the Mind* (London: James Currey, 1986), 68.

MUSEUM COULD HAVE AVOIDED CULTURE CLASH

Four museums, including the Natural History Museum of Los Angeles and the Albuquerque Museum, have recently refused to stage the Royal Ontario Museum exhibit, *Into the Heart of Africa*.

The acting director of the ROM, John McNeill, was recently quoted as saying that the "controversy which surrounded the exhibition and led to the cancellation of this tour impinges on the freedoms of all museums to maintain intellectual honesty, scientific and historical integrity and academic freedom."[1]

With very few exceptions, all the media, print and electronic, have at one time or another echoed those opinions, and have portrayed African Canadians who challenged the ROM exhibit as being irrational, emotional and unable to grasp the irony that very quickly became the linchpin to a proper understanding of this exhibit.

The greatest irony of all, however, is that through the words of its guest curator, Jeanne Cannizzo, in the accompanying catalogue to the exhibit, the ROM had been uncannily prescient in describing the issues this show would generate. Both the ROM and the media missed this irony. The tragedy is that the ROM was unable to recognize the opportunity presented to it to do exactly what it said the show was intended to do.

Jeanne Cannizzo writes, "By studying the *museum as an artifact, reading collections as cultural texts*, and *discovering life histories of objects*, it has become possible to *understand something of the complexities of cross-cultural encounters*"[2] [my emphasis]. With these words, Cannizzo, in fact, describes a framework for interpreting the exhibit and the response to it in a less adversarial way than it has been understood to date.

What follows is an analysis of the component sections of Cannizzo's statement, which, had it been truly understood, could have allowed for a more informed understanding of the exhibit and the intensely negative response to it.

"Museum as an artifact." For Africans, the museum has always been a significant site of their racial oppression. Within its walls, reasons could be found for their being placed at the foot of the hierarchical ladder of human evolution designed by the European. Proof could also be found there of the "bizarre" nature and "primitive" anatomy of the African. Where else could you find the preserved genitalia of the Black South African woman, Saartjie Baartman, known as the "Hottentot Venus," but in the Musée de l'Homme in Paris?

The museum has been pivotal in the expansion of the West's knowledge base about the world; it has been seminal in the founding of its disciplines—ethnography, archaeology and anthropology; and it has been indispensable in Europe's attempt to measure, categorize and hierarchize the world with the white male at the top. And all at the expense of the African, Asian and the Indigenous peoples, raw material for these processes.

Those who objected to the ROM's display were, in fact, showcasing the *museum as an artifact* for its uncritical and traditional presentation of these objects—the booty of soldiers and spiritual "exotica" collected by missionaries. The larger and more significant gesture of the opposition to the display lay in challenging the museum and its roles, particularly as it has affected African peoples. The potential—never realized—in this challenge was that the ROM *could* have found another way of looking at these objects.

"Reading collections as cultural texts." The African Canadian demonstrators and other objectors *outside* the museum were, in fact, an integral and indispensable part of the cultural text *inside* the museum that Cannizzo and the ROM expressed interest in reading. In this instance, the cultural text extended beyond the walls of the museum.

The ROM argued that this was a part of Canadian life that Canadians did not know about. This immediately begs the question as to which Canadians the ROM had in mind. European or African Canadians? Or was the ROM perhaps defining "Canadian" as someone of European heritage?

This exhibit was, however, also about African history *and* African Canadians, some of whom have been here for centuries. African Canadians know the history of colonialism in a painfully intimate way; they often live its implications and repercussions every day of their lives in this country. It is, of course, a not-so-astonishing *and* racist oversight that the ROM would assume that the only meaningful audience of this exhibit would be white Canadians.

The same text resulted in contradictory readings determined by the different life histories and experiences. One reading saw these artifacts as being frozen in time and telling a story *about* white Canadian exploration of Africa; the other inserted the reader—the African Canadian reader—actively into the text, who then read those artifacts as the painful detritus of savage exploration and attempted genocide of their own people.

"Discovering the life histories of objects." On one level, this collection represented a victory of the British Empire in Africa. The presence of these objects as colonial booty was, however, balanced by and resonated with that of African Canadians who represent a victory of another sort—the survival of African peoples in the New World, in the face of some five centuries of racial abuse and oppression. To discover the life histories of the objects on display, it was imperative that one also understood the *life of histories of Africans in the New World and Canada.*

Understanding the *"complexities of cross-cultural encounters."* What the ROM was not prepared to accept was the fact that, for the first time, a mirror was held up to its actions, and what was reflected there was an image of the museum as the cultural arm of the same powers that had exploited and continue to exploit African peoples.

The ethnographic "Other" in this case was the white Canadian fossilized in his or her bed of unconscious racism. Very much in keeping with that now-notorious picture of the white missionary woman teaching African women how to wash clothes, the *cross-cultural encounter* that the curator saw as a possibility could only happen if it went in one direction—from the repository of knowledge and power (the ROM) to the subject peoples—irrational and unsophisticated African Canadians.

And in this cacophony of racism, with its rhythms and counter-rhythms of allegation and denial, the media, while pretending to air both sides, uncritically supported the institutions of the dominant culture. African Canadians who objected to the display were, in fact, presenting a *different*, not *an inferior*, way of knowing from that of the museum "expert." For the African Canadian, those objects are still connected to them as part of an ongoing struggle against white supremacy.

In response to the controversy, Cannizzo wrote in the *Toronto Star* (June 5, 1990) that "the exhibition does not promote colonialism or glorify imperialism…it should help all Canadians understand the historical roots of racism." So what went wrong? As long as institutions and individuals fail to understand how thoroughly racism permeates the very underpinnings of Western thought, then despite all the goodwill in the world, catastrophes like *Into the Heart of Africa* will continue to happen. Intentions, particularly the good ones, continue to pave the way to hell. And to Africa.

The challenges to *Into the Heart of Africa* were intended to have the ROM look at these objects in another way—a way that would both reveal to white Canadians what their history has been, *as well as* support and validate the struggle of African Canadians for equality and respect, and celebrate their dynamic and astonishing survival in the New World.

Despite the recent rejections of the display by other museums, the attitude remains that those objecting to the show were wrong. If the ROM wished to show that it understood what its curator wrote in the text accompanying the display, which I have analyzed above, it could donate a portion of the proceeds of the gate of this exhibit to helping to set up, *with African Canadian involvement*, a permanent collection of African art and artifacts in the City of Toronto, preferably under the aegis of the ROM. The ROM could also donate some of these pieces to the African Canadian community in Ontario and offer to store them on the latter's behalf. On appropriate occasions, those communities could then display these pieces. Those objects are part of the cultural and spiritual patrimony of Africa and Africans that European Canadians stole, and compensation is warranted.

Gestures like these would serve to show that the ROM was beginning to understand the life histories of those objects, as well as making an attempt at a more equal cross-cultural encounter.[3]

CODA: Abiswa Visits the ROM

May 18, 2017

Dear _____

Thank you for your responses yesterday to my queries. I must confess to it being very emotionally and spiritually taxing to ask to perform in the presence of objects that belong to my Ancestral culture and which were brought to the West, like the people, as a result of colonial exploits. All I can do is breathe into the pain. We shall no doubt have further conversations.

Would love to come to the lecture. Is it at all possible for a comp +1? Would be great to have some company.

NourbeSe

This is an email I sent to a ROM employee—I will call him John-from-Sussex, the metonymical representation of the colonial project—with whom I had met to ask whether I could perform *Zong!* in the presence of some of the artifacts and objects that were taken out of Africa and are now stored in the basement of the ROM.

I attended the November 2016 event at which the ROM offered an apology to the Black community for the 1989 *Into the Heart of Africa* exhibit. I had initially been skeptical that anything of value would happen, but noted that a traditional priest from Ghana opened the event; I noted also that there were a number of high-level board members in attendance. I heard, with surprise, the ROM's spokesperson name what had happened as anti-Black racism that had negatively impacted the community. I noted that there were also commitments to improve access for African Canadians in the form of an upcoming show by Black artists, as well as internships and so on. Overall I was impressed, and this was what prompted me to visit the ROM to ask for what I should never have had to—permission to perform in the presence of the tangible and material legacy of the spiritual heritage of Africa.

I notice, with a pang, the various masks and artifacts in John-from-Sussex's office as I enter, no doubt collected as part of his job. I am not entirely at ease as he talks to me about the different kinds of collections—the ones that can be touched and that can travel to schools and so on, and the organic ones made from wood or fabric that must be kept in a controlled environment at the museum. I already knew this and I sense a certain reservation on his part. Those, of course, are the ones I am interested in, and I had anticipated this response. I explain that *Zong!* is a work in which the voices of those Ancestors thrown overboard from the slave ship are allowed to surface and breathe and be heard and that it would be significant to perform that work in the presence of those objects which were stolen and brought out of Africa as the people were, and suddenly Abiswa is in the room. I feel her presence and all those who are trapped in basements of museums, on the ocean floor, in unmarked graves along the many slave routes. It was as if the spirits in the basement of the ROM had risen and come up to the modest office we were meeting in. I place my open hand over my heart as if to calm myself: I can feel something, I say to him, and he says he can feel it as well, and I hear him saying excitedly that I should perform *Zong!* in the presence of those objects! We conclude the conversation and I leave, but am aware that I am upset, deeply upset. I want to weep but not in front of John-from-Sussex, who is escorting me to an exhibit I want to visit. I spend a few minutes walking around the exhibit to calm myself but I am feeling a deep, anguished sense of loss—that I have had to ask permission of John-from-Sussex to bring together the stolen legacy of Africa and the lost voices of the Ancestors. I should not have done it—*on these exact places of exacted grief / i placed mint-fresh grief coins / sealed the eyes with certain and final;*[4] I had re-incised the scars, opening them up as they do in traditional African cultures—*oath   moan   mutter   chant / time grieves the dimension of other...* except in those cultures the opening of cicatrices is ritual, often done to beautify or to mark social status or belonging within community—these scars marked me as Other—a quantity of minus; I had reawakened the memory of the loss and the trauma—*babble curse chortle sing / ...one word erect the infinite in memory.* I feel a sense of shame along with the loss.

The sunlight on Bloor is blinding as I exit the shadowed interior of the ROM, and suddenly the craving for bread and cheese is overwhelming—my body advertising, as it always does when I'm deeply upset, that it needs the comfort of carbs and milk—the latter the first food drunk from a mother's breast, the former, bread, a metonymical stand-in for all food, as in Biblical exhortation that humans cannot live by bread alone.

I sent the above email in response to a query from John-from-Sussex about comps for a ROM lecture. I felt I needed to share with him how I felt. John-from-Sussex never responded. Not even to let me know whether there would be one or two tickets.

Abiswa waits. Always.

NOTES

1   Christopher Hume, "U.S. Tour Cancelled for ROM Africa Exhibit," *Toronto Star* (Nov. 29, 1990), A6.

2   ROM catalogue *Into the Heart of Africa*, 92.

3   In January, 1992, the ROM opened a permanent gallery on Egypt and Nubia.

4   All quotations are from the title poem, "She Tries Her Tongue."

SIX MILLION DOLLARS
AND STILL COUNTING

Six million dollars! As of the week before the October 17, 1993, opening of *Show Boat*, this was the amount reportedly sold in advance ticket sales. The *Globe and Mail* described these figures as "encouraging," given that *Show Boat* was a revival and not a "much-bally-hooed new work."[1] ("Much-ballyhooed" is, in fact, exactly how I would have described the media coverage of *Show Boat*.) On Friday, October 16, 1993, Livent share prices closed at $16.00 on the Toronto Stock Exchange, reflecting a $1.50 increase.[2]

Alongside television images of opening-night festivities reflecting with the theme of travelling up the Mississippi, this sort of hard factual information (or is it disinformation?) representing tangible evidence of Garth Drabinsky's and Livent's "success," could very easily have the impact of making those who opposed this production of *Show Boat* feel that they had lost the fight. Not to mention the chortling on the part of the media, including dismissive references, at the small number of demonstrators at the previews and the opening night. In these zero-sum games, there appear to be only winners and losers, and the Coalition to Stop Show Boat (the Coalition), along with those opposing *Show Boat*, certainly appear to have lost.

Imagine for the moment, however, the following scene and its development: it has come to the attention of the Black and African Canadian communities that the well-known impresario Garth Drabinsky and his company Livent are producing the musical *Show Boat* in which they have already invested a considerable sum of money. Various members of the Black communities meet with him and, through a series of meetings, he is convinced that the production of *Show Boat* will create great pain and hurt to African Canadian communities. He is concerned that he and his company might be associated with a show that is racist, and whose production will affect

African Canadians negatively. He meets with his shareholders and with the mayor of North York. With the exception of a few shareholders, there is general agreement that this show cannot go on. Drabinsky realizes that the opening of the North York Performing Arts Centre (NYPAC) will have to be postponed for another six months, while he arranges for another musical to open the Centre. North York has agreed to bear 50% of the financial cost of this postponement.

> Fairy tale? Yes.
> Romantic hogwash? Yes.
> True or False? False.

Would that such a scenario could play itself out in the Toronto of the '90s. It would be illustrative of a very different society from the one in which we presently live; it would be representative of a society which valued all its peoples equally. A society which didn't need the lubrication of power or money to work. As this one does. A society which understood the collective pain of African peoples. But if we lived in such a society, then Black children would not be being streamed into vocational programs; we would need no affirmative action programs to ensure that African Canadians were hired; we would not have Black people being shot by the police in circumstances which did not warrant it; nor would we have strip searches of Black women in public.

What has played itself out over the last several months in North York and Toronto around the production of *Show Boat* is all of a piece with how African Canadians are positioned in a society which consistently dismisses them and their concerns. For instance, in the October 16, 1993, issue of the *Globe and Mail*, William Thorsell, editor in chief, writes that the only game in town is one of power—"The apparent issue is race—the allegation by some black people in Toronto that *Show Boat* demeans them. But the real issue is power. *Show Boat* is really just a vehicle to advance the campaign of some blacks in Toronto for more power in the life of the city, in particular the City of North York."

Thorsell not only dismisses the most consistently and publicly expressed concern of all those opposed to *Show Boat*—its demeaning treatment of Blacks—he also suggests that in expressing this concern, Blacks are being less than honest, and, as all good white fathers are wont to do, he tells his audience what the *real* issue is. Power.

Accepting for the moment Thorsell's argument that power is the issue, there is a further implication by him that there is something amiss in Blacks seeking to gain power. In as rapacious a society as ours, where power—and primarily financial power—*is* the only language understood, surely its pursuit would be seen as a respectable and acceptable act. Not, however, when it comes to Blacks. The acquisition, maintenance and abuse of power by individuals like Garth Drabinsky and his corporation are commendable and remain unquestioned; the acquisition of power by Blacks—whether or not we agree with Thorsell's analysis of the issues behind the opposition to *Show Boat*—always remains questionable. Once again we see the double bind of being Black: not only are we dishonest in identifying what we find demeaning in a show, but we also have no business trying to achieve power.

ALL THE WORLD'S A PLAY

There have always been two "plays" in rehearsal around the present production of *Show Boat*. One is the Garth Drabinsky/Livent-produced show; the other, the "play" of events around the production.[3] At issue in the latter "play" have been the following: the inappropriateness of using a racist production to open a multi-million-dollar, municipal flagship which was also publicly funded; the public and private challenges and objections to the production made by Blacks and African Canadians; and the whole-heartedly negative responses to those challenges by the producers and the media—in short, by the powerful.

The nub of the issue in this latter production is the refusal on the part of Canadian society to take seriously the issues Blacks and African Canadians define as important to themselves, including their histories, their cultures and their representation in society. This refusal is integrally linked to their social position in Canadian society.

With the opening of *Show Boat*, Garth Drabinsky and Livent have attempted to shift the ground of the debate from this central issue to whether or not the production is racist. This being a democratic society, the argument goes, we must see for ourselves and make up our own minds. The unstated corollary to this argument is that if you decide the play is, as we have been told repeatedly, a paean to racial tolerance and anti-racism, then the issues which have been the focus of the "play" around the play immediately become non-issues. They fade to black with the last curtain call.

It is, therefore, crucial that we look backwards and forwards simultaneously in order to remain centred on the issue—that even if the present production of *Show Boat* were *the* most anti-racist piece of work since *The Autobiography of Malcolm X*, it in no way alleviates the up-front-out-there racism on the part of the producers, the media, and other institutions like the United Way during its production.[4] It in no way cures the disrespect meted out to Blacks and African Canadians, nor does it repair the grave damage done to race relations in this city. The black of $6 million does not appear on the only relevant balance sheet—the one that tallies relations between whites and African Canadians. By my reckoning, this balance sheet remains deeply in the red to Black and African Canadians.

If we see this struggle as merely one between winners and losers and believe that winning equates with the opening of *Show Boat*, then we have, indeed, lost. Those losses, however, translate into gains when we acknowledge the strenuous work on the part of the Coalition in a variety of areas, including making presentations to various school boards. Further gains are to be found in the individual and collective acts of resistance and courage, in the face of powerful institutions, resulting in mass resignations by Blacks and African Canadians from the United Way committees and board.

There are also some lessons to be learnt. While physical demonstration of Black protest is important, to rely primarily on public demonstrations to convey our concerns is, to some degree, to speak a language that can be easily dismissed as outmoded—particularly if numbers remain small. The weekly pickets demonstrated an overwhelming commitment and helped to keep attention focused on the issues. Strategies like boycotts, lobbying and legal actions need to become a greater part of how Black communities function in their struggles. The Coalition's attempt to have criminal charges laid under hate-crime legislation and to involve the Human Rights Commission represents a welcome development. A mass return of American Express credit cards and a one-day-a-week boycott of the *Toronto Star* were among some of the possibilities raised in discussions I have had with others. Such actions, however, require a great deal of coordination and work to convince Black and non-Black people of their appropriateness. At the higher levels of the economy, Blacks as a group may not exert much economic leverage, but our purchasing power is by no means insignificant. It is a weapon we should focus on increasingly; it speaks the only language this society understands.

As we tally the balance sheet, we notice that overt government support for the position of those opposing the production of *Show Boat* has been virtually non-existent, although the absence of the Ontario premier, Bob Rae, from the opening-night celebrations represents a small public relations victory. The Anti-Racism Secretariat has made no public statement on the issue. While giving money to the Coalition, it has remained assiduously low-keyed, not wishing to be seen to be taking sides. This *is* the Anti-Racism Secretariat after all.

At a recent lecture in Toronto, sponsored by the Garth H. Drabinsky Lecture Series, Harvard professor Henry Louis Gates Jr. described this production of *Show Boat* as "a victory of tolerance and sensitivity to the feelings of an important segment of the community."[5] In his May 12, 1993, written presentation to the North York Board of Education trustees, however, we can see what Garth Drabinsky and Livent thought of the concerns of this "important segment of the community." In his submission, Drabinsky describes those opposing the production as "using *Show Boat* as a platform to promote their own agenda and causes which have nothing whatsoever to do with this show."[6] He dismissed legitimate concerns as "shouted slogans, mob rule and wild accusations which have no substance behind them." In an accompanying document in which he responds to community concerns, he writes: "We believe that the protests that have been raised about the script's purported racial stereotyping and its alleged contribution to the perpetuation of negative images of people of African-American ancestry, are *vague, misconceived, and inaccurate*" [my emphasis]. Drabinsky criticizes those opposing the show *prior* to its staging. "[W]e have the right to be judged on our works," he argues, "only after they have been presented for public scrutiny…and not a minute before." Simultaneously, Drabinsky uncritically accepts the support of "the media, the general public and…even educators, [who] have expressed their full support of this production." *This without their having seen the Livent production.*

According to Drabinsky, those objecting to a show which had already been performed countless times, filmed three times, and based on a book which is undeniably racist, indulge in "mob rule" and "wild accusations," while those supporting a yet-unproduced show are a "largely silent majority" supporting the "right of the free exchange of ideas, opinions and information."

Despite his condemnation of those criticizing *Show Boat*, within the same document Drabinsky writes that "all of the concerns which have been raised about *Show Boat* have been and will be considered as our production is developed," a production which, he assures us, will carry a "message of racial harmony and understanding."

If there were no validity to the arguments of those challenging *Show Boat*, if those concerns were "vague, misconceived and inaccurate," if those challenging this production are interested in "mob rule," why did Livent think it necessary to state that it would consider all the concerns raised and to emphasize the show's "racial harmony and understanding"? Why has Livent produced a television program on the making of *Show Boat*, narrated by Black actor James Earl Jones, which tries to show how racially sensitive and respectful it has been to issues around race?[7] Why was it necessary to bring in personalities the stature of Oscar Peterson to validate the show and the production? If accusations were "wild" and lacked substance, why go to the trouble and expense? If nothing else, Livent and Garth Drabinsky owe an apology to those who have opposed this show for the kind of contemptuous statements Drabinsky and Livent have written about them, since from all reports the production now seems all set to win a Tony for the most socially acceptable if not politically correct version of *Show Boat* ever produced.

Further to the issue of the dismissal of Black concerns and requests, Drabinsky, in his response to community concerns mentioned above, gave reasons for refusing to release the script for public scrutiny. To do so, he argued, would be an "abrogation of the right of free speech… [W]hat the show will be, cannot be fully ascertained from the script alone," since levels of meaning could be added through "directorial embellishments, underscoring, stage action and other theatrical techniques." How then do we explain the fact that *without having seen the show* and *only having read the script*, Henry Louis Gates Jr. was able to declare the show non-racist?

Despite protestations to the contrary, Livent's attempts to discredit the protesters and their opinions, and to take the high moral road. have been driven by the morality of the bottom line. With $8 million at risk, not to mention the possibility of a Broadway run, the juggernaut that is Live Entertainment Corporation of Canada could not risk the possibility that "shouted slogans," "mob rule" and "wild accusations" might hinder its progress. And so, despite the genuine and very real concerns of African Canadians, advance ticket sales have reached $6 million and Livent share prices have increased.

THE CULTURE OF CONTEMPT

In a racist society such as Canada, it is a common practice to isolate issues of racism so that they appear to have relevance only for Africans, Asians or First Nations people. Links between these groups and the larger society only surface when the need arises to manipulate the latent and, more recently, not-so-latent racism around issues of immigration and crime and welfare fraud. While the issues around *Show Boat* may appear to have relevance primarily for African Canadians, its opening during the height of the 1993 election campaign has highlighted the connections between apparently 'Blacks only' issues and the seemingly larger issues like the deficit.

These links and connections have to do with how ideas are legitimizd or delegitimized, and while I have more questions than I do answers, it is all the more important to ask these questions. For instance, how does one explain the apparently meteoric rise of the Reform Party? Is it simply populist fervour, or are there other factors at work? How have the ideas of a party that, not too long ago, the media presented as fringe, racist, sexist and fundamentalist, become mainstream? How has a party that many in the media appeared to have to hold their collective noses in order to write about, become the main player in the 1993 elections? Did the media malign them in their earlier coverage? Or, is it that the media have realized the error of their ways and now understand the validity of what the Reform Party truly stands for? Whatever the reasons, what is almost miraculous is how a party like the Reform Party has been able to come in from the cold to a position of respectability, where reporters have by and large failed to challenge its spokespeople on issues that as little as two years ago were grounds to dismiss it. Where have all the investigative journalists gone? Why hasn't there been a major article about the racist roots of Reform? Or, was discussion of the deficit—that supposedly colourless, classless, genderless issue—sufficient to legitimize its more unsavoury antecedents?

Since beginning this epilogue, the Liberal Party has become the government of Canada with an overwhelming majority. The Conservatives—may they rest in peace—have been vanquished, and Reform, some two seats short of the official opposition party, the Bloc Québécois, will remain a significant force in Parliament.

What does all this have to do with *Show Boat* and opposition to its production? A great deal, indeed. Alongside the redemption, sanitizing and recuperation of socially repugnant ideas, such as those espoused by the

Reform Party, have been the demonizing and discrediting of ideas such as anti-racism, feminism, and respect for one's history and culture—despite the fact that all levels of government pay lip service to these ideals, not to mention those of multiculturalism. The success of these processes runs the gamut from the national to the local level, so that the Reform Party is now a major player on the national scene, while one of the most blatant exercises of how the powerful trample on the concerns of the powerless—the production of *Show Boat*—is heralded as the second coming.

With the catch-all epithet and slur, "politically correct," the media—no doubt speaking for their readers—is able to effectively discredit and dismiss every progressive idea and ideal. And they do. Could it be because those so-called politically correct ideals can only be realized with real and fundamental change—the yielding of power to the powerless; the democratic control of the powerful, and a more equitable distribution of power? Is it that these ideas truly challenge the powerful, while the ideas of the Reform Party, all talk of populism and the deficit to the contrary, appeal to those who see the powerful as victims of the "politically correct" and the powerless as deserving of, and at fault for, their position in life.

All this constitutes the backdrop, setting and context of the 1993 production of *Show Boat* and its sycophantic support by the media. "When the NYPAC opens on October 17, the self-proclaimed City with Heart will become the City with Culture." So wrote Christopher Hume in an advertising section of the October 2 edition of the *Toronto Star*, masquerading as news. With the building of the new Princess of Wales Theatre for the Canadian launch of *Miss Saigon*, and now NYPAC, culture has become synonymous with big buildings, just as it did during the heyday of imperialism. It is an impoverished definition of culture that fails to encompass those artists who, year after year and with very little funding, make their art, put on their plays, perform their dance and keep the cultural heart of this city beating. Caribana, for instance, remains *the* most outstanding example of culture without walls or buildings. With very little support from either government or the private sector, in excess of a million people are entertained and some $200 million pumped into the economy within a week to ten days.

The equation of culture with big buildings is an integral part of a long and imperial tradition that equated civilization with big stone edifices. By this definition, India and China were "civilized," while Africa was not. At least south of the Sahara. When great stone buildings stopped (beyond

Egypt), so did civilization. The only explanation, therefore, according to European scholars, for archaeological ruins of great stone buildings such as Great Zimbabwe found in sub-Saharan Africa, must be that non-Africans had built them. Despite evidence to the contrary—that Africans had, in fact, built these buildings—this remained the entrenched and irrational belief of many European scholars. The script has remained the same: Europeans are civilized and Africans not at all. Consider the language used by Drabinsky and Livent to describe Blacks objecting to the production: "mob rule," "wild accusations," "vague, misconceived and inaccurate." All connoting qualities of the primitive, the uneducated, and the unsophisticated—in general, an absence of civility.

Culture is, however, far broader than the arts—big buildings included; it includes the mores, customs and behaviour of individuals in society— how we settle disputes; how close we stand to people when we talk to them; how we marry; and so on. We in Canada believe our culture to be a kinder, gentler one than America's, where violence appears to be more endemic. The hotly defended right to bear arms and the frequency of assassinations are but two examples of this culture of violence. Within the context of a shift to the right of the entire country, as reflected in the success of the Reform Party in the 1993 federal elections, the "play" of events around the opening of NYPAC and the production of *Show Boat* symbolize, if not represent and illustrate, the development of a different kind of culture in Canada—the culture of contempt.

This culture of contempt is a burgeoning one: it sees the weak, the helpless, the unemployed, the aged, the sick and the potentially sick as being at fault for their plight; immigrants, women, lesbians, gays, Africans, Asians, and First Nations are parasitic groups feeding off the country. It is a culture of the powerful dismissing the powerless, a culture that says the less powerful can be ignored and dismissed with impunity. The very ideals that Canadians cherished, which they saw as setting them apart culturally from Americans, for instance—the culture of caring, of compassion, if you will; the culture of the peacekeeper (now also damaged, perhaps fatally, by the killings of Somalians by Canadian peacekeepers)—are now all under threat if not permanently destroyed. Many, if not all of these beliefs were myths in the first place, but myths are the lifeblood of cultures and no less powerful for it. Their value lies in their ability to generate a certain belief system that shapes a culture indelibly. These myths—the myth of multiculturalism included—have now all been exposed for what they are, at least in relation to Black and African Canadians; they have been effectively laid to rest with the production of *Show Boat*. May they rest in peace. Long live the culture of contempt—Canadian-style!

NOBODY KNOWS THE TROUBLE I KNOW

When his father wrote "Ol' Man River," a sombre-faced William Hammerstein (Oscar Hammerstein's son) told the audience during the October 26, 1993, CBC special,[8] he "expressed things that nobody had expressed before." Hammerstein was gracious enough to qualify this statement by adding, "certainly no white man." Naturally creativity only begins when the white man or woman creates or composes. Not a minute before. But who composed the spirituals and gospels? Nobody, of course. Who sang them? Nobody. From whom did Magnolia learn her "coon" songs? From Nobody, naturally. And Kern himself, when he used Black syncopation and gapped sevenths to convey the Black melodies and rhythms in *Show Boat* and in particular "Ol' Man River," from whom did he learn them? Why, Nobody! Since Blacks were all Nobody. And Nobody knows the trouble I know. The words of the spiritual by the same name take on a new and deeper meaning if we understand Nobody to mean not "no one" but Blacks themselves, since in the hearts and minds of most whites they were all, individually and collectively, Nobody. And isn't this still the case today, where we remain Nobody in trying to get our voices and concerns heard. And Nobody knows the trouble I know—words bearing the possibility for generating solidarity work in two senses: (a) only other Nobodys will understand the trouble Blacks experience—through similar suffering, and (b) to understand the trouble Blacks experience, one has to be prepared to risk becoming a Nobody.

It is probably unlikely that Hammerstein junior consciously *intended* any deliberate disrespect for Blacks. It is also irrelevant. What *is* relevant is how statements like these reveal the commonsensical and organic nature of racism, resulting in racist statements even when individuals are trying to show how kind and good they are or were toward Blacks.

FALSE NEWS SYNDROME[9]

Newspaper reports to the contrary, the production of *Show Boat* is not a victory for free speech and freedom from censorship. Rather, it is an expression of how money talks, of how when one is able to control the media, one's position can be articulated—apparently endlessly—in advertisements masquerading as news specials. The press, both print and electronic, have slavered over this production of *Show Boat*. Even *Share* newspaper: "[I]f there are the equivalents of Oscars for theatre set designers…then Eugene Lee, who conceptualized, designed and developed these *Show Boat* sets, should get *two*."[10] For $8 million what did we expect? And can form be so neatly separated from content? While the verdict of this newspaper was that *Show Boat* was "implicitly" racist, it failed to explain how, suggesting instead that we not take the writer's word for it but look to the *Globe and Mail*'s review for verification.

The overall effect of media response to the production, including articles such as this, was to make one wonder what all the fuss had been about. Garth Drabinksy and Livent had urged us to have faith in them, assured us that they knew what was best for us, and promised us that they would clean up the production so that Blacks would find it acceptable. And so they have, from all reports to date.

As argued earlier, the issues have shifted ground. Instead of the focus being on the racism inherent in using this type of production to open a publicly funded arts centre, *over the legitimate objections of African Canadians*, or the racism manifest in the dismissive attitudes shown toward Black concerns on the part of institutions like the United Way, the issue has been transformed into a debate: is or isn't the Hal Prince–Garth Drabinsky production of *Show Boat* racist? (I too have gone through the should-or-shouldn't-I-go arguments with myself—how else could I critique it if I didn't see it?) Further, the implication is that if you can only get enough people to come forward and say that the production isn't racist, then that will lay the issue to rest. Particularly if you can get enough "respected" and respectable Black-skinned people to argue how ill-informed and misguided those who object to the production are, and a few powerful whites to urge Blacks to spend their time doing something else.

The spectacle and farce of newspapers quoting other newspapers to prove the racist or non-racist nature of the show would be risible if it didn't underscore the essential colonial status of Canada. How many drama critics does it take to convince us that this performance is truly non-racist? Sid Adilman of the *Toronto Star* quotes five—the *New York Post*, the *New York Times*, the *New York Daily News*, the *New Yorker*, and *Variety*.[11] Does the recommendation carry more weight if its source is American? Possibly, since received opinion holds that their experience with racism is far more extensive than ours. And can you score extra points if the recommender/critic is Black? Like James Earl Jones, Henry Louis Gates Jr., Sandi Ross, or Lonette McKee? Does an American Black carry more weight than a Canadian Black? There could be a whole new genre of light bulb jokes: how many critics does Garth Drabinsky need to convince us that *Show Boat* is not racist? The process is as whimsical as the s/he-loves-me-s/he-loves-me-not daisy test. Depending on which petal remains, you have your opinion.

Racism, however, is not merely a matter of whimsy and unsubstantiated opinion. It is a highly developed, finely tuned system; it is a matter of historical fact as well as present-day reality. If we understand how it has worked and continues to work right up to the very present reality of Black concerns around *Show Boat* being dismissed, then we understand how this production is all of a piece with the tradition and practice of racism. In its very underpinning, the work remains what it has always been—a work *by* white people who have used Black creativity to enrich themselves; a work *about* white people whose very lives as characters depend on their Black characters, whose function is to sing and dance and disappear so that whites can prosper.

"Censorship is to art as lynching is to justice," Henry Louis Gates Jr. is reported as saying. "We ought to fight the former as ardently as the latter."[12] Many see this production of *Show Boat* as a successful fight against censorship. For others it is a victory of right thinking (no pun intended) over the forces of political correctness and "mob rule." The media's insistence on the unblemished quality of this production, their role in attempting to convince the public that Blacks and Africans are ill-informed about protesting this production, and their insistence that *Show Boat* is a miracle of tolerance, underscore the adage that he who pays the piper calls the tune.

Promotion of *Show Boat* has relied heavily on the use of "specials," which cloak advertisements in a news format. As mentioned above, the *Toronto Star* Special Section in its October 2, 1993, issue was entirely devoted to NYPAC, *Show Boat* and Garth Drabinsky. What was essentially advertisement for Garth Drabinsky and Livent was presented by the *Star* to the public as news, with articles by art critics like Christopher Hume. Given that the *Toronto Star* is one of the investors in this production, it calls into question the objectivity of the "reporting."

On October 18, 1993, during its *Prime Time* news, CBC aired clips of the opening-night festivities, along with interviews of some of the main "players" in the play around the "play." With the exception of Jeff Henry, chair of the Coalition, all the "players," Black and white, expressed support for the production and contempt for the position of those opposing it.

On October 26, 1993, CBC television featured a special, produced by Garth Drabinsky and narrated by James Earl Jones: *Show Boat: Journey of an Epic Musical.* The unrelenting message presented to the audience by individuals of the stature of Oscar Peterson was that *Show Boat* was non-racist, and that this production had gone to great lengths to redeem the negative stereotypes. In an attempt, no doubt intended to show how generous the production team was in giving credit where credit was due, choreographer Susan Stroman tells us that African Americans created the Charleston dance, along with many other American dance styles. "Whites," she adds straightfaced, "stiffened it up and *took it to another dimension.*" Is this theft masquerading as appropriation masquerading as imitation being the highest form of praise? Or, just theft. Or is it, as Ntozake Shange writes in *For Colored Girls Who Have Considered Suicide When the Rainbow Is Enuf,* that "somebody almost walked off wid alla my stuff...you cant have them or do nothin with them / stealin my shit from me / dont make it yrs / makes it stolen / somebody almost run off wit all my stuff."[13]

On October 29, 1993, once again in its *Prime Time* slot, CBC television aired yet another program on *Show Boat,* billed as a feature on Hal Prince. The latter suggested that there were better things that African and Black Canadians could be doing than protesting *Show Boat.* Lonette McKee, the mixed-race African American actress who plays Julie, assured listeners that because she was Black *and* performing in *Show Boat,* this meant that there was nothing wrong with it! Ms. McKee may be Black and American, but her comments reveal an astonishing lack of knowledge about a significant development in Black politics—Black conservatism, as epitomized by Clarence Thomas. Black skin is no longer a marker of anything except Black skin. No longer can we assume that because someone is Black their actions will be helpful to Black people. As in the case of Clarence Thomas, the work of such people will often be actively harmful to Blacks. At best, Ms. McKee's position is problematic; her Blackness neither explains nor justifies anything.

The mutual back-scratching between the *Toronto Star* and Livent, while not acceptable, is understandable. The one-sided and therefore biased coverage by our national broadcasting agency, CBC, is entirely unacceptable and must be in breach of both CBC guidelines for fair coverage and CRTC licensing requirements. These advertisements, masquerading as news, all feature spokespeople for Livent with Nobody representing the position of those opposed to the production. The one exception to this was Jeff Henry's appearance on the October 18, 1993, feature, but he was entirely outnumbered. The format requires that questions are put to Livent supporters on behalf of Nobody, and the answers come back rejecting Nobody's position. Nobody, of course, never appears to speak for him or herself.

Surprisingly, there has been some criticism of the present production of *Show Boat* in the mainstream press, surfacing in the most unexpected of places—the *Globe and Mail*. Critics of the present production of *Show Boat* do not necessarily agree on the reasons for objecting to it, however Bronwyn Drainie's objections to the overwhelming American nature of the production (*Globe and Mail*, October 30, 1993) bears noting. So too do Michael Valpy's strongly worded criticism of the production for its insensitivity (*Globe and Mail*, October 19, 1993), and Liam Lacey's targeting of the blurring of the lines between news and advertisement that the CBC has indulged in (*Globe and Mail*, November 2, 1993).

The *Globe and Mail* has, in fact, gone on record as identifying the show as racist: "Is the Hal Prince-directed *Show Boat* racist?" theatre critic Jack Kirchhoff asks.[14] "Sure, and probably sexist and ageist, too," he answers. Could this statement be used, I wondered, to launch a complaint with the Ontario Human Rights Commission? My mind buzzed with possibilities. I read on in surprise, recognizing many of the arguments, albeit unacknowledged, made in *Showing Grit*.[15] But. And there is always a but. "Is *Show Boat* appropriate for the 1990s?" Jack Kirchhoff asks again: "I think so," he answers, "at least as much as any other sixty-five-year-old piece of theatre." I was to hear others—on CBC radio, for instance—repeat this argument. Age, it appears, has now become the rationale for racism and sexism. The argument, astonishing in its banality, goes something like this: what do you expect from something that is sixty-five years old? Would such an argument be acceptable enough to justify the republication and distribution of works such as *Mein Kampf* today? Or, is it because *Show Boat* is a "work of art" that such arguments apply? There are some who might object to the comparison between a work of reprehensible hate literature and a piece of theatre, but the argument holds.

If age becomes the primary criterion by which we assess the acceptability of material around us, then even the very society around us should escape our judgments. In seven years, the year 2000, racism, classism and sexism and their manifold practices will be at least two millennia old. Ought we to use the age of these belief systems to excuse them today? Surely, the relevance of the age of these system lies in helping us to understand how embedded they are in the cultures of the world and, therefore, how difficult it is to eradicate them. To use age to excuse the inexcusable—the present production of *Show Boat*, for instance—is, at best, lazy thinking; at worst, it is to be an apologist for Livent and Garth Drabinsky.

Before leaving the subject of the media, it is worth noting the double standards that are blatantly applied when issues of concern to Blacks arise. The *New York Times* dismissed the protesters against *Show Boat* as "ill-informed," individuals who "accused the show of racism without bothering to see it."[16] *Show Boat* has had a sixty-five-year track record of indisputably racist productions, of which at least three versions are preserved on film. Despite this we remain, according to the *New York Times*, "polite, ill-informed local protesters."[17]

Be it American or Canadian, white society, by and large, ignores the concerns and issues of its African citizens. This remains *the* central issue around this production of *Show Boat*—that the concerns raised by many African Canadians were dismissed as "mob rule" and "wild accusation." The concerns of other groups are always seen as more important, more valid, more worthy than those of Blacks and African Canadians and Americans. The approach of the *New York Times* underscores this fact.

TO REDEEM OR NOT TO REDEEM

There has been much talk about the redemption of stereotypes regarding *Show Boat*. Did I think negative stereotypes could be redeemed, a reporter asked me recently. In other words, did I think that Garth Drabinsky could sufficiently "clean up" the negative stereotypes in *Show Boat* to make it acceptable to those who were objecting to the production. If we accept that the central issue in this particular set of events is to be found in the "play" around the play—namely the dismissal of Black concerns—then this question becomes irrelevant. Within the context of the larger issue of "race and representation," however, the issue does bear some looking at.

The first issue that comes to mind is whether a white person can ever redeem a stereotype about Black people, or whether a white person should even be trying to do so. Some years ago, the African American artist Betye Saar "liberated" the image of Aunt Jemima in a work in which the latter carries a broom *and* a machine gun.[18] The image, at once powerful and immediate, completely subverts and, therefore, redeems the stereotype of the mammy, the fat Black woman, whose role is one of universal nurturer. In its subversion, the image is overwhelmingly empowering.

Any redemption of stereotypes that may have taken place in *Show Boat* has only taken place *because* of the outcry around this production. Livent's aim has always been to make money for Livent and Garth Drabinsky, *not* to redeem negative stereotypes of Black people, as in the case of the Betye Saar's work. And most certainly not to empower Black people. Being concerned only about box-office profits, Garth Drabinsky and Livent had no recourse but to minimize the financial effect of those criticisms. Hence the company's attempts to discredit critics of the show and "prove" how non-racist *Show Boat* is.

What has *always* been at stake here is the bottom line: the Livent corporation has never been concerned about the feelings, opinions, concerns or pain of Black people, except as these might prove to be inconvenient for them and lose them money. Black pain, provided it doesn't become Black anger, is tolerable, particularly if it reinforces the liberalism of whites. This explains the existence and persistence of the language of handouts and charity, rather than reparations in matters relating to Africa and Blacks. Black pain is acceptable if it can be turned to a profit for whites, as all productions of *Show Boat* have done. Black pain is unacceptable if it turns to anger and demands not pity but respect, as the Coalition and other African Canadians have done. The only opinions of Blacks that Livent and those supporting this production, such as Mayor Mel Lastman, have been willing to listen to were of those who supported their position.

There is, however, another sort of bottom line—another type of tallying—that needs must happen. On the one side of the balance sheet are the powerful with their advance ticket sales of $6 million, the increase in Livent share issue prices and news that *Show Boat* will open in New York the spring or fall of 1994. On the other side is the heightened tension and anger on the part of many Blacks in this city, at the flagrant disrespect and disregard for their concerns. *No one* should equate the paucity of numbers at the demonstrations and pickets—more a reflection of overextended activists—with a lack of support for the issue by many, many people in Black communities. For instance, the annual cricket match, a major fundraiser by the United Way, and organized by Black member organizations of that organization, did not take place this year. Contrary to what many want to believe, there *has* been a cost—a cost in social tensions that Toronto will have to bear long after *Show Boat* has gone to the Big (rotten) Apple. Which was always the goal of this enterprise. The deficit that presently exists in the provincial and federal economies is paralleled by the even larger social deficit that has been created in relations between Blacks and whites in Toronto.

NOT WITH MY CHILD

While tallying balance sheets, we must keep in mind the attempts being made by Livent to expose students to this production. If the issue around this production of *Show Boat* continues to focus on whether or not the production is racist or whether Livent has adequately cleaned up the stereotypes, the larger *and more important issue* of how Blacks and Black concerns are treated will be lost. Once that happens, and it is in danger of happening, then it all becomes a matter of whose opinion carries more weight. Further, an entire struggle will be obliterated and the impulse to social amnesia so pervasive in modern society will carry the day. In the vacuum so created, it will be extraordinarily easy to justify taking students to this show.

Garth Drabinsky's and Livent's response to community concerns, presented to the North York Board of Education and mentioned above, states that it "offers comprehensive educational programs to students from across Canada and the U.S. border states."[19] According to Livent, "(m)ore than 400,000 students have participated in these programs." Livent considers it important that young audiences be given an opportunity to experience the world of live theatre"? Given the exorbitant price of tickets to these shows—an average of $50—and given that it is only the well-to-do who can afford them, is this an accurate experience of "the world of live theatre." Isn't this a brazen attempt to influence the thinking of students so that they come to equate live theatre with these "blockbuster" types of shows—often American and transatlantic imports? This type of experience fails to provide students with an understanding and knowledge that much good, and often great, theatre takes place around them month after month, year after year, put on by small and often struggling theatres like Tarragon, Theatre Passe Muraille, or the now-defunct Black Theatre Canada and Theatre Fountainhead.

For teachers, many of whom are already juggling several tasks, the ready-made packages provided by Livent are undoubtedly attractive. The preparatory work is already done for them and school boards will already have approved the shows, so the possibility of offending parents is lessened.

In the case of *Show Boat*, the "world of live theatre" to which Garth Drabinsky and Livent wish to expose Canadian students comprise an imported show, thoroughly American in its racist script, its cast and its production team, not to mention the racism in the "play" around this production. And to explain it all to Canadian students, no less a figure than the eminent Harvard professor Henry Louis Gates Jr., with his educational "anti-racist" material paid for by Livent and Garth Drabinsky.

Corporate involvement in schools has gained increasing acceptance over the last few years, particularly in the U.S. This involvement includes food concessions and direct linking of curricula to business needs. The most reprehensible of these incursions take the form of companies contracting with schools—for which schools are paid—to have students watch televised material, complete with advertisements prepared by them.

The process is not so far along in Canada, but with school boards facing shrinking budgets, pressure mounts for them to seek this solution. There is, in fact, at least one recorded attempt to introduce advertisements into the school system in Alberta. At present, the linking of business and education in Canada manifests itself primarily as the tailoring of curricula at the secondary and university levels to fit the needs of business.

Livent represents the cultural manifestation of this now-burgeoning movement of corporate involvement in schools. In their own words: "As government arts programs have been drastically cut back due to budgetary constraints, Livent considers it important that young audiences be given an opportunity to experience the world of live theatre."[20] "Budgetary constraints" and cuts are the very arguments used by businesses and schools as rationales for forging closer links. While the dangers of this new alliance appear sharper with respect to business, it *appears* to be less so in areas of culture—it is, after all, only entertainment. But culture "works" best when it does not appear to be "working" at all. In racially toxic societies such as Canada and the U.S.A., shows like *Miss Saigon* and *Show Boat*, both implicitly and explicitly racist, become even more pernicious. To allow corporations like Livent, which have demonstrated contempt for concerns of Blacks and African Canadians, to control anti-racist education of students is a frightening and unacceptable development.

THE EMPEROR HAS NO CLOTHES

A great deal more than negative factors exist on the Black side of the balance sheet, however. Despite all that has been written about the evils of political correctness, including the media attempts to dismiss the protests and protesters, the latter have had an impact: the sheer amount of media time spent justifying the production is proof of this. The Coalition, which kept up pressure through weekly demonstrations, must be given credit for this. If opposition to the show had no effect on public opinion, Garth Drabinsky and Livent would not have spent money producing a show to prove how entirely non-racist this production of *Show Boat* is. Neither would he have brought Henry Louis Gates Jr. to Toronto to tell us country, Canuck, Caribbean Blacks just how ill-informed we really are. Nor would that backsliding anti-Semite William F. Buckley have come, courtesy of B'nai Brith, to tell us why Jews deserve special treatment and Blacks don't. Neither of these individuals comes exactly cheaply.

Those of us—African, Asian, First Nations and white—who have opposed the productions of *Show Boat* and *Miss Saigon* have succeeded in pushing the boundaries of the debate concerning issues such as racism and culture and that post-modernist mantra, "race and representation." In short, we have collectively put the issue of culture, one of the linchpins of racist structures, on the table. The mandarins of high culture and the media can try, and how they have, to dismiss us as typifying "mob rule" and rabid purveyors of political correctness. They can no longer ignore the arguments, rooted as they are in fact. The best the *Globe and Mail* could do, after admitting that the show was racist, was to drag out the age of the work to justify it.

One argument, however, made earlier in *Showing Grit* bears repeating. It is the argument, made equally often by Blacks and whites, that *Show Boat* is acceptable because it is historically accurate. The history that *Show Boat* reflects is a one-sided history, written, as often history is, by the victors. It is a history that omits—deliberately—the anguish, the pain and the trauma of a people. It is a history that, in an attempt to cover its bloody tracks, portrays Blacks as happy, singing "darkies." It is a twisting and warping of history that in 1993 results in the son of Oscar Hammerstein, William Hammerstein, describing his father as having a strong sense of "unpleasant experiences such as being Black in the South 100 years ago."[21] Somehow the words "unpleasant experience" do not begin to capture the experience of the holocaust that was slavery in the South and its aftermath. It is but a short step from "unpleasant experience" to portraying Blacks as essentially happy-go-lucky workers content with their lot.

While we continue to engage in the debate about whether or not *Show Boat* is racist, we continue to play by the rules of the game laid down by Garth Drabinsky and Livent. It is crucial that we not lose sight of the larger issue located in that "play" around the play—the adamant refusal of white Canadian society to take seriously, or treat with respect, the needs of its Black citizens and residents. This is manifest in *all* aspects of Canadian life—beginning with the education of Black children, through issues of policing and the justice system, to larger issues like immigration. This ought not to surprise us, when we reflect on how Canada, a white supremacist society, has treated, and continues to treat, its First Nations people. The benchmark for the treatment of all other peoples of colour coming to this land is the attempted genocide of Indigenous peoples by Europeans. *That* is what links this struggle by Blacks and African Canadians against the production of *Show Boat* to the opposition to *Miss Saigon* and to the many struggles of Asians, First Nations, and other peoples of colour—the struggles of all Nobodys—against a system and systems that appear poised to claw back the tiny and very recent gains made by them.

These systems *are* powerful; they appear to have unlimited financial resources and, allied as they are to the mainstream media, they seem invincible. They are, however, morally repugnant, politically bankrupt and spiritually dead. Despite the many, many tailors—the Emperor has no clothes.

No walls will come toppling down with the death of capitalism; there will be no media gathered to witness its demise. But we *are* living it, if not witnessing it, as economies shrink, unemployment rolls grow, violence multiplies and poisons our environment. Hence the need for anodynes like *Show Boat* and *Miss Saigon*.

The fairy tale described above of Garth Drabinsky cancelling the production of *Show Boat* would have had astoundingly long-term benefits for race relations in this city; it would have gone a long way toward convincing Blacks that lacking financial clout does not mean that they are at the mercy of the powerful. What we have had instead is an exercise of raw, naked power—*Show Boat* must open and hang the costs of increased resentment and anger on the part of African Canadians—masquerading as a "victory of tolerance and sensitivity." In their gospels of power, the powerful always win; the powerless remain losers. However, the powerful are not the only ones who tally balance sheets: resentment, anger, perceived contempt, and limited educational, social and employment horizons eventually and inevitably lead to explosions. Unfortunately, rioting is still one of the most frequent ways in which Blacks attempt to exercise power and exorcise the disrespect and abuse meted out to them in white societies. Yonge Street was just such an attempt to balance these inequities. And while that "ol' man river" of racism continues to run, other Yonge Streets are inevitable.

To ensure a balance sheet that results in the Black, it is essential that those opposed to *Show Boat* continue their opposition during the run of this show. Since there has been so much talk of redeeming the stereotypes of *Show Boat*, I determined to explore the possibilities of truly subverting these stereotypes. The play *The Redemption of Al Bumen*[22] is the result of that attempt. I hope it succeeds, as "The Liberation of Aunt Jemima" has, in empowering readers and revealing the emancipatory possibilities when we take control of our own images. The following are other suggestions for continued resistance.

1. Parents should refuse to allow their children to attend *Miss Saigon* and *Show Boat* if their school organizes such a trip. They should also make their protests known at the school and board level.

2. Individuals or groups should write to the Anti-Racism Secretariat *and* the Minister of Citizenship to express their concerns and opinions over *Miss Saigon* and *Show Boat*, including the treatment of Blacks and Africans in the events leading up to the production of the latter.

3. Individuals or groups should complain to the CBC's ombudsman and the CRTC regarding the lack of representation of the views and opinions of the Coalition and those opposed to the production.

4.   Contact the Coalition or the Black Secretariat to see how you could be of assistance.

5.   Continue to educate yourself and others about the issues.

CODA: God Don't Like Ugly

In August 2009, Garth Drabinsky was convicted of fraud and forgery related to management of his theatrical production company Livent and sentenced to seven years in jail. Drabinsky had been accused of defrauding his investors of some $500 million. After serving time for those convictions, Drabinsky returned to his role as impresario in 2016 with a new musical, *Madame Sousatzka*, spanning at least two continents, complete with a multiracial and multicultural cast. The show opened in Toronto in February 2017 to poor reviews and low attendance numbers prior to its transfer to Broadway.

My path crossed with Drabinsky's many, many years earlier when he and I attended law school at the University of Western Ontario. He and I were in the same year (1970) and I recall playing table tennis with him on a couple of occasions in the rec room at the law school. I doubt he would remember me, although I was the only Black student in a school of some 200 students and one of only seven women. I remember him because he walked with a distinct limp. Who would have predicted that many years later, arcs of our respective lives would have me protesting a show he was producing on a sidewalk outside of a building site, or that I would be writing about the moral failure he displayed in his contempt for the concerns of the Black community in Toronto.

NOTES

1   *Globe and Mail* (Oct. 16, 1993).

2   Ibid.

3   This idea of the "play" within a play came after a discussion with Enid Lee. Credit for the idea rests with her.

4   Summarizing the controversy surrounding the United Way, Lincoln Alexander writes, "In 1993, when the United Way and the Canadian National Institute for the Blind presented a revival of the musical *Show Boat* as a fundraiser, it prompted different reactions from blacks, some of whom charged that it portrayed racist stereotypes that were best left buried. Ruth Grant, the United Way chairwoman, acknowledged the 'heartfelt concerns and issues that have been raised by members of the black community' but contended that shutting down *Show Boat* was not

the answer." Lincoln Alexander, *Go to School, You're a Little Black Boy* (Toronto: Dundurn Press, 2006), 213.

5 *Toronto Star* (Oct. 29, 1993). The B'nai Brith Garth H. Drabinsky lecture series invited Dr. Henry Louis Gates Jr. to speak in Toronto on October 28, 1993.

6 "Statement by G. H. Drabinsky to a Meeting of the North York Board of Education Trustees, Wednesday, May 12, 1993" and "Community Concerns and Live Entertainment Corporation of Canada's Responses."

7 CBC Television, October 26, 1993, *Show Boat: Journey of an Epic Musical.*

8 Ibid.

9 This expression was coined by the artist Robin Pacific and plays off the expression "false memory syndrome."

10 *Share* (Oct. 21, 1993).

11 *Toronto Star* (Oct. 25, 1993).

12 Ibid.

13 Ntozake Shange, *For Colored Girls Who Have Considered Suicide When the Rainbow Is Enuf* (New York: Macmillian Publishing Company, Inc., 1977), 50.

14 *Globe and Mail* (Oct. 18, 1993).

15 M. NourbeSe Philip, *Showing Grit: Showboating North of the 44th Parallel* (Toronto: Poui Publications, 1993).

16 *New York Times* (Oct. 20, 1993).

17 *Ibid.*

18 "The Liberation of Aunt Jemima," 1972, Mixed Media. Joe Overstreet and Murry DePillars have also produced work on Aunt Jemima in 1964 and 1968, respectively. See also "A Battered Woman Rises." See Cathy Campbell, *Voice*, (Nov. 7, 1989), for a discussion of the changing image of Aunt Jemima.

19 See note 5.

20 See note 5.

21 *Toronto Star* (Oct. 29, 1993).

22 M. NourbeSe Philip, *The Redemption of Al Bumen*, in *Showing Grit: Showboating North of the 44th Parallel*, 2nd edition (Toronto, Poui Publications, 1994).

DISTURBING THE PEACE

[I]t is true that the nature of society is to create, among its citizens, an illusion of safety; but it is also absolutely true that the safety is always necessarily an illusion. Artists are here to disturb the peace.
—James Baldwin[1]

Disturbing the peace. That was what a small group of writers, artists, and supporters were doing outside Roy Thomson Hall on the evening of September 24, 1989. We were "disturbing the peace" by leafleting the guests as they attended the gala of the 54th PEN Congress. To describe us as an odd bunch would not have been amiss. We comprised an Anglo Canadian, teenaged student doing a project on racism and writing; a South African refugee; an African Canadian employee of the Women's Press; a Chinese Canadian playwright; an Anglo Canadian adult educator; an Asian Canadian writer; two Anglo Canadian volunteers from the Rape Crisis Centre; an African Canadian writer and critic; an Anglo Canadian writer and critic; an Irish Canadian writer; and myself, an African Canadian of Caribbean background.[2]

Some of us were members of a fledgling group, Vision 21: Canadian Culture in the 21st Century, which had been formed in July 1989 around issues of multicultural representation, racism, and the arts. Some were members of Multicultural Women Writers of Canada, a group formed in May 1989 in response to the failure of the Writers' Union to deal with issues of racism and sexism.

The more immediate context to our presence outside Roy Thomson Hall on the evening of September 24, 1989, reached back some eighteen months to the split of the Women's Press over the issue of racism in writing and publishing. The debate generated by these events swirled in the media as well as the writing community for many months, only to surface once again at the annual general meeting of the Writers' Union in May 1989. At this meeting, certain members of the Union brought a motion to set up a task force to look into racism in writing and publishing in Canada; the motion failed to carry, leading to no little debate and even dissension.

These events were but the high points in a long-standing struggle on the part of many artists and writers across Canada against racism and its manifestations, both in the various disciplines of art and in the structures managing these disciplines, such as arts councils and associations. The faceoff between the League of Canadian Poets and De Dub Poets several years earlier was one of the more notorious manifestations of this reality.[3] Prior to that there was the *Fireweed* issue, edited by women of colour, which dealt with these issues.[4] Makeda Silvera's address at the 1983 "Women and Words" conference also raised the issue of racism.[5] In writing and publishing in Canada, racism was by no means a new issue.

As a poet and writer, my own personal involvement in and contribution to this struggle has primarily been as a critic and writer, always attempting, in the words of James Baldwin, to disturb the peace of those invested in maintaining the status quo.

The aim of this involvement has always been to articulate the nature of racism in the arts, to reveal the profound injustices that result from the systemic practice of racism, and to push those who try to manage and diffuse the effects of this practice to respond to the legitimate needs and demands of African Canadian writers and artists in Canada. Based on this involvement, there was, in fact, a certain inevitability to my standing outside Roy Thomson Hall, along with fellow artists and supporters, holding signs and placards and giving out leaflets that challenged PEN Canada for locking out writers of colour, and thereby using up our fifteen minutes of Warholian fame.

The fundamental purpose to our leafleting campaign was, and always had been, to advance the state of the debate concerning racism and the arts here in Canada. Our aim was not to change PEN Canada or PEN International. We merely used the ethnic and racial composition of the Canadian contingent as a startling yet predictable example of the official face of racism in the arts in Canada. None of the individuals demonstrating outside Roy Thomson Hall wanted to be invited to participate in the 54th PEN Congress. What we did want to do, however, was bring to the attention of *all* PEN delegates, both from Canada and from abroad, the fact that there was and is a very real problem with racism in writing and publishing here in Canada which, in many instances, serves to silence African, Asian, and First Nations writers. We argued in our leaflet (see appendix below) that such silencing of writers, while in no way equivalent to the imprisonment of a writer, was serious enough to warrant the attention of an organization such as PEN and the delegates to the congress.

There was an unusual lack of pre-publicity about the 54th PEN Congress; however, in the week immediately prior to the congress, *NOW Magazine* published a schedule which revealed that most of the writers and moderators comprising the Canadian delegation were white. The schedule also mentioned "Next Generation" readings, but the individuals taking part in this event were unnamed.

Our first response to this schedule was a letter to *NOW Magazine* (September 21, 1989), signed by myself, Kass Banning, Cameron Bailey, Winston Smith, and Enid Lee, protesting the under-representation of writers of colour at the congress. During that week there was much discussion about whether we should do anything further, and if so, what the best plan would be. Because of lack of time and bodies, we eventually decided that the best approach was that of leafleting. The leaflet we designed provided information to delegates about racism in writing and publishing in Canada: it gave a background to the issue by outlining the official policy of multiculturalism and the latter's relationship to racism, as well as describing the more recent events in writing and publishing relating to these issues. Through the leaflet, we welcomed the presence of "Third World" writers in Canada, and supported PEN's work on behalf of imprisoned writers. We also pointed out the peculiar form of silencing of writers that takes place in Canada as a consequence of racism and drew attention to the overwhelmingly white, Anglo-Saxon, Protestant composition of the Canadian delegation as an example of this racism. We argued that this was tantamount to the exclusion of Black writers and writers of colour. We asked delegates to raise these issues in their panels.

Unaware that there was a reception (courtesy of *Saturday Night*) being held prior to the concert, we arrived at Roy Thomson Hall on the evening of September 24, 1989, only to find that many of the delegates had already entered the hall, although we had allowed ourselves at least forty-five minutes to leaflet. However, we were still able to leaflet a number of guests as they entered the hall.

Some guests supported us, others quite clearly disapproved of us, and still others stopped to argue with us, challenging us to prove our "allegations."

The most common objection we heard was that it was "inappropriate" for us to be there—read impolite; this is Canada, eh! That appropriateness had become one of the trappings of democracy, was a revelation to me that evening. At the end of that stint of leafleting, we all felt exhilarated and believed that despite missing many of the delegates and guests, we had accomplished something.

We returned after the concert to leaflet the guests we had missed on their way in, and found very much the same responses among the departing guests as there were earlier. Some guests, having sat through the concert, now agreed with our interpretation of the event; others asked for bookstores where they could find the books of the writers of colour; there were also those who continued to disapprove of us. One guest even pointed to a typographical error in the leaflet and, with great malice, said that since we couldn't spell we could not be taken seriously.

By about 11:00 p.m., our already small group had dwindled to about five or six tired but satisfied leafleters. We were collecting our signs and preparing to leave when we noticed two people coming through the front doors of Roy Thomson Hall. I approached the couple and, as I had done on many, many occasions that evening, held out a leaflet to the woman who preceded her companion. I do not recall that I even had a chance to say what I had customarily been saying to guests—"Have you had one of these?" The woman's response was swift as it was vicious.

"Fuck off!" she said to me. That woman was June Callwood, the then-incoming president of PEN Canada. Sheelagh Conway—member of Multi-cultural Women Writers of Canada—who was standing next to me, told Callwood that she ought to be ashamed of herself for what she had just said, to which the latter once again replied, "Fuck off." As she passed the other members of the group (some three or four people who were merely sitting quietly), June Callwood once again told us to "fuck off." During the course of that entire evening, Callwood had been the only person who responded in such an abusive manner. The irony is that, as president of PEN Canada, Callwood is head of an organization whose members are sworn to uphold freedom of speech, particularly for writers, the world over.

Contrary to the *Globe and Mail* article (September 26, 1989), no member of our group accosted anyone that evening, including Callwood. We were a small, low-key group of people who merely handed out leaflets. Occasionally the odd voice or voices would be raised in a chant challenging PEN to "do the right thing." Contrary to the *Globe and Mail* editorial of September 27, 1989 ("PEN Pals"),[6] Callwood was not "tormented" by anyone, nor was there a "heated altercation." Altercation suggests at least two people engaged in discourse. No one said anything to Callwood before she abused us. Contrary to the suggestion in the September 30, 1989, *Globe and Mail* piece by Bronwyn Drainie, no one drove June Callwood to obscenities or profanity. Her verbal attack on us, for that was what it was, was unprovoked and unwarranted.

Callwood said "Fuck off" in public and thereby used up *her* fifteen minutes of Warholian fame. In that her profanity and abuse garnered Vision 21 more media attention for its issues, her response, albeit personally distasteful to me, could be seen to be helpful.

However, because Callwood is an iconic representation of liberalism in Canada, the media, after the immediate news coverage, rushed to find excuses for her abuse of us. As mentioned above, use of words like "accost," "tormentor" and "heated altercation" was prevalent, and in a more recent article, the *Toronto Sun* described us as a "gang." These are all examples of damage control on behalf of Callwood by the media.

In the more extreme cases, such as the *Globe and Mail* editorial and the *Sun* piece, there was also an attempt to discredit us and our arguments about racism in Canada.

The reason for Callwood's response to us, however, is not hard to find. In a *Marxism Today* (August 1989) article on racial turmoil between British Muslims and English people in Bradford, journalist Simon Reyell writes that there is a "fundamental intolerance which ordinarily lurks beneath the surface 'as long as they keep themselves to themselves,' [which] erupts whenever a minority culture impinges on the day-to-day life of the majority culture."[7] And that was what Callwood's "Fuck off" was all about—minority culture impinging on majority culture. In the media's rush to protect her, however, the legitimate issues concerning racism in Canada have tended to be discredited along with us as individuals. The corollary of this is that responsible media coverage, both of the issues we raised and Callwood's response, has been virtually non-existent.

MEDIA COVERAGE

The *Toronto Star* gave the leafleting and demonstration a few lines in its September 25, 1989, issue. It did not mention the event again, nor did it mention the Callwood incident. It did, however, in a later piece (*Toronto Star*, October 2, 1989) refer, in terms very disparaging to Sheelagh Conway, to an interaction between her and Betty Friedan, that took place on September 27, 1989, at Union Station.

CBC Radio carried the item about the demonstration and Callwood's profanity twice on the morning of September 25, 1989, on its *On the Arts* program. Significantly, in its September 29, 1989, *Morningside* coverage and summing up of the events in Toronto, and the train trip to Montreal, there was no mention made of the leafleting campaign or Callwood's abuse of the individuals handing out leaflets.

The *Village Voice*, in its November 1989 Literary Supplement, described us as "local writers from the immigrant community" who were picketing "alleged racism." The article conceded that "the protesters had a point"; that "the [Canadian] mosaic...could have been more variously represented"; and suggested that we "could have been invited to attend the Congress as observers."

Neither *Share* nor *Contrast*, the two newspapers serving the African Canadian community in Toronto and with whom I spoke, took any interest in the issue, nor did they cover the leafleting or the issue of Callwood's response to us.

Surprisingly, however, the *Globe and Mail* was the exception to the studied indifference of the media, and the only organ of the media, print or otherwise, mainstream or marginal, that gave the demonstration any reasonable coverage or treated it with the seriousness it warranted (Tuesday, September 26, 1989). Reporters H. J. Kirchhoff and Isabel Vincent must be given credit for this. However, the *Globe* editorial of the following day, "PEN Pals," did an impressive job of damage control; in its tone, it attempted to make light of Callwood's behaviour, euphemistically referring to her abuse as an "Anglo-Saxon expletive." Clearly, the editorial's intent was to excuse her actions by suggesting we were at fault.

NOW Magazine was helpful in allowing us to deliver two letters to them after their deadline; beyond that, they gave no coverage of any of the events we had been involved in, nor did they in any of their articles deal specifically with the issue of racism which we raised.

TVOntario, the publicly funded television channel, on its *Imprint* show (September 9), featured Graeme Gibson and Callwood who, in discussing the issue of our leafleting the gala, suggested that we were witch-hunting, that we were not writers and that we had not done our homework. TVO did not, as it ought to have done, provide us with an opportunity to put forward our position or to rebut the inaccurate statements that were being made.

The media have, in fact, effectively censored the expression of our views concerning the composition of the Canadian delegation to the 54th PEN Congress, as well as the events that took place outside Roy Thomson Hall. Whether or not this was intentional is irrelevant. The result of this censorship has been protection of the image—I am tempted to say the illusion—of Canada as non-racist and, in the words of Graeme Gibson, the then-president of PEN Canada, an "indecently rich Third World country."

The irony of all this is that the explicit mandate of PEN Canada and PEN International is the opposition of censorship wherever it occurs. Clearly, the maintenance of a certain image is far more important to the media than the significance of Callwood's abusive response to our very small demonstration against racism. The cumulative result of this approach is, once again, a complete denial of the existence of racism in Canada and a dismissal of the issue.

AFTERMATH

As representatives of Multicultural Women Writers of Canada and Vision 21 respectively, Sheelagh Conway and I called on Callwood to take responsibility for her actions and to apologize for swearing at us. In a letter to the *Globe and Mail* on September 29, 1989, I personally called upon her to apologize to me for her abuse. We have also called for her resignation as president of PEN Canada. To date, there has been no response from her. Her silence speaks more than the clichéd volumes.

On the morning of September 26, 1989, the morning on which the first *Globe and Mail* piece appeared, I received an anonymous phone call from a male calling me "nigger." I cannot hold Callwood responsible for this reprehensible type of behaviour. I do, however, believe that when individuals of her stature in this country take a dismissive approach to issues of racism, sinking to the level of profanity, when a *Globe and Mail* editorial excuses this attitude with euphemistic platitudes and patent inaccuracies, the result is a climate in which this more extreme type of behaviour begins to surface.[8]

Callwood has been quoted as saying she was "outraged" (*Globe and Mail*, September 26, 1989) that we had "got our facts wrong," and that we hadn't "done our homework." Surely, her response—as incoming president of PEN, with access to the facts—ought to have been one in which she demonstrated *how* we had gotten our facts wrong.

Subsequent "corrections" of our "wrong facts" by John Ralston Saul, then-secretary of PEN Canada, stated that "more than 20 Canadian writers of minority or ethnic background participated" (*Globe and Mail*, September 28, 1989). These figures have since been adjusted downward to give us the most recent and final "correction" of our facts (*Globe and Mail*, October 2, 1989), "At least five of the congress' 51 invited Canadian guests were 'ethnic,'" or as many as ten or twelve, depending on how you figured it. This would be entirely risible if it weren't so serious.

The Ontario government now has in place policies which make a distinction between multiculturalism, which deals with *all* ethnic minorities, and race relations, which address the issue of race and colour, a distinction which appears to have escaped those involved in the *Globe and Mail* pieces mentioned in the previous paragraph. Vision 21's leaflet identified five or at most seven writers of colour.[9]

I had always understood the phrase "writer of colour" to have a specific meaning—those writers who are not white. It is a catch-all and therefore, at times, inaccurate phrase including, but not exclusively, African, Asian, and Indigenous writers. While we raised the issue of ethnicity in our leaflet, our arguments were directed primarily at racism affecting African, Asian, and First Nations writers in Canada, as exemplified by their underrepresentation at the congress. Nothing in the "corrections" of our facts in any way contradicted what we observed and had noted about the composition of the Canadian delegation to the 54th PEN Congress—that it contained five and possibly seven writers of colour.

The emphasis laid by many spokespersons for PEN Canada subsequent to our leafletting, on the presence of writers from developing countries, exemplifies a particularly pernicious form of Canadian internationalism, which promotes Canada as an international do-gooder while, as in this instance, practising a racism at home as virulent as any found in the U.S. Neither is this fork-tongued practice restricted to issues of racism. Canada's handling of the South African situation is symptomatic of this behaviour: while talking about the need for sanctions against South Africa, Canadian trade with that country increased dramatically. While mouthing platitudes about human rights violations, Canada, under the guise of private enterprise (Armx), hosted a major arms fair in spring 1989 that welcomed many of those very countries (with the exception of Eastern bloc countries) that Canada condemned for human rights violations. The presence of writers of colour from overseas and from developing countries at the 54th PEN Congress was intended, and is now being used, as an answer to a critique of Canadian racism practised against African, Asian, and First Nations Canadian writers. It is not, nor can it ever be, an acceptable answer.

We Canadians live in a society where racism permeates the very fabric of our society; the arts, and in this case writing and publishing, are in no way immune to this particular problem. Like an alcoholic who will not accept that he or she has a drinking problem, Canada cannot be helped until it accepts there is a problem. The response to our leafleting and demonstration by Callwood and the media (except for the *Globe and Mail*'s initial piece) is an example of this dissimulation and self-delusion.

There is a vast chasm that presently exists between the rhetoric of politicians who chorus the existence of a multicultural, multiracial society and the reality for African, Asian, and Indigenous Canadians in this society. And rhetoric it will remain as long as organizations such as PEN Canada fail to turn that rhetoric into something more substantial. We have come to expect rhetoric from politicians, but the existence of that rhetoric usually means that the politician is responding to a felt need in the society. It behooves organizations to respond to those needs. Many government agencies, organizations and departments funded the 54th PEN Congress. One would have thought that ministries like the Ministry of Culture and Communications would have insisted that before being able to obtain funding, the Canadian delegation reflect the makeup of this province and country. This did not happen, and PEN Canada was able, with the assistance of public funds, to put together a Canadian delegation that was fundamentally non-representative of Canada's peoples.

Small as it was, I believe our group accomplished what it set out to do, although I *am* aware that there is a personal cost to this—the bringer of bad news is seldom, if ever, welcomed. Our intention was to conscientize the larger society to the presence of racism in writing and publishing here in Canada *and* to advance the debate on racism in those areas. Already, I have seen changes that are the direct outcome of our work around the 54th PEN Congress.

James Baldwin argues that our role as artists is to disturb the peace, and this is not only, or necessarily, in the political sense. What we were doing on Sunday, September 24, 1989, was, I believe, a natural outcome of our lives as artists committed to creating a more equitable world in which the practice of our art can continue; our actions reflected, in fact, a profound commitment to this country, its future and the future of our children.

As artists we must continue to disturb the peace in whatever ways we are most comfortable with. For some of us, it might mean living the most honest life possible, a difficult thing in today's world; for others, in a society that seems so satisfied with mediocrity, it might mean writing as excellently as possible. For still others, it might mean becoming more active, if only temporarily.

The peace Baldwin refers to often means the status quo, controlled and/ or legalized oppression, or a self-satisfied smugness so prevalent in Canada. When peace means those things, not to disturb it means to collude with it. The writer has an obligation not only to disturb but even to destroy that sort of peace.

APPENDIX: PEN Canada Locks Out Writers of Colour

IN-VISIBLE INK: CANADA

1.   Canada is a multiracial, multi-ethnic society. Multiculturalism is the official policy of the governments of Canada, Ontario, and Metropolitan Toronto.

2.   At its lowest common denominator, multiculturalism means the equal access of all ethnic, cultural, and racial groups to the resources that the Canadian society has to offer.

3.   Contrary to the policy of multiculturalism there is a dominant culture in Canada which is white, middle class, and Anglo-Saxon. Racism, in fact, permeates all aspects of Canadian life including writing and publishing.

WRITING AND PUBLISHING IN CANADA

1.   In September 1988, the Writers' Union censored the resignation statement of a female member relating to the presence of sexism

within the Union membership, by disallowing publication of this statement in the Union newsletter.

2.   In May 1989, at the Annual General Meeting of the Writers' Union, the Union refused to look at the issue of racism in Canadian publishing and writing.

3.   A significant number of the Canadian organizers of PEN Canada are also members of the Writers' Union.

4.   African, Asian, and Native Canadian writers are consistently underfunded by arts councils; publishers are reluctant to publish their works, and when published, their works are often ignored by reviewers.

5.   Some Indigenous Canadian writers have also expressed concern about the use of their myths, legends, and tales by white writers, while their own work remains unpublished.

6.   The Writers' Union of Canada is an organization which purports to represent most of the writers in Canada today. Its role is to represent writers and advocate on their behalf. Membership of the Union is almost entirely white.

The 54th PEN CONGRESS

1.   Fifty-one Canadians are scheduled to take part in the 54th PEN Congress at Harbourfront, Toronto. Only seven of these participants are Asian, African, or Native Canadian. There is also a marked dearth of Canadians from ethnic backgrounds which are not English.

2.   The overwhelming majority of the white Canadian participants reflect what is, in fact, the dominant culture of Canada—white, middle class, and Anglo-Saxon.

3.   These latter writers all appear in events for which an admission fee is charged; with the exception of one Black and one Native writer, all other Canadian writers of colour have been scheduled to participate in panels or readings described as Next Generation events, all of which are free.

4. In the two years PEN Canada has had to organize this event, its organizers have made no attempt to involve writers of colour. There have, for instance, been no membership drives among such writers, the result of which is the overwhelmingly white membership of PEN Canada, which is in turn reflected in Canada's representation at the 54th PEN Congress.

5. While the numerical representation of women at the congress is an accurate reflection of Canadian society, this representation is, however, overwhelmingly white, middle class, and anglophone.

FREEDOM AND POWER

While the presence of writers from Asia, Africa, the Caribbean, and Latin America is a welcome one, when these writers leave, African, Asian, and Native Canadian writers continue to face the implacable face of racism in writing and publishing here in Canada.

While we appreciate our relative freedoms here in the West, freedoms which are, at best, limited, we also wish to point out that freedom and power can be effectively and efficiently curtailed without the physical imprisonment of a writer. If the so-called freedom of the marketplace works to silence you as a Black or Indigenous writer, so that what you have to say never reaches your audience, then your freedom and power as a writer is, in fact, thwarted. The writer is imprisoned—albeit metaphorically. The Canadian composition of this 54th PEN Congress is a telling example of the silencing of writers of colour. These writers who live, work and struggle in Canada have been made invisible by this conference. Not only is the representation of African, Asian, and Native Canadian writers or moderators appallingly and unacceptably low, but the corralling of the majority of the visible Canadian writers into Next Generation events is a form of cultural apartheid. In this respect PEN Canada has replicated the First World/Third World or North/South polarity. We deplore this fact; we deplore the fact that this conference was funded by various levels of government whose policies specifically espouse, and at times even attempt to foster, a multicultural, multiracial and multi-ethnic society. The 54th PEN Congress is a travesty of these policies; it makes a mockery of any commitment to eradicate racism or classism in this society.

RECOMMENDATIONS

We urge delegates to keep these facts about Canada in mind as they debate the plight of writers in other countries. While it is important to consider the case of writers who are physically imprisoned, it is also important to think of writers of colour in Western democracies such as Canada, who often face racism in their daily and writing lives. These writers often live a "Third World" reality in the affluent Western democracies. There is often, in fact, a direct link between the power structure that supports the privileged position of white writers in countries like Canada, the circumstances of their own writers of colour, and the existence of regimes which imprison writers in other countries.

Since the issues raised above relate directly to your commitment as PEN members to "oppose any forms of suppression of freedom of expression," we urge you to raise these issues whenever you can at your panels and readings.

Vision 21—Canadian Culture in the 21st Century
Multicultural Women Writers of Canada

Vision 21: Canadian Culture in the 21st Century is a multiracial, multiethnic group of artists (formed in July, 1989), working in different disciplines; their commitment is to eradicating racism, sexism, and economic inequities from Canadian culture.

CODA: Hairline Fractures

This small demonstration and the fallout from it had a significant impact on Canadian culture. The furor over this went on for quite a while. The fact that June Callwood was involved in it seemed to create seismic shocks. Joey Slinger, who wrote op-ed pieces for the *Toronto Star*, constructed a farrago of lies around me in defence of Callwood about what had happened. After I launched a lawsuit against him and the *Toronto Star*, they settled and printed a correction. It would also surface in Michael Coren's racist, sexist diatribe against me.

In the meantime, anytime Callwood was involved in a situation that attracted negative attention, and there were a couple, the reporting would always include mention of me. A friend joked that there was a new genre being created—the linking of my name with Callwood's.

The more lasting impact, however, came in the wake of the high-profile, public standoff between PEN Canada and Vision 21 and could be seen in the fact that the arts councils began striking committees to look at diversity issues—not called that back then. Coincidentally, it just so happened that the following year PEN Canada brought to Canada an Oromo journalist who had been jailed for ten years in Ethiopia. Oddly and serendipitously enough, she and I became friends.

I support the work of PEN and am not at all suggesting it is an oppressive organization, but my involvement in this small demonstration and its aftermath taught me something: sometimes all we can do is put hairline fractures in the institutions and organizations that need to change. With enough hairline fractures, when the time is right, the structure will come down.

NOTES

1   James Baldwin, *Conversations with James Baldwin*, ed. Fred L. Standley and Louis H. Pratt (Jackson: University Press of Mississippi, 1989), 21.

2   Unfortunately, many other African Canadian writers and artists who had been invited to distribute leaflets with us were unable to participate.

3   In 1984, the League of Canadian Poets refused membership to three leading Canadian dub poets. Lillian Allen, a major Canadian dub poet and writer, responded to the refusal: "When the dust of discourse settled the verdict was unaccommodating: de dub poetry triple menace of Clifton Joseph, Devon Haughton and myself failed to satisfy 'standards' of the League of Canadian Poets. The official line? We are not 'poets,' but 'performers.' So we asked, What do you think we perform, newspaper articles?!" (Lillian Allen, in *Dub Poetry: 19 Dub Poets from England and Jamaica*, ed. Christian Habekost (Neustadt: Michael Schwinn, 1986), 14.

4   *Fireweed: A Feminist Quarterly of Writing, Politics, Art & Culture* 16, "Women of Colour."

5   Speaking at the conference at UBC in July of 1983, Makeda Silvera "unambiguously addressed the question posed to all five of the opening night speakers—how far have we come? 'I could simply answer that question in 30 seconds by saying "not far enough,"' she said. 'As black women we have had to fight, cuss and kick to let our voices be heard'"; In her work, "[Silvera] challenged the audience—'(Women of color) wonder if you women understand your power and your privilege as whites. Many times you say our work is unpublishable. We demand that you stop imposing your standards on our work.'" Julie Wheelwright, "Women and Words: One Thousand Gather to Celebrate Writing," *The Ubyssey* 2, No. 2 (July 6–12, 1983), 1.

6   In 1990, M. NourbeSe Philip lodged a complaint with the Ontario Press Council against the *Globe and Mail* for the inaccuracies contained in the article. The Council held for M. NourbeSe Philip that the *Globe and Mail* had erred in its presentation of the facts.

7   Simon Reyell, "Tale of Two Cities," *Marxism Today* (Aug. 1989), 9.

8   Today we witness a similar phenomenon as people in the highest offices express opinions that are racist and discriminatory. As *Time* notes, "In the days since the presidential election, states across the country have seen increased incidents of racist or anti-Semitic vandalism and violence, many of which have drawn directly on the rhetoric and proposals of President-elect Donald Trump." Katie Reilly, "Racist Incidents are Up Since Donald Trump's Election," *Time* (Nov. 13, 2016), <http://time.com/4569129/racist-anti-semitic-incidents-donald-trump/>.

9   Two names suggested that the writers were neither Anglo- nor Franco-Canadian; we were, however, unsure of the race of the writers.

LETTER, SEPTEMBER 1990:
AM I A NIGGER?
INCIDENT AT CONGRESS

Globe and Mail:

A m I a nigger because I exercised my democratic right to express my opinion outside Roy Thomson Hall on September 25? Am I a nigger because I dared to challenge the organizers of PEN Canada on the representation of writers of colour? Am I a nigger because I merely handed June Callwood a leaflet explaining our position? Or, am I a nigger because Ms. Callwood told me to "fuck off" ("Charges of Racism Spark Protest at Writers' Congress," September 26)?

On September 26, 1989, an early-morning telephone caller with a male voice called me a nigger—my six-year-old daughter was on the extension. On September 26, 1989, the *Globe and Mail* carried fairly extensive coverage of a small demonstration I took part in, challenging the under-representation of Canadian writers of colour at the 54th PEN Congress. This article also described an incident involving the incoming president of PEN Canada, Ms. Callwood, myself, and other members of our group, Vision 21.

While I cannot and do not hold Ms. Callwood responsible for this phone call, I wish to point out that when someone of the stature of Ms. Callwood contemptuously dismisses allegations of racism in the manner she did, as well as being verbally abusive to a Black woman, such behaviour gives licence for individuals, such as that early-morning telephone caller, to do what he did. By its frivolous treatment of the subject, replete with euphemisms, the *Globe*'s treatment of this incident in its editorial "PEN Pals" (September 27) compounds this problem. It suggests that Ms. Callwood was tormented, and that lack of information on the part of the

169

protesters was sufficient to provoke and, therefore, excuse her response. This may be what the media pundits call spin control, but to my mind it is irresponsible journalism. Ms. Callwood's response to us, combined with the *Globe*'s editorializing, is tantamount to declaring open season on individuals like myself.

I strongly object to the *Globe and Mail* calling me a tormentor. I merely approached Ms. Callwood and handed her a leaflet; we now know her response. Some guests supported our presence; others were displeased with us; still others engaged in debate with us, challenging us to prove what we claimed. Such is the nature of democracy. Ms. Callwood was the only one who became verbally abusive. Surely if she had information that revealed our lack of information, in her role as incoming president of PEN, she ought to have challenged us with this information and not abused us. This was essentially an irrational response to legitimate protest.

I respect the invaluable work Ms. Callwood has done on behalf of the underprivileged in this country. Her election as president of PEN Canada was seen as a welcome development. All the more reason why her response to me and the other protesters outside Roy Thomson Hall on the evening of September 25 was appalling and ought not to be excused. Ms. Callwood ought, in fact, to take responsibility for her actions. I once again call upon her to apologize. Such an apology would go a long way toward clearing the path for a more enlightened debate on racism in writing and publishing in Canada. It might also dissuade callers hell-bent on persuading me that I am a nigger.

M. NourbeSe Philip

LETTER, JANUARY 1989:
HOW DO YOU EXPLAIN?

Toronto Star:

How do you explain to an eight-year-old why, for the first time in the twenty years of living in Canada, his mother is afraid as a Black woman?

How do you explain that the year you came to this country was 1968, during one of the long, hot summers in the United States, when dogs, hoses, mace, and batons were used indiscriminately against Black people who dared to demand that they be treated with respect and dignity—as members of the human race—and that never having been in a predominantly white country, his mother was afraid? Were these white Canadians going to turn on her for being Black? They didn't, for this was Canada after all, and although she would come to understand that the history of racism was as deeply embedded in this country as in the U.S., overt racism appeared invisible.

How do you explain to an eight-year-old child that despite the fact that over those twenty years, the myth of a non-racist Canada has been exploded time and again, as a place to raise young children in such a way that they grow up respecting themselves for what they are—African Canadians, respecting others and their differences, and most importantly taking pride in themselves and all their heritages, African, English, Caribbean, and Canadian—Toronto was close to exceptional when compared with other large metropolitan areas in the U.S.?

How do you explain to a child that Black people do not want special treatment—they want to be treated as others are treated—that if seventeen-year-old white boys are not shot for stealing cars, then seventeen-year-old Black boys should not be shot. That's all. And how do you explain that when

171

you get the feeling that the police consider you the enemy, merely for asking for that equality of treatment, it is very hard not to feel afraid?

It is very hard not to feel afraid and to teach your children not to be afraid when it appears that the police are angry with you as a group, because you demand what you ought not to have to demand—equality of treatment. It is very hard not to feel afraid when you read of threats by the police not to respond to incidents involving Black people—isn't this encouraging Blacks to be scapegoated, and in an already racist society, isn't this singling out an already vulnerable group and setting them up as potential targets for bigots?

How do you explain all this to a child, and the fact that as a group Blacks have little or no power in this society, that there have been no major or massive demonstrations recently in response to the most recent shooting of a Black youth; that despite this, Blacks have again been incorrectly accused of bringing pressure to bear to have a police officer charged? How do you explain that to want justice as a Black person in this society is to be described as an activist, which now appears to have the connotation of a four-letter word?

And finally, how do you explain to a child how alone it is to be a Black person in Canadian society today—that there has not been much or any support from other groups in this society—where are the Jewish, Japanese, Chinese, or South Asian Canadians; where the churches? Where the political leaders in this faceoff between the Black community and one of the most powerful institutions in this city—the police force?

But explain I shall and explain I must—to myself and to my children, small as they are—that racism is a scourge on any society and that *everyone* is victimized by it; explain I shall and explain I must, that we as African Canadians must and shall overcome.

Yours truly,
M. NourbeSe Philip

CODA: Fear-filled wardrobes

I now have a twelve-year-old grandson and I have the same fears for him that I had for my children. Black children living in a society that is often hostile to them, their dreams and their hopes. Consider that in 2016 the medical school at the University of Toronto had admitted one Black student in its first-year class. As a parent who had immigrated here, I believed that if my children were clean, tidy, well-spoken and polite, it would be sufficient. Of course growing up in a Black society where Black doctors, nurses, teachers and policemen were the norm rather than the exception instills a tremendous confidence and belief in one's ability. I, like many other parents, hadn't realized that the game was a very different one here in Canada. I heightened the fears I had for my children and channelled them into the young adult novel *Harriet's Daughter* because there were so very few books for young Black children. Then, I had to confront the fact that publishers admitted to having a problem with the characters—read: Black characters. I eventually sent the book to England where it was immediately accepted by Heinemann Publishers. It was later published here.

The fears for my children and now grandson are indubitably shaped by gender, for this white, patriarchal society perceives Black men as presenting a particular threat. The mistakes young, white men are allowed to make— the natural result of adolescence—are not permitted young, Black men. And so I worry. Young Black boys like my grandson often do not get a second chance when confronted by the police. Sometimes that confrontation is fatal. The continued surveilling of young, Black people, male and female, as well as gay and trans youth, continues through carding or in other forms. A friend shared with me once a story she had heard from another friend— that the latter had hanging in her closet the clothes she would wear if she ever got that late-night call to attend the police station because her son had been arrested. A poignant story about the fears Black parents live with.

What would I tell my grandson who is bright, intelligent and outspoken? What can I tell him other than what I told my children some twenty years ago.

LETTER, JULY 1990:
CONVERSATIONS ACROSS BORDERS

Yo Jan!

If anyone had told me, on coming to Banff, that the person I was most likely to have hard, political conversations and dialogue with was a white, American woman from San Diego, I would have said, "No way." And I'm not sure why I'm surprised—maybe I let labels get in the way. On thinking about your being gay and the experiences you've shared with me, I see reasons why we would understand each other's experiences and understand how difficult it is to resist becoming what the dominant culture defines you as—nigger, fag, or dyke.

Over the last few weeks here I have heard myself raising the issue of the absence of Indigenous people from the residency on border cultures and, at the last meeting, I explained why it was important for me to address that question. I am going to try to again, but before going any further I do want to say that what I have observed is that Indigenous people are not exactly absent from Banff; in fact, their presence increases commensurately the lower down the staff hierarchy you go. I have noticed quite a few among the staff that clean the rooms, and to complicate matters immediately, I've also noticed that the presence of francophones increases among the lower ranks.

Let me be upfront and straight: the absence of Indigenous artists in the Border Culture Residency is, in my opinion, a form of silencing of the Indigenous voice in Canadian cultural practice, as well as a reflection of that silencing. To continue being upfront and straight, I recognize that the expression of my concern comes too late. I had noticed this absence when I received the list of participants; the principled thing to have done then was to have raised it as an issue and taken some action on the matter.

We are all implicated in this silencing, whether or not we agree with it—I don't believe anyone in our group does—just as we are implicated—

whether we like it or not—in certain inequities in this world. By virtue of our relatively privileged existences here in the West, *all* our hands are soiled—the coffee we drink; the cheap clothes we wear; the computers we use are but three simple examples of this privilege which has been bought at the expense of others. The problem is that no matter how much we want to, we can do little about this form of exploitation. To stop drinking coffee, wearing cheap clothes, or using computers made by the exploited labour of women somewhere in the Global South in no way means that those exploited women or men will be guaranteed a better life, or any life at all. There is always another consumer out there to buy these products. I believe, however, that what we must do, those of us who understand the price others pay for our often undesired privilege, is position ourselves or use our position here in the belly of the whale—*in the Global North*—to critique and challenge the assumptions by which the Western world fuels itself; we must prevent the miasma of smug I'm-O.K.-rhetoric from spreading more than it has already spread. This is fundamentally where my concern about the absence of the First Nations presence is coming from.

If I understand that the ideology of white supremacy which decimated the Aboriginal peoples in Canada and the U.S., not to mention the Caribbean, Central and South America, was the same which enslaved my people in Africa and the Caribbean, and attempted to obliterate our culture; if I understand that white supremacy, as practised here in Canada against the Indigenous people, set the stage for the treatment of Black immigrants to this country; if I understand how white supremacy continues to wreak havoc today against the Indigenous peoples of Canada, how can I be silent about their absence? Their Silence (as in the sense I use it in *Looking for Livingstone*[1]) has a grammar and a poetics, can be parsed, and quantified, and has spoken volumes to me at this site—one of the largest and most powerful site-specific installations of Eurocentric culture outside Europe.

I cannot presume to speak on behalf of Indigenous artists and will not. I only have the facts. Consider the high rates of unemployment, and the high incidence of infant mortality, wife and child abuse, and alcoholism among First Nations communities; consider also the fact that not too long ago a young Indigenous child burnt to death on a reserve in this part of the country, because the fire department refused to come to the reserve—they claimed the reserve hadn't paid their fees;[2] consider the fact that a recent inquest into the murder of a young Indigenous woman by white men many years ago revealed that many people, including police officers, knew who was implicated in the murder and did nothing about it for several years.[3] Consider, finally, a recent report from a commission of inquiry into the justice system and the wrongful incarceration for murder of a young Mi'kmaq, Donald Marshall, in Nova Scotia, which stated that there were two systems of justice operating in that province—one for whites and one for First Nations.[4] Nova Scotia is not unique in Canada, Jan—merely typical. I could go on and ask you to consider also the forced sterilization of Indigenous women. I could go on, but I won't.

What I will do, however, is call attention and describe the silence I feel created by the omission of the Indigenous tradition from a gathering of outstanding artists around the concept and idea of borders. For me to say nothing, which is not the same as being silent, would be to collude in that silencing, which would make me even more derelict in my responsibility as a writer, particularly since I believe that the social context within which one practises one's art is as important as, in some instances more than, the skill involved.

I acknowledge that the creation of a space in an institution such as this, to allow issues and questions like these to be raised, is something of a breakthrough, or, to be more accurate, a hairline fracture, in the massive structure of Eurocentric culture. Our gratefulness for this ought not, however, to work to silence us about very grave issues such as those Rasheed Araeen[5] talks about. I believe we have determined the source of domination at the Banff Centre—Eurocentric culture and all its assumptions, even when disguised in po-mo (postmodernist) rhetoric—and we would not be amiss in concluding that the effect of the "power relations," to use Araeen's phrase, in terms of "production, recognition and validation," works to silence Indigenous artists within this context.

Inertia is a powerful force, and postmodern capitalism would very much prefer us to accept its assumptions unquestioningly, consume a bit more and leave everything to Big Daddy Reagan or Maggie. After all, who would want to disturb the contemplation of nature, or sully this paradise, albeit bureaucratic and artificial, with crass thoughts about racism—and in Canada, at that? Laughing and talking about Mount Rundle appears a far more rewarding activity. And doesn't "great art" get created in environments like this, where the artist can go on a hike and commune with nature? Romanticism is alive and well. In Banff! Because before you know it, you have suspended your critique forged in what is essentially a hostile, racist, and sexist environment, and you forget to question how and where a place like Banff fits in the cultural practice of Canada.

While the receptivity—or lack thereof—of a Eurocentric institution to non-Europeans is an important issue, we cannot, however, let the apparent impenetrability of the Banff Centre prevent us from asking pertinent questions about the absence of Indigenous artists from the Border Culture Residency, where they would appear to fit most naturally. One of the markers of oppressed groups is the fact that their members have had to learn how to cross borders and boundaries; functioning in a white world or workplace and then returning "home" to the ghetto or to the family is all of a piece with Black life. I am convinced that Indigenous people have been making similar journeys across boundaries of race and culture to earn a living or merely to survive, from the time the European landed on these shores. So the argument which has been made, that the Banff Centre *first* has to become receptive and sensitive to Indigenous artists *before* they can be invited, is to wait for hell to freeze over.

Furthermore, if no one invites them, who will speak on their behalf; who will challenge the racist practices? Neither is it sufficient that an Indigenous artist will be coming to talk to the artists in the residency. The issue belongs *inside* the residency. It is only when shifts in power are made at the level of curating, for instance, that any possibility of true change is possible. I would argue that it is now fairly received opinion that women ought to be in charge of events that relate to them specifically. I have found, however, that when it comes to race, the same understanding and acceptance of this principle doesn't exist.

I keep coming back to responsibility and the practice of art—if we claim certain privileges and rights as artists (Do we? The existence of the Banff Centre certainly suggests that we do), and if we accept that just by virtue of where we live, the language we speak, the education we've had, we *are* privileged, then we must ask ourselves what the concomitant responsibilities are. And in this setting, one of my responsibilities is to question, question, and question further. Is the absence of Indigenous artists from the residency and the silence about the issue but another manifestation of Canada refusing to deal with its own domestic racism, but only too happy to focus on racism practised by its big bad neighbour to the south—the United States of America? What types of borders does the present Canadian fascination and flirtation with multiculturalism elide and what sorts of borders does it erect? How do multicultural organizations in Canada, such as arts councils, all of which manifest forms of systemic racism, deal with issues of race and the borders between races, particularly when certain races, and therefore their cultural practices, are considered to be superior?

Racism is a growth industry in today's world and, like the multinational, knows no boundaries. Hearing about cross-border racism and imperialism between the U.S. and Mexico ought naturally to lead to questions of cross-"border" racism and imperialism here in Canada. Starting with the First Nations issue. But the response has been a general anti-Americanism. And silence. Neither of which is going to lead to fruitful dialogue. Both of which work to leave things as they are. CONSIDER INSTEAD THE LANDSCAPE! AND THE ELK AND THE MOUNTAINS!

For many artists from less materially privileged countries, the material plenitude offered by Banff is a welcome change, and I am happy that Canada, through Banff, has provided an opportunity for me to meet artists like Magda and Jose and Leonora and Angel. My responsibility to them as a Black writer in Canada is to let them know that there are realities right here in Canada, this country of the Global North, that are the same as those of the countries of the Global South; that Banff is an aberration in the cultural practice of African, Asian and Indigenous artists in Canada. Artists from these communities have been engaged in a protracted struggle to resist appropriation of their cultures; to eradicate racism in funding and cultural practices, such as book publishing and curating; and to develop strategies that ensure cultural institutions treat them and their work with respect.

I wish them to know the contempt which the literary establishment of this country has for Black writers like myself, as manifested recently by George Bowering, one of the pre-eminent members of this establishment, writing and publishing in the *Globe and Mail* that he had read my poetry and was very surprised to see that I was a good poet! I want them to know that racism is alive and kicking shit all across this country; that in Toronto, for instance, four Black people have been shot by the police in the last two years, in situations that didn't warrant those shootings; that similar shootings have taken place in Montreal; not to mention the long history of racism in Nova Scotia against the oldest Black population in this country—Blacks who came to Canada from the U.S. as Loyalists. (In exchange for their loyalty to the Crown, Black Loyalists were promised land and other benefits. Those promises were never kept.) I could go on about studies showing that Blacks are three times as unlikely as whites to get jobs, but I won't.

As I have been writing this, Jan, I have been asking myself whether my concern with the First Nations issue raised here at Banff is merely a displacement of my concern with issues having to do with Black people—but no, I do believe profoundly that we can't build our new realities on the oppression of others, and equality, dignity and respect gained at the expense of someone else's respect and dignity is a chimera. And I have just turned on the radio and heard something that confirms for me that the Indigenous issue is pre-eminent in this country. The Nova Scotian government has just awarded Donald Marshall, whom I mentioned above, a substantial settlement for the eleven years he spent in jail for a murder he did not commit. I have also tuned in to the end of a phone-in show on the Meech Lake Accord with Elijah Harper, the Indigenous MP who did a Rosa Parks on Meech Lake. In response to a caller who said that First Nations were promised that once the Quebec issue was settled the Indigenous issue would be "high on the agenda"—yes, his words, Harper said that *for several centuries* they had been "promised" certain things, and those promises had never been kept.

Wherever he strayed outside Europe, the European was met with generosity; he has always returned this by speaking with forked tongue and for once he's been called on it. It sometimes only takes one honest man or woman, eh! It's not that I don't accept that the French have been screwed and ROYALLY, and they ought to be able to preserve their culture and language, and have their own country, if that is what they want, but again to position myself as I did at the beginning, it seems to me that what we have are two European peoples arguing over land that was stolen in the first place. And surely we've got to deal with that initial theft and compensation for it *before* we deal with anything else. And speaking of First Nations people and reserves and Canada—how many Canadians know or care to know that the South Africans got their ideas for Bantustans and homelands from Canadian reserves?! A group of South Africans visited Canada to look at how the system of reserves worked—the year escapes me—and returned home and set up the homelands! Mandela ought to have met with the First Nations chiefs in Alberta—the links are deeper than many of us think.

What more can I say? What does all of this have to do with art? Everything. And nothing. Everything—in the sense that these are facts against which (in both senses) I write. Nothing—in the sense that for many of us, to write or practise our art requires a supreme act of belief in ourselves, in the face of a system and culture that conspires to silence us, to make us believe that we are nothing. And in believing in ourselves, we have to assign the value of zero (= nothing) to those other beliefs. In your quotation by Araeen, he talks of the European practice of documenting and studying the cultures of those to whom they ascribe the status of Other. I believe that we too are engaged in a similar documentation and study. But of European cultural practices, from an entirely different perspective and with an entirely different aim. Our correspondence is an important part of this documentation, since Banff is a significant marker of cultural practice here in Canada. We ought to put our writings—our markings—into the box that the Border Culture residents have committed themselves to putting together. When Banff changes, as it most certainly will, it will be an important record, from our perspective, of what it was all about. For too damn long we have had to read their records on us. It is about time they begin to read our records on them.

All the best in your work and my love,

NourbeSe

P.S. Jan—

How difficult it is to believe in ourselves—to not dismiss our dreams as merely rant. We are only a minority in this country, after all. The question is, how did certain groups get to be a minority in this country? First Nations—genocide; Black people—slavery and racism. I'm writing this postscript because since writing the letter I've been walking around the campus and hearing voices. The two people whom I identified in "Who's Listening"[6]—the Oxford-educated, Englishman, John, and the wizened, old, Black woman, Abiswa. He tells me that I'm full of shit—that this place is built on excellence and that colour and race are immaterial. He tells me to pick up the brochure on the summer festival and read the president's welcome—"artists…who have come here to stretch their imaginations and their skills into a tautness as tough as iron and supple as leather." He shows me the opera rehearsal studio, points out the two Black performers—asks me what more I want and tells me that what people said about me was true—"You're a troublemaker!" And all I want is to crawl away and cry and forget it all, because I didn't want to see any of this when I came here—I came only to write, I told myself—only to write, to escape politics and politicking.

The image that comes to mind, strangely enough, is the temptation of Jesus in the desert—where the devil offers him cities and principalities, if he would just admit that he, the devil, was the head honcho. In my case, this cultured, urbane Oxonian wants my silence and shows me the Banff Centre as proof that he is the boss and my silence will confirm it. Through my tears I notice Abiswa, the little old lady, laughing and laughing, then she starts twirling and spinning as she sings a low, melodious tune in a language I don't recognize. When she's done she calls me over and says—"Chile, there was many a day during slavery time when we did wish we could tell others who were lucky enough to stay back home in Africa what was happening to us—the drums didn't travel that far across the ocean. All you have to do is tell it like it is, so we remembering. You see how he gone—like the devil, he don't like hear the truth." I laugh and look around, and John has disappeared. So maybe, Jan, I was right after all about documenting and recording and telling it like it is—despite the consequences. Stresses and problems there have been in the residency—we are all aware of them—but nothing that is worthwhile gets born or created easily, and a space has been created for debate, dialogue and conversation. What we have to do is make the space larger and wider so our voices—*all* our voices—can be heard. And this is happening through vehicles like Angel's paper, the radio station and this correspondence. I hope you can continue the debate with the other residents—they are a fine group! Once again, my love to you and all the others.

From correspondence between M. NourbeSe Philip and Jan Schaefer at the 1990 Border Culture Workshop held at Banff, Alberta, and published in the Border Cultures newsletter.

CODA: The Unsettled Truth

The Truth and Reconciliation Commission into Residential Schools was long overdue. It provides a road map to a more just society, but my concerns, some of which are expressed in my conversation with Nasrin Himada in *Bla_K*'s final chapter, remain. What I think about is this—in the contexts in which we have had these kinds of commissions there has usually been armed conflict, and the Truth and Reconciliation Commission becomes an alternate model, particularly after South Africa, to the Nuremburg-style reckoning. There has been a war against the Indigenous people in Canada, but with the exception of events like Oka, there has not been armed conflict. It concerns me that it seems almost too easy for the dominant culture to articulate the liberal discourse of "truth and reconciliation." Take the current practice of stating before every public event that we are on Indigenous land, or a variant of that, while Grassy Narrows is still not cleaned up. I know that there have been some changes—the Ontario government has just agreed to fund an Indigenous education system in which teachers will be paid the same as teachers in the dominant system. Despite this, I still am wary and rightly so because the colonial state still exists. Unlike in Africa, with the exception of Zimbabwe and South Africa, the colonizer never left, and in both those cases they are in a minority, unlike in the Americas. It all feels too easy. Perhaps I am too skeptical.

I am relieved, however, that the absence that I was so aware of at Banff, and that I struggled with, is now being loudly named in different ways.

NOTES

1   M. NourbeSe Philip, *Looking for Livingstone: An Odyssey of Silence* (Stratford, ON: The Mercury Press, 1991).

2   The death of this child is not an isolated event; Indigenous people on reserves have much higher rates of fire-related deaths than the rest of the Canadian population living off reserves. This repeating, ongoing problem faced by First Nations communities is due to the absence of adequate housing and adequate fire protection. In 2015, two toddlers died in a house fire on the Makwa Sahgaiehcan reserve in Saskatchewan when the fire station refused to come to the fire because of a funding dispute. Chinta Puxley, "Little to No Fire Protection in Almost Half of First Nations Reserves: Report," *Globe and Mail* (Dec. 21, 2015).

3   The Canadian government opened a national enquiry into the Missing and Murdered Indigenous Women of Canada on September 1, 2016. The CBC reports: "Activists working for the Walk 4 Justice initiative started collecting the names of indigenous women who are missing or murdered—they stopped counting when they got to 4,232." John Paul Tasker, "Confusion Reigns Over Number of Missing, Murdered Indigenous Women," *CBC News* (Feb. 16, 2016), <http://www.cbc.ca/news/politics/mmiw-4000-hajdu-1.3450237>

4   Nova Scotia, *Royal Commission on the Donald Marshall, Jr., Prosecution: Digest of Findings and Recommendations* (Halifax: Office of the Lieutenant Governor in Council, 1989), <https://www.novascotia.ca/just/marshall_inquiry/_docs/Royal%20Commission%20on%20the%20Donald%20Marshall%20Jr%20Prosecution_findings.pdf>.

5   Rasheed Araeen, "From Primitivism to Ethnic Arts," *Third Text*, Vol. 1 (Autumn, 1987).

6   See "Who's Listening? Artists, Audiences & Language," elsewhere in this collection.

LETTER, JUNE 1991: JAMES BALDWIN

Dear James—

How did you survive it—did you, like me, find the woods cleansing of the pollution of racism—did you go for long walks exploring yourself as you did the paths? Maybe you sat exactly where I did in the woods, just before you crossed the planks over the brook—did you? Sit there and feel the specialness of creation—the gift that this world is and wonder just how it got so fucked up? And here I am in this country—the one that drove you out and away. I understand it so much better now and I've only been here two weeks plus two days—that's all it took to look the beast that's American racism in its face. How so, you might say—being with some of the best and finest any society can produce. True, but at what cost—the stillbirth of all the dreams of the sixties and seventies. And don't get me wrong, but read me right—I am not talking about anyone being unkind, unpleasant, or even openly racist—quite, quite the contrary—but there *is* an apartheid in this country, all the more profound for the apparent freedom and lack of rules. Two realities—two solitudes, to borrow a phrase from Canada's own political morass. My mind turns to you and to the work of one of your peers, Ralph Ellison's *The Invisible Man.*

I am an invisible man...a man of substance, of flesh and bone, fibre and liquids—and I might even be said to possess a mind. I am invisible, understand, simply because people refuse to see me... When they approach me they see only my surroundings, themselves, or figments of their imagination—indeed, everything and anything except me... That invisibility to which I refer occurs because of a peculiar disposition of the eyes of those with whom I come in contact. A matter of the construction of their inner eyes, those eyes with which they look through their physical eyes upon reality, I am not

complaining, nor am I protesting either. It is sometimes advanta-
geous to be unseen, although it is most often rather wearing on the
nerves.[1]

There is nothing more to say, is there—as often happens with good
writing—Ellison has said it all. And more. But let me continue. I think of
you, James, with your face remarkable in any language, but your remarkable Black face, all angles and lines, your wide, wide mouth, and those eyes,
those eyes that seemed to register the worst and the best of what America
is—the cesspool and the heaven, both materialist. I think of you, James,
taking that face into town—were some eagerly friendly as they are with
me?—just a half beat too quick with their hello—as if...*almost* as if they
were both trying to prove that it didn't matter you had a Black skin, *and*
to subvert their own fear of you you see reflected in their eyes, exactly and
precisely as the camera registers the image, albeit reversed, on its lens. But
that's just it—we are reversed, aren't we, in their sights. Did anyone offer
to take you swimming—or were the invitations such that you had to say
no? Did anyone ask what you were doing or writing and show interest in
it, or were you on the horns of a dilemma—made too much of as a kind of
aberrational one of a kind?

I walked through the woods today, James, the woods of New Hampshire, thinking of you, and there was and is a certain logic to my thinking of
you beyond reading your quotation in the Colony newsletter: "The Colony
has, for many years, lived in my mind as a refuge."

If Beale Street Could Talk, it would tell of the tears I shed for the woman
in that book, whose name I now forget, and of the flame of recognition that
came alight within me when I realized that literature could be peopled with
those like myself—plain people, Black people, single women—yes, from
this you could weave stories not just make news. I didn't have to be Russian
like dear Anna, or English like Tess, with a mouth I could never have, or
American like Zelda, but she wasn't really a character, only Scott's wife. I
could be Black *and* female *and* plain *and* have a life worth writing about,
and now I would add worth writing. And isn't that what this sometimes
gut-busting, tear-jerking, son-of-a-bitch art that we practise is all about—
simply, yet profoundly and with great care, reflecting back to people their
lives—their very own lives, which they can then reclaim.

Dear James, I only saw you once—at the infamous Harbourfront Reading Series—but I thought of you today—here in New Hampshire—New

England—Yankee country. Oh, James, so much and so very little, so very, very little, has changed.

NourbeSe

CODA

Dear James, when I visited Switzerland for the first time some years ago, you were on my mind. Despite your self-acknowledged difference, you found a haven, a quiet place to write. I visited the Montreux Jazz Festival, and in the little town that lends its name to the festival there is an artists' walk—the Poets Ramble—along which there are plaques and monuments with the names of different artists who have visited the Montreux-Vevey area. Queen's lead vocalist, Freddie Mercury, is among those honoured. You are not. I was surprised—perhaps you never visited. I was quite sure I had written to you after that trip but could not find the letter. Perhaps I had written to you only in my mind.[2]

I recently listened to a lecture and Q & A you gave at a college in the U.S., and the continuing relevance of what you had to say then remains with me, as does the way in which you opened the students' questions so that you didn't give them predigested answers but cut a path for them to explore, if they so cared. The young need your guidance now more than ever as the MAGAites (**M**ake **A**merica **G**reat **A**gain) close in.

NOTES

1   Ralph Ellison, *Invisible Man* (Toronto: Random House of Canada, 1995), 3.

2   I did find notes I had made in preparation for a letter never completed.

Kwame Anthony Appiah's Cosmopolitanism: Ethics in a World of Strangers *(2006)[1] is perhaps more necessary than ever in these times in which politicians talk more of building walls and expelling or rejecting "the stranger." While I am entirely in support of increased interactions between individuals, groups and nations, my concern with his work was the entirely ahistorical and apolitical nature of it.*

THE WARM-AND-FUZZIES, OR, HOW TO GO TO THE OPERA AND NOT FEEL GUILTY

There appears little to take issue with in Kwame Anthony Appiah's model of cosmopolitanism; its pedigree, he argues, is long and distinguished: it influenced the Enlightenment and the Universal Declaration of the Rights of Man, not to mention Kant's proposal for a "league of nations." According to Appiah, cosmopolitanism and Christianity share a desired and desirable universality, which for the latter meant that there was "neither Jew nor Greek...bond nor free...male nor female...all [were] one with Jesus Christ" (xiv). Fellow travellers along the cosmopolitan path made by Appiah include Virginia Woolf, who desired "freedom from unreal loyalties," and Leo Tolstoy, who was opposed to the "'stupidity' of patriotism" (xvi).

Pluralism and fallibilism (awareness of the imperfection of our knowledge); recognition of one's obligations to others, particularly those less well off; acceptance of difference and of "obligations to strangers" (158) beyond family and ethnicity; the need to "take seriously the value...of particular human lives": cosmopolitanism is all these things, according to Appiah, and more (xv). It is about "intelligence...curiosity [and] engagement" (168) in "conversation" with the stranger; it believes in "universal truth," and its slogan is "universality plus difference" (151).

Very few concerned with the plight of the world today and issues of social justice could argue with these values. And herein lies one of the central problems of *Cosmopolitanism*: the version of this philosophy Appiah touts is a large and capacious portmanteau carrying anything and everything that anyone with a scintilla of conscience would value. And, despite his stated objections to a description of cosmopolitanism as generating the "warm-and-fuzzies," in many, if not most, instances, that is exactly what this work offers (157).

Despite Appiah's advocacy of the sterling virtues of cosmopolitanism, however, he appears to sit on the fence, advocating instead a "partial cosmopolitanism"—this after setting up a false dichotomy between nationalists, who are indifferent to strangers, and "hard-core" cosmopolitans, who view "friends and fellows with icy impartiality" (xvii). He then acknowledges that a belief system that spurns the "partialities of kinfolk and community may have a past, but it has no future" (xviii).

Cosmopolitanism may have a long pedigree, but in the hands of Appiah it is an ahistorical one. In his attempt to force his arguments into the cosmopolitan glass slipper, Appiah ignores the contradictions of history, so intent is he to prove the beneficial nature of cosmopolitanism. In his reference to St. Paul's exhortation about the universality of Christianity, Appiah makes no mention of the various divisions within Christianity, one of the most glaring being the role of women. Christians may have been "all one with Jesus Christ" but women were certainly not the equal of men, nor African slaves the equal of their white masters. He fails to address the fact that being one in Christ, more often than not, meant the destruction of Indigenous communities and cultures the world over. Neither the French Revolution nor the Declaration of the Rights of Man meant that the French state was prepared to accept that "men are born and remain free and equal in rights" when it came to the enslavement of Africans. More particularly, post-revolutionary France was prepared to go to war against Africans in Haiti to prevent them from liberating themselves. Within European nation-states, the Enlightenment coexisted comfortably with involvement in the transatlantic slave trade by those very countries who prided themselves on the advancement of reason. This is not to deny the importance of these developments in the history of human thought, but to cite these events as evidence of the significant role of cosmopolitanism without identifying the contradictions at the heart of these movements is dishonest scholarship. It is a simplistic, *Reader's Digest* approach to history and philosophy. As are Appiah's attempts to use literary figures like Virginia Woolf to bolster his argument. In addition to her innovative fiction, Virginia Woolf is remembered not for her desire for "freedom from unreal loyalties," but for her literary polemic, *A Room of One's Own*, an articulately passionate and urgent call for women—not humanity—to have a room of their own and an annual income.

The obligation to the stranger that Appiah identifies as one of the central planks of cosmopolitanism is not unique to that philosophy. Such an obligation to others was on full display during encounters between the European and Indigenous populations in the Americas, Africa and Asia. If otherwise were the case, the European would have received very short shrift during such meetings, where host populations expressed a deep and inherent courtesy to the stranger. There was a saying in southern Africa, for instance, that the village ate well when a stranger visited because a cow would be killed and cooked to honour the stranger.

Appiah makes statements that are astonishing in their silliness: "Thoroughgoing ignorance about the ways of others is largely a privilege of the powerful. The well-traveled polyglot is as likely to be among the worst off as among the best off—as likely to be found in a shantytown as at the Sorbonne" (xviii). I know no residents of "shantytowns," nor, I am sure, does Appiah, but I do know of the forces that help to create and sustain "shantytowns," and it would surprise me to find "well-traveled polyglots" in the "shantytowns" of Manila, Rio, Mexico City, Lagos, or Johannesburg.

Then there are the statements which state the obvious: "when the stranger is no longer imaginary…if it is what you both want, you can make sense of each other in the end" (99); or, "[P]oints of entry to cross cultural conversations are things shared by those who are in conversation" (97). Others border on the absurd: "[W]e can fully respond to our art only if we move beyond thinking of it as ours" (135). This is a presumptuous statement and one beyond proof, since Appiah has no way of judging how "fully" or not someone is responding to a work of art.

Appiah may not be expected to have wondered "as a child, why" the Lebanese, Syrians, South Asians and Europeans had "traveled so far to live and work in [his] hometown," Kumasi, but surely as an accomplished academic he must know that these occasions for "conversations across boundaries" as he describes it, were for the most part the direct result of colonialism, which was not a tea party (xix–xx). Not for the Indigenous, at least. And the "conversations," which is his metaphor for engagement, took place against the backdrop of a system that was brutal and exploitative. Appiah appears not to care to remember that earlier practice of globalism, which lasted some 500 years, the fulcrum of which, at least for Africa, was the transatlantic (and trans-Saharan) slave trade. His hometown, Kumasi, was an important slave-trading area and the Asante, his father's ethnic group, were deeply implicated in this trade that transformed bodies into things, which were shifted around the world in that particular and peculiar practice of globalization, with very little concern for the cultures and peoples that were being destroyed.

Today's globalization is no less destructive, and the evidence is all around us—loss of jobs to cheaper outsourcing; inequitable wages in the developing world for workers producing things for the affluent West; the refusal of Western countries to pay fair prices for Third World commodities—the list is a long one. But none of this fazes Appiah: instead, he pooh-poohs the analysis of how present-day capitalism works to the benefit of the West and dismisses the arguments delineating the effect of cultural imperialism on local cultures and societies. His proof for the absence of harm done? Wherever there was a local, cultural product, the local populations preferred it, and local populations often took different lessons from Western shows—lessons that fit more with their cultural norms: "Cultural consumers are not dupes. They can resist" (110). Surely, the fact that people may have an alternate interpretation of Western television shows or cultural products does not in any way mean that cultural imperialism is not happening. What does it do to people in Swaziland or Uganda, for instance, that CNN is beamed to them twenty-four hours a day and their local programming is on for a couple of hours in the afternoon? In the world according to Appiah, cultural imperialism does not exist—"it isn't true," and to believe otherwise is to be "deeply condescending" to local populations (111).

His ahistoricism is wedded to a type of social conservatism that results in statements that are startling in their failure to come to grips with the social and economic issues that plague the world today. The best possible interpretation is that he appears to live in a never-never land of wishful thinking. How else is one supposed to interpret the following statement: "The juxtaposition of Western affluence with Third World poverty can sometimes lead activists to see the two as causally linked in some straightforward way, as if they are poor because we are rich" (172). One is tempted to respond, "Duh?!" He continues: "So it's worth remembering that poverty is far less prevalent today than it was a century ago" (172). Even if we accept his last statement, it in no way negates the argument that there is, indeed, a causal link between the wealthy West and impoverished Third World. One only has to look at the struggles that have taken place over the last few years to establish more equitable trading practices between the wealthy North and the impoverished South. Further, there is no disputing the fact that the world has become far more economically inequitable, *even in the West,* than it was a century ago, with CEOs making fabulous salaries far in excess of what their workers make. Indeed, more and more wealth is being concentrated in fewer and fewer hands. He does acknowledge that there exists a "complexity of problems facing the global poor"— those "well-traveled polyglots," no doubt—but he absolves the West of any responsibility (171). Appiah acknowledges that the goals of the Monterrey Consensus[2] agreed to years ago to deal with the "grinding poverty" of parts of the developing world have not been met, but lauds it as a "truly cosmopolitan conversation on a matter of central cosmopolitan concern," and he urges further such conversations and, finally, concedes that it should move beyond conversation (173). I'm not sure what is gained by calling it a "cosmopolitan concern," except that Appiah gets to include it in his grab bag of cosmopolitanism. Alleviating poverty in the developing world has to do with economics and politics, on national and international levels; it is integrally related to fair-trade practices, and many of the issues hark back to the inequitable relationships established during the period of rampant colonialism, when the colonies were seen as simply the source of raw materials for the West. In these times of rampant globalization, very little in this approach has changed.

On issues of cultural appropriation, Appiah is consistently contradictory in his arguments and, at best, conservative in his approach. "[I]t is exactly right," he writes, that the British Museum should be the "repository of the heritage…of the world." The museum's only obligation, according to Appiah, is to make the collection "more widely available" (130). He appears to sidestep the issue of how much of the museum's collection came into its possession as booty and spoils of war, or just plain theft. But if the objects were stolen, he adds later, they should be returned, but only some items, and we shouldn't ask for what's stolen to be returned because they won't return them in any case. Except where the artifacts "were stolen from people whose names we often know," whose descendants would like them back, then repatriation is recommended (132). This is an abjectly self-serving argument, complete with a parenthetical thank-you to Prince

Charles, regarding claims for the return of certain items made by the King of Asante, hereditary monarch of the Asante people, the ethnic group of Appiah's father.

The contradictions continue: "Humanity isn't an identity," he asserts, a statement no one would argue with (98). However, the Nigerian government cannot claim that Nok sculptures be returned to them as part of their patrimony: since Nigeria did not exist when they were made, he argues, they were made neither for Nigeria nor Nigerians, and the latter cannot therefore claim them, except as "trustees for humanity" (125). He argues that "connection through local identity may be as imaginary as the connection through humanity," but it was the connection through "local identity" that produced the art and other cultural artifacts we value today, and while globalization puts us in greater contact with each other, emphasizing our common humanity, we still, for the most part, begin at the local, whether that local be neighbourhood-based, urban, or regional (135). And within those aspects of the local will be other locals—religion, ethnicity or culture.

Humanity might not be an identity, but in Appiah's world, it trumps the local when it comes to artifacts, except when "an object is central to the cultural or religious life of the members of a community" (132). In this case, there "is a human reason for it to find its place back with them" (132). But much, if not all, of what the West defined as art from Africa and Oceania during the heyday of empire, when these objects were being stolen, was integrally linked to cultural and religious practices and performance of the various communities. Art in Africa did not exist as a separate category over and apart from spiritual practice and performance. Further, the destruction of those communities by the various European powers through colonialism means that it is now even more difficult for those communities to argue for the return of those objects.

In his desire to reduce the particularities of difference, Appiah caps his argument about the need to privilege "humanity" (despite asserting that "humanity is not an identity") by stating that "[his] people—human beings—made the Great Wall of China, the Chrysler Building, the Sistine Chapel" (135). When the Taliban announced that they would be destroying certain ancient religious statues, there was a worldwide outcry. I had never seen the statues myself but confess to feeling a sense of sadness at their destruction. It appeared wanton. This sadness, however, had less to do with "my people" making those statues and more to do with the destruction of something beautiful in a world where humans have already destroyed so much that is beautiful, and much of it not made by humans either. And, as a further cautionary, there were some people who pointed out that there was far more of an outcry at the destruction of the statues than there was at the oppression and abuse of women.

The problems that Appiah attempts to deal with are grave ones—how do we, particularly those in the West, live responsibly in a world that is being destroyed by a lifestyle run amok, that is rent by divisions of religion, ethnicity, culture and economics? How can we come to an understanding so cogently and powerfully expressed by John Donne that "[n]o man is an Island, entire of it self" and live that truth?[3] It is so self-evident as to be clichéd to say that the challenges facing the world can only be solved by the peoples of the world working together. Yet it remains so difficult to achieve. In a world brutalized by the forces of capitalism, Appiah asks whether one should go to the opera knowing that the price of admission could save a dying child. A sticky question and one to which the hard-core cosmopolitan would answer, "No." But Appiah, as mentioned before, is a "partial" cosmopolitan, and in trying to have his opera and assuage his guilt, he has written a work that fails to do justice to these issues. *Cosmopolitanism* is, fundamentally, an unsatisfactory work, precious and banal at times; it attempts a feel-good philosophy intended to make the reader less guilty about living in the privileged West in a world riven by inequalities of income, life expectancy and quality of life. It fails to engage with the legacies of colonialism or the ill effects of present-day capitalism. What Appiah appears not to understand is something the poet and novelist understand only too well: the only chance we have of approaching the universal is through the particular. The danger, of course, is that the particular can often remain just that—the particular—and lead to a turning inward, to an us-and-them approach. But that is a danger that we as humans have always and will always face. The anthropologist Wade Davis writes: "The world in which you were born is just one model of reality; other cultures are not failed attempts at being you, they are unique manifestations of the human spirit."[4] Indeed, the courtesies of Indigenous peoples to strangers offer as viable an approach to conversation and engagement with the stranger as Appiah's grab-bag version of cosmopolitanism.

CODA: What's in a Word?

In an August 2017 press conference, Stephen Miller, senior policy adviser in the Trump administration, called out critics of Donald Trump's plans to change the U.S. immigration system and described them as having a "cosmopolitan bias," which I have come to learn is a dog-whistle word for the alt right when it wants to identify someone as un-American. The word was also used in Nazi Germany to refer to Jews, especially those who claimed their Jewish identity. Stalin also used it around 1946 as a criticism of foreign, anti-communist elements, many of whom were Jewish.

NOTES

1   Kwame Anthony Appiah, *Cosmopolitanism: Ethics in a World of Strangers* (New York: W.W. Norton & Co, 2006), xiv. All further references to this text are from this edition and are parenthetically incorporated in the body of the essay.

2   The Monterrey Consensus was agreed upon at the 2002 United Nations International Conference of Financing for Development, held in Monterrey, Mexico. Among the Consensus's goals are promotion and regulation of international development primarily in countries of the South.

3   John Donne, *Devotions upon Emergent Occasions*, ed. John Sparrow (Cambridge: Cambridge University Press, 1923), 98. I have modernized the original spelling, which reads, "No man is an *Iland*, intire of it selfe."

4   Wade Davis, "The Wayfinders: Why Ancient Wisdom Matters in the Modern World: 2009 Massey Lectures," *Ideas*, CBC (Nov. 2, 2009).

PEACEFUL VIOLENCE

Along with a friend, my partner, and my thirty-year-old son, I attended the rally and march at Queen's Park on Saturday, June 26, 2010, in response to the G20 Summit which was being hosted at the Metro Convention Centre in Toronto. I confess to being somewhat fearful about attending, what with all the warnings about the expected violence and public safety, but it was exactly because of that fear that I felt I had to attend. I decided that I did not want to feel afraid in my own city, in the place that has been my home for some thirty-five years. I love Toronto with a passion—its cool ravines, shady parks, the hard white of winter, not to mention the incredible music scene that this city has developed over the last couple of decades. I stayed here rather than move to the U.S.A. because I always found it a livable city. There was good, available and affordable daycare—at least there was some twenty-five years ago. And although there is an incredible shortfall between the reality and the many touted glories of multiculturalism, there is still a profound pleasure to live in a place that is home to so many people from so many different backgrounds. To see so many peoples of colour on the streets is a joy. I feel at home.

So, when on Thursday evening, two days earlier, a friend and I walked along the entire security fence that stretched along Front Street, I felt a mixture of emotions. I was astonished, angry and saddened. I looked up at the fence stretching some one and a half metres above me: it looked to be of some sort of mesh but was entirely hard to the touch. I began to believe I was in a Kafkaesque or Orwellian nightmare: How could this happen, here in this city? Who was the architect of this?

We walk east from Bathurst, passing policemen and women along the route, some writing in notebooks, others talking on walkie-talkies. A couple of them acknowledge us by saying hello; I nod, my friend answers. We get the once, twice, sometimes three times over from others. Little did we know then that had we been stopped and asked for identification, and had we refused, as we then believed we had the right to do, we could have been arrested and detained. What we hadn't known is that four days earlier, on June 21st, the Ontario government had passed a regulation granting the police the right to do just that within five metres of the security fence. The residents of Ontario would only become aware of this on Friday the 25th, the day *after* my friend and I visit the fence. The regulation also gave the police the right to declare huge areas of Toronto "public works" within which the same requirements for identification and possible arrest would apply. (A later update stated that some of the information released about this regulation was deliberately inaccurate.) As we head north on Bay at Queen, we observe a security guard removing a man who was attempting to bed down for the night outside a Starbucks.

The Harper government's decision to defund abortion counselling or services as part of its international maternal care aid package had incensed me. Even more so, the shut-the-f-up comment by the Conservative, pro-choice senator, Nancy Ruth, to aid groups. Her concern that criticism by aid groups could have led to a backlash on the part of Harper is understandable, but her use of the "us-versus-them" tactic—"us" being so-called First World women and "them" being the poor women of the world—disturbed me deeply. I know what a Third World back-street abortion looks like. It is not pretty. I also know how much it differs from an abortion in a sterile environment. So it was thrilling to attend a meeting earlier in the week leading up to the G20 at which maternal health, including abortion, was the topic and to find that Canadian women would not allow themselves to be divided from women in those places that have been impoverished through a combination of colonialism, imperialism and discriminatory, exploitative economic practices. Our rights here cannot be taken for granted, particularly under a Conservative government; an attack on women's health through defunding abortion in Africa or Pakistan means it becomes easier to strip us of that right here in Canada. Such practices have to be named for what they are—racist. And lest we think that all is well here in Canada—there are no surgical abortion services provided women in Prince Edward Island,[1] not to mention the reduced availability of abortion services for rural and First Nations women on reserves. In keeping with these concerns, the unions had asked women to lead the march on Saturday, and that seemed to be the place to be, sound cannon and police notwithstanding.

Was I nervous? Very much so, because everything I was hearing or reading seemed to suggest that it would be unsafe to be at the rally and march. There is talk of sound and water cannons. On the CBC, Police Chief Bill Blair warns about violence, and although his warnings appear to be addressed to those whom he anticipates will be there to wreak mayhem, one can't avoid the feeling that he is suggesting that it would be better if we all stayed away. But this is my city, I tell myself, where I have demonstrated countless times, so why shouldn't I be there? I worry about the potential effects of the sound cannon if it's used and am relieved to hear that the courts have ruled it can only be used to make announcements. But I will and must go, because if I let myself be afraid in my own city, then where will it end?

We arrive at Queen's Park just as the various groups are moving off, and I see a banner for keeping our education public and free and suggest we join that group. Being there is energizing, as demonstrations always are: there are drums and other musical instruments; there are chants. "What does democracy look like?" the chant goes up. "This is what democracy looks like," we chant as we move down University Avenue. And I think, yes, this is what it looks like—messy, a bit disorganized, but with a principle at the core—that we all matter. Equally. I notice an elderly woman holding the hand of an obviously mentally disabled woman as they make their way through the crowd. Mother and daughter, perhaps, and I am moved that they, too, are here. This, indeed, is what democracy looks like.

We are overtaken by a group chanting, "No one is illegal!" I join in. Barricades and police prevent us from going south on University directly in front of the U.S. embassy. The area around it is cordoned off, and the show of police force is massive, many of the police standing with their hands on their batons, glaring at us. Some of us approach the metal barricades telling the officers that we are there for them and for their children as well. "Do you have children?" we ask. They remain impassive. "Whose streets?" the chant rises up. "Our streets," we answer. Among ourselves we question the reason for this display of raw, brute force as we continue on our way down to Queen Street. At one point, we see to our left a group of young people clad in black running alongside the march, but think nothing of it. A man does yoga postures perched on the head of a female figure that is part of a monument to the Boer War at Queen and University. People laugh and cheer him on, while fearful that he might fall. It is here, however, that we are met with one of the most awesome displays of police power I have ever witnessed. Police extend across the entire southern boundary of the intersection; behind them are phalanxes of officers, helmeted and at ready.

At each southerly intersection of the march went along Queen Street this is the scenario, cutting the city off south of Queen. It is disturbing and confusing: "Why is this necessary?" we ask each other. People are stunned and angry at the display of force. At every intersection south from Queen Street, black-clad, helmeted police can be seen running along the streets. There is talk along the march that they are clearing out the alleyways. We continue west along Queen to Spadina, where the march seems to have come to a stop. Everyone is milling around, wondering where the march is going next. Some people go south to Richmond, where the police have blocked the street. We mill around outside the café Lettieri, use the bathroom, buy an espresso and wonder what to do next. There is an announcement by someone on a megaphone that the peace march is going north along Spadina and the justice march is returning east along Queen Street. The march has split. We, along with hundreds of people, simply continue to stand around chatting and talking, primarily about the massive police presence. At one point, a pink flare is released too far away for us to see who is responsible, but strangely enough, there is no panic. Smoke rises, people continue talking.

Suddenly a line of police mounted on bicycles emerge out of the crowd and aggressively move east along Queen. We aren't sure what that means, but something is happening, we conclude. We aren't sure what to do, but then decide to walk back east along Queen. There is no longer a march as such, simply people walking or talking in groups. At the Rivoli, a confrontation occurs between scores of police officers and what appear to be young people who had been in the demonstration. There are no black-clad people here, and a police car with smashed windows is in the middle of the street. I still can't figure out why the police would need to bring a police car there, given that there are police—scores of police, in fact—at each and every intersection within easy reach. This is one of the cars that will be burnt later. Why was it left there in the middle of the street, and, having been set on fire, why didn't it explode? For that matter, why didn't any of those cars explode? Were their gas tanks empty? People come out of their stores to watch what is happening. I do not observe any aggressive actions by the crowd, but the police form a circle in the middle of the street and begin aggressively shoving people back against the storefronts; they don gas masks, which makes us think things will be getting out of hand, if not ugly, so we head further east.

For some five hours, we walk the streets of downtown Toronto, covering some eight to nine kilometres, and at no time do we witness what the media refers to as the rampages that took place in Toronto.[2] Also, the streets north of Queen are eerily absent of police officers. At University Avenue, on our return journey, I witness a brilliant intervention by a young man who holds a microphone and in a soft, almost intimate, voice asks questions like, "Will you remove your facial recognition security cameras after the G20?" It is powerful and effective: this quiet voice against this massively brutal array of force. I myself challenge individual officers at the barricades, asking why it is necessary for such a show of force, insisting that this is my city, too. I feel strongly that their foreboding presence says that I am a threat, that I don't belong there, that I am somehow illegal. And I resist accepting that. They remain stone-faced, these men and women in blue whose function, I am told, is to serve and protect. Why do I feel that they don't mean me any good, let alone serving and protecting me. Further east, still on Queen, we good-naturedly tease a group of officers from Waterloo and get some five of them to smile—we applaud. A group of clowns bring a delightful sense of whimsy and humour as they balance on an imaginary tightrope in front of this same group of officers; as the clowns make it to the other side of the tightrope, the people standing around applaud them. These interactions aside, however, the overwhelming image that I am left with, in this city of astonishing ethnic and racial diversity, is a virtually monolithic, white and male police force suited up for war against its inhabitants, most of whom are peoples of colour. And that is a sea change in this city.

All of which brings me to the property damage, which becomes obvious as we walk east along Queen, starting with the Starbucks and TD Bank at Queen and University. At Queen and Bay there is more evidence of it. The very Starbucks where the homeless man was moved on two days earlier has been smashed. The bank next door as well. North along Yonge from Dundas, the property damage is more widespread—de Boers, American Apparel, Tim Hortons—very few independent mom-and-pop stores appear to be damaged. Someone has brought a tall coffee table out from a Tim Hortons and placed it in the middle of the street with coffee cups on it. Zanzibar, the seedy exotic dancing lounge, has had its windows smashed. Is this intended as a feminist gesture, perhaps? There is a Second Cup with a sign advertising (incorrectly, I might add) that the business is independent and Canadian-owned. Its windows remain intact. Essentially, the violence appears to be directed against franchises and banks. Right across from the police station on College, where a line of poker-faced police officers stand at attention, the windows of the Winners store are shattered, as is the bank machine next door.

Most of the people on that march were not involved in acts of violence against property. The debate has raged on as to whether the property damage justified the one-billion-dollar price tag for the G8 and G20 meetings. Many, led by Stephen Harper, believed that to be the case. I have no doubt that in among the crowds demonstrating were some who had come with the intent to destroy—to mash up the place, as they say. Violence, I believe, should only be a last resort, but it is endemic to us as humans, and it has been used for good and ill. The French and Haitian revolutions as well as the armed struggle against apartheid, are but three examples of the former that come to mind. There is also a long tradition in this country of allowing a certain amount of rioting by young, white males in celebration of sporting victories. Acts similar to the vandalism carried out at the G20 march occur almost annually in Montreal related to sports events. In 2008, for instance, a string of police cars were torched in Montreal during celebrations after a sporting event,[3] and as recently as May 2010, when Les Canadiens beat the Pittsburgh Penguins, the Montreal Gazette stated that "rarely had so much testosterone been unleashed onto Montreal's streets with so little consequence"; the article also reported that police in Montreal emptied and removed beer bottles and generally tried to allow people to enjoy themselves without harming others.[4] And in June 2011, there was the infamous Vancouver Stanley Cup riot.[5] In all these cases, there is no redeeming social agenda other than boys just wanting to have fun.

As a Black person, rioting white people, particularly males, conjure images of lynch mobs, and helmeted white police in full riot gear remind me of how African Americans were attacked in the streets by police using water cannons and attack dogs. I would certainly prefer to know who this group is that is now labelled as the Black Bloc and who has been identified as being responsible for some of the violence.[6] What is their agenda, what their aim? Are they being elevated by the media to a stature beyond what they actually are?

We live in societies that are profoundly violent in their acts against many people and groups—we need go no further than to think about the overwhelming nature of state-sanctioned violence against Indigenous and Black people. We tolerate it not because we want to—those of us who long for social justice—but because, for the most part, we don't have a choice but to live with what Franz Fanon calls the "peaceful violence that the world is steeped in."[7]

Government and media response to these acts has been to deplore violence out of hand—after all, peace, order and good government is one of the founding principles of this country. Our mayor raced to suggest that it was all outsiders who were to blame for the destruction, and I am reminded of how the Canadian sprinter, Ben Johnson, was disavowed and became Jamaican as his steroid use was revealed. As if violence and the propensity to violence exist elsewhere, and we in Toronto somehow are not capable of being violent. This country has carried out unspeakable acts of violence against its First Nation peoples. That violence continues today in many, many ways, not least of which can be seen in the disproportionate numbers of Indigenous women who go missing and are believed murdered, and in the breakup of Indigenous families by the removal of their children. There is the daily violence with which communities of colour are policed here in Toronto and Canada-wide. There is the everyday violence against women in virtually every area of their lives: from the harassment on the street to the justice system. There is the violence wreaked on low-income families in this very city when their dietary allowances are cut. And whenever some big attraction rolls into town, whether it be the Vancouver Olympics or the Toronto G20 conference, it is perfectly acceptable to move the homeless, the poor, the downtrodden out and away. This too, is violence, perpetrated against people, not property, but very few people complain about it. And when, through the actions of speculators, bankers and investment houses, thousands lose their homes or their jobs because someone somewhere thought it was oh-so-clever to develop some new way of bundling and selling mortgages, that too is violence. Much has been made of mom-and-pop stores that have been damaged this weekend past, but many of those very stores have had to close—there are several in my neighbourhood—because of the havoc and violent upheaval wreaked by a financial system untrammelled by regulation. A financial system that those selfsame powers—the G8 group—turned a blind eye to and then bailed out with taxpayers' money. Not to mention the enormous violence, with fatal consequences for species, if not life itself, that corporations are allowed to unleash on the world under the guise of projects like the tar sands, offshore drilling, or logging. And many, many of those who smugly decry the violence of the Black Bloc, or whoever it was, who this weekend vandalized property, which on a scale of things was minor, live comfortably with these acts of violence and seldom if ever raise their voices in opposition.

Have we as a community of people ever demanded to know how many Iraqis were killed in the U.S.A.-led invasion? Do we know how many Pakistani civilians are being killed by drone aircraft or other acts of war? We are told whenever a Canadian soldier dies, but never how many Afghanis are killed. Do we even care to know? And, when we use our cellphones to take all those pictures as part of what the media now refer to as "riot tourism," do we think of the internationally supported violent struggle taking place in Congo for minerals, not least of which is the coltan so essential to the construction of cellphones. When our children play violent war games on PlayStation, Xbox and Nintendo, do we think of the real war raging in Congo that results in many violent deaths—real deaths—not to mention the rape of Congolese women? Even as I write, there are some eight to ten Canadian mining companies operating in Congo. This is the "peaceful violence" we all live with.

I have felt for a while that the entire exercise of holding the G20 in downtown Toronto was a dress rehearsal of sorts: perhaps I have watched too many MI-5 shows. The massive display of intimidating police force has to be seen as a provocation, even an incitement to respond to or challenge them; the earlier subterfuge in passing the regulation granting the police special powers during a period of time that had not been declared a state of emergency showed a contempt for the rights of the residents of Toronto. The Harper government's attempted end runs around long-established, democratic practices, such as proroguing Parliament, its avoidance of transparency and public accountability, all point to a disregard for the populace which the events of June 26, 2010, illustrate.

There is talk that the messages of the demonstrators were drowned out by the violence, but in the week of demonstrations and meetings leading up to the G20, the media paid scant attention to the issues raised by these groups, and had the violence not occurred, there would have been no greater coverage of the issues and demands that these groups care so passionately about. I for one am guardedly hopeful about the future of the world and, therefore, the future of my five-year-old grandson because of what I saw on Saturday: young people who care passionately enough about this world to take to the streets with their messages of hope and struggle. Maybe he will learn the lesson of speaking truth to power, which is what the demonstration was all about. "Whose streets?" the young Asian woman on the megaphone calls out. "Our streets," we yell back. These *are* our streets. This is *our* city and, therefore, our home. We should never have been held hostage in it by police forces that presented themselves as an invading army. Nothing, not even Stephen Harper's dislike of Toronto, warranted that.

CODA: Talking the Talk

Whose streets? Our streets! A familiar chant as we take our bodies to the street, but as I write this, the shadow of what happened in Charlottesville in August 2017 lurks. White supremacists and neo-Nazis displayed their evil intentions on the streets and were met by those who refuse to allow racial hatred to spread. When I initially thought of what I would write as a coda, I reflected on the idea of how we humans, despite our highly technological society, continue to put our bodies on the line. It is an activity that only makes any degree of sense only in areas that are built up, like villages, towns or cities. I cannot imagine our cave-dwelling ancestors demonstrating against the animals that may have preyed on them. But through outdoor ritual, they might have understood how to move through space and how that impacted them and their bodies. I think of all the times I have taken to the streets—over apartheid, the arms race, and against police shootings of Black men. I think of that with pride, believing myself to be a part of a long legacy of those literally walking the walk. After Charlottesville, however, I no longer feel so sanguine—perhaps the optimism will return. What I had seen as a progressive act has somehow been sullied by the acts—the same acts that I have carried out over the years, taking to the streets and shouting slogans—of the racist right wing. These were people who, if they dared to march, marched in hoods, hiding their faces. Trump and his band of haters have made hate legitimate, however, and they will be out in full force for the foreseeable future. Exercising their democratic rights to free speech and assembly. I have to tell myself that the cause is what makes it different and that we are on the side of good; that we owe it to ourselves to take our beliefs to the streets even in the face of hate.

NOTES

1   Prince Edward Island will pay for the service in Moncton, N.B., and Halifax, N.S.

2   For just a couple of references to the "rampages," please see "American G20 Rioter Who Threw Rock at Police Car Sentenced to 7 Months," *Globe and*

Mail (Feb. 3, 2014). See also "G20 Police Officer Guilty of Misconduct Over Bandana arrest," CBC (Dec. 17, 2013), <http://www.cbc.ca/news/canada/toronto/g20-police-officer-guilty-of-misconduct-over-bandana-arrest-1.2468333>

3   "Police Cars Burned, Stores Looted in Montreal Hockey Riot," *CBC News* (April 22, 2008), <http://www.cbc.canews/canada/montreal-policecars-burned-stores-looted-in-montreal-hockey-riot-1.757821>.

4   Catherine Solyom, "Fears of Riot Prove Unfounded," *Montreal Gazette* (May 13, 2010). Despite its title, this article concludes, "The celebration deteriorated as the night went on. After midnight, the display window of the SAQ store on Ste. Catherine near Stanley St. was smashed and the contents looted, police said. The hard-core hooligans then turned their attention to three boutiques on Ste. Catherine, and police resorted to tear gas to break up the crowd." Another article on the Montreal post-win riot identifies the rioters as "rowdies" in its title and refers to them as "youths" in the article: "Montreal police regained control of the downtown core early Thursday after firing tear gas at hundreds of bottle-tossing youths, many of whom looted businesses following a stunning playoff victory by the Canadiens." Nelson Wyatt and Alexander Paneta, "Rowdies Put Damper on Montreal's Win," *The Globe and Mail* (May 13, 2010). These "rowdies" performed acts of violence similar to those of the "rioters" in the G20 march that would occur a little more than a month later in June 2010.

5   "Riots Erupt in Vancouver after Canucks Lose," *CBC News* (June 15, 2011), <http://www.cbc.ca/news/canada/british-columbia/riots-erupt-in-vancouver-after-canucks-loss-1.993707>. Despite Canada's history of sports riots, the police in Vancouver didn't identify the hockey fans as a threat and adopted a different style of policing than that deployed by Toronto police officers at the G20: "Using 'meet and greet' tactics that worked successfully during the Olympics and run-up to Wednesday night's game, which had police mingling with the crowds and high-fiving celebrants, police were confident they had turned the corner at avoiding violence." Rod Mickleburgh and Justine Hunter, "What went wrong in Vancouver?" *The Globe and Mail* (June 16, 2011).

6   Ciara Burn, "Black Bloc Stragety Has Been Used for Decades," *Globe and Mail* (June 26, 2010).

7   Franz Fanon, *The Wretched of the Earth* (New York: Grove Press, 1963), 81.

CARIBANA:
AFRICAN ROOTS AND CONTINUITIES

PROLOGUE

Black bodies in public spaces are always policed and restricted: from regulations related to noise levels pertaining to Black and African music, through locations of gatherings and routes of parades, to more overt policing. The annual version of the Trinidad Carnival, formerly known as Caribana, which takes place in Toronto, began fifty years ago.[1] Its initial route, like the Pride parade, was through certain downtown streets of the city. Over the years, the route of the parade has been moved, finally ending up on Lakeshore Boulevard in 1992, with increasingly tall fences cordoning off the spectators from the masqueraders.

Some experiences demand a faithfulness to the language in which the experience happens, and Carnival does not happen in standard English. For this reason, I chose to make my arguments in "Race, Space and the Poetics of Moving" in one of the Caribbean demotics of English—the Trinidad creole or vernacular, which bears the influence of French, English, Spanish and African languages. The strength and beauty of the demotic lies in what I call its kinetic qualities—its kinopoesis.[2] It is a language that brings over into English the "relationship between the dynamics of speech and the dynamics of action" that is to be found in at least one West African language, Yoruba.[3] The Trinidad demotic moves, like the Carnival band, through space rhythmed by time. It is, therefore, eminently suited to capturing the moving at the heart of Carnival. Traditionally, this vernacular has been used publicly and almost solely for humour, satire and entertainment; I have, however, over the years been challenging myself to make argument in the Caribbean demotic. This essay is illustrative of that project.

RACE, SPACE AND THE POETICS OF MOVING

Creole gaiety at its most exuberant can be the most depressing experience in the world. How so when its wildest display is at Carnival, "a Creole bacchanal"?... Carnival is all that is claimed for it. It is exultation of the mass will, its hedonism is so sacred that to withdraw from it, not to jump up, to be a contemplative outside of its frenzy is a heresy.
—Derek Walcott[4]

Carnival represents an ancient and recurrent rite of passage. It is a festival which occupies a certain space, neuter time. You suspend what you are, what you do, who you are, for a space. Sometimes we perform behind a mask and symbolically become another personality. We put on a ritual mask. It happens in all societies.
—Gordon Rohlehr[5]

Oh, he danced. He danced pretty. He danced to say, "You are beautiful, Calvary Hill, and John John and Laventille and Shanty Town. Listen to your steel bands how they playing! Look at your children how they dancing!.. You is people, people. People is you, people!"
—Earl Lovelace[6]

Carnivalesque discourse breaks through the laws of a language censored by grammar and semantics and, at the same time, is a social and political protest.
—Julia Kristeva[7]

        sweat and jostle and
        jostle and push
        jostle and jostle
        push and jostle and
        and shove and move
        to the pulse
        riddim pan
        riddim and beat
        the beat
        sweat like a ram goat
        sweat for so

and push and shove and jostle and shove and move hip sway hip wine[8] in your wine and look how we enjoying we self—move hip sway hip slap hip big hip fat hip flat bottom big bottom sweet bottom wine-your-waist bottom. Look we nuh, look how we enjoying we self right here in Canada self and Toronto sweet sweet too bad—but look me crosses! Is not Totoben that? Begging your pardon, Mr. Emmanuel Sandiford Jacobs himself, right here in Canada if you please, carrying on as if he don't give a damn blast or shit. Watching him play marse[9] nobody believing he putting up with shut up and go back where you come from in this mine-yuh-own-business catch-arse country where the living hard like rock stone and police shooting you dead dead and leaving you stone-cold in the street like dog. For six cold-no-arse months he up at five cold or no cold, travelling for two hours straight, punching a clock, working like a robot: punch a clock eat, punch a clock pee, punch a clock work, punch a clock leave—clock the punch! Two more hours, underground and over ground is all the same, it dark like hell self, till he back in his basement where the sun on long-leave.[10] But he don't mind, not Totoben, not today—he not giving a blast, damn, or shit if they calling him nigger, for today Emmanuel Sandiford Jacobs dead dead and Totoben in full sway, riding high, riding hard on University Avenue,[11] T-shirt pull up high high over his belly which big, round, black and shining like it carrying six months of baby in it—a real don't-give-a-damn belly that walking down University Avenue past all them war memorials celebrating empire which is nothing but shooting and looting dress up in fancy costume. Past the Immigration Department where all like Totoben visiting plenty time and coming out feeling like they don't belong in Canada, past all those hospitals like Sick Kids and Mount Sinai and Toronto General where plenty Black people like Totoben working and not like doctor or nurse either, past the court houses that Totoben and others like him knowing only too well, and the police station just over there on Dundas Street, and don't forget the American Embassy either that marking another empire, except this one living and not dead yet. Totoben walking down University Avenue, drinking some rum with the boys, playing some marse and feeling like he not back home.

Look! Is not Boysie that, the little Indian boy from down the lane—look how he get fat eh—you see how he working himself up on that woman? Uh uh. I hear he doing well for himself, but Lord help me he should be shame to let anyone see what he doing with that woman, eh eh! you notice she not Indian neither—his poor mother putting she orini[12] over she head and bawling—is a good thing she not alive, god rest her soul, and seeing this shame. He should wear a mask the way he wining and wining on that woman…but I never know Indian could wine so—I thought was only Black people wining like that, well I think my eyes seeing everything today—but wait! is not Bluesman that in the band behind? Lord, he up here too!—I wonder if Immigration knowing that. Is what Canada coming to? Every piece a riff raff up here and look how he cocking a leg over that woman—Lord preserve me! is Gloria that and she coming from a decent home. Her mother dying from shame if she seeing her daughter today— look how he jerking up himself—oh my blessed Saviour! you don't see it look like she enjoying sheself—uh uh, her poor mother! I telling you is this kind of behaviour that giving Black people a bad name. But wait—look, is Maisie that! Is long time since I see her—Lord, but she get even bigger— life up here must be agreeing with her. She still pretty though and it looking like she still liking man and man still liking her huh! Now see here! look at what she doing, wining her all, every and what-you-may-call-it round and round that bottle, and is like she seeing heaven—is like these people losing all shame (if they ever had any) right here on University Avenue. Is like marse gone to their head and is mad they gone mad to marse in your marse and rum sweet, woman sweet, man sweet, and life sweeter still today and is sweat and jostle and push and…

We keeping our eyes on Totoben dancing down University Avenue and Maisie wining and wining her all around that bottle, but we leaving them up in Toronto for a while and looking back, back to where they coming from and how it is they doing what some calling this commonness on University Avenue in the white people country that more than a million Black people invading on the first weekend every August.

On ships the slaves were packed in the hold on galleries one above the other. Each was given only four or five feet in length and two or three feet in height so that they could neither lie at full length nor sit upright… In this position they lived for the voyage, coming up once a day for exercise and to allow the sailors "to clean the pails." But when the cargo was rebellious or the weather bad, then they stayed below for weeks at a time. The close proximity of so many naked human beings, their bruised and festering flesh, the foetid air, the prevailing dysentery, the accumulation of filth, turned these holds into a hell. During the storms the hatches were battened down, and in a close and loathsome darkness they were hurled from one side to another by the heaving vessel, held in position by the chains on their bleeding flesh. No place on earth, observed one writer of the time, concentrated so much misery as the hold of a slave ship.[13]

What connecting Maisie and Totoben on the slave ship to Totoben and Maisie on University Avenue up in Canada is moving—the moving of their bodies. And the stopping of that moving. From the very first time when the Europeans putting them in the slave coffle in Africa, holding them in dungeons all along the coast of Ghana, and forcing Maisie and Totoben onto the slave ship, the owners trying and controlling their moving—where they going, what they eating, who they sleeping with. When Totoben and Maisie entering the slave ship, they having nowhere to move, and once again they moving under heavy manners. Once they landing in the New World—Brazil, Tobago, the United States—anywhere, it don't matter—is the same thing. They living on plantations where massa watching and trying to control all their moving, the moving of their thinking, their speaking and their singing, the moving of their hands on the drum skin giving praise to their gods, even the moving of their feelings, so that mothers finding their loving toward their children coming to nothing when massa taking them away and selling them. Totoben and Maisie seeing the moving of their loving going nowhere when massa selling them one from the other, even their moving toward their gods—their drumming, their dancing, and the movings of their tongue—all these massa trying and controlling. The only moving massa wanting is when Totoben and Maisie working for him in the fields, and when they not moving as he wanting he using the whip.

The crossroads! Where the world of the living bucking up the world of the spirit and filling up with the what could be happening in every meeting. Is early early in the morning—fore day morning at jouvay time[14] and four bands meeting and colliding at the crossroads! Their sounds embracing every living thing and the sound of steel pans beating its way up and out of the holds of slave ships, beating its way up and out from slaving into the freedom of sound wrested from oil drum and steel pan into the new new of music. At the crossroads! What you hearing is the sound of Africa cutting loose and moving across the Atlantic to surface again and again in the music of the boys from "behind the bridge"[15] striking fear in the hearts of whites and middle-class Black people; the boys from behind the bridge who hiding their cutlasses inside their steel pans and when the time right is take they taking them out and chopping their way to supremacy and everybody running, pants tearing as they climbing walls and fleeing the sound of Africa turning and turning around and across the Atlantic.

The crossroads! Where tongue licking up against tongue and Yoruba meeting English meeting Ga meeting Twi meeting French meeting Ibo meeting Spanish. The crossroads! Home of Eshu-Elegbara[16] where all things happening and the present, past and future coming together, and out of them coming what nobody never seeing before, but which plenty more than the future, and what wasn't there before appearing and becoming more than what was there and time lasting as long as when you blinking your eye, or as short as the age of the time self.

Totoben and Maisie carnivalling and playing marse in Brooklyn; they playing marse in Montreal, in Toronto and Miami, they playing marse in Calgary, and in Antigua, in St. Lucia, and Jamaica; they playing marse in New York and Notting Hill, moving and moving and in the moving they defying the holding in the ships crawling across the Atlantic with them and their brothers and sisters.

Some calling this thing that Totoben and Maisie doing, this playing marse, European; some saying is Indian, and others saying is a creole thing—all mix up mix up. And then again some saying is a African thing. If you wanting you could be starting with the French who running coming to Trinidad from Grenada, Guadeloupe, and Martinique in 1784. The Spanish awning the island and passing the Cedula of Population[17] that saying that as long as you white and Catholic you can be coming to Trinidad. The Spanish giving away to French people land they stealing from the Native[18] people and they hoping that this stopping the British from invading the island. Then again in 1789 more French people fleeing Haiti and the rising up of Africans against Europeans; they fleeing the example Toussaint and Dessalines[19] setting when they insisting that Africans must be having their freedom to move and move and move out of the nowhere of slavery into history. Toussaint and Dessalines playing Ole Marse[20] with history and making bassa bassa[21] with the plans of France; they beating Napoleon at his own game and driving the French right out of Haiti. Then they putting on the costumes of the Jacobins and with their Napoleon hats and coattails they turning themselves into Black Jacobins and parading through history and ending Napoleon and his empire earlier than he expecting.

Although Spain bringing plenty French people to Trinidad with Totoben and Maisie as their slaves, the British still taking over the island in

1797. When the French people coming they bringing their carnival with them and every year around Christmas time the governor declaring martial law and the white French people going from house to house singing Christmas songs; they going into streets and dancing and wearing masks and costumes; and they dancing at parties. Although massa letting Totoben and Maisie have some free time and they dancing in their yard and eating, all at massa expense, is only white people and free coloured people who having Carnival. Sometimes free coloured people breaking out of their colour and dressing up like king and queen and lord and lady. And white men blacking up their faces and playing *negue jadin,* which taking the garden negro in *negre jardin* and turning it into garden nigger, and the white women dressing up like the mulatto and Black women their husbands sexing and sleeping with, and all the while the white people dancing to the music that Totoben and Maisie making on their drums because that is the only way Totoben and Maisie taking any part in the white people Carnival.

Then again maybe we could be starting in Africa with the Yoruba and Ibo of Nigeria, the Ashanti and Fon of Ghana, Dahomey and Guinea and their dances, their masquing, and the rituals they performing and keeping their gods happy. In the New World Totoben and Maisie remembering these in the "Bamboula" "Ghouba" and the "Kalinda"[22] stick dances, and even if they not dancing in the streets because the French not wanting them nowhere round them, the remembering running deep and strong and they only waiting for the right time.

Sometimes Maisie and Totoben hiding their dreaming for freedom behind Carnival time at Christmas and in 1805 they gathering together in regiments with kings, queens, princes and princesses and they dressing up in fancy costumes and singing songs rebelling against their not moving and they plotting their overthrowing of massa. And when massa finding out he punishing them bad bad. But in 1838 slavery and its half-sister, apprenticeship,[23] really over and Totoben and Maisie saying: "Ah hah! is free we free now," and all the free-up Africans taking their new new moving onto the streets and celebrating and the white people not liking the bacchanal of Totoben and Maisie and pulling right back.

"Nothing but the vilest of the vile...now think of appearing in the streets. Why not forbid it altogether?"[24] Is so the *Port-of-Spain Gazette* talking about carnival in 1856. But Totoben and Maisie celebrating their moving for the first time in the New World, and they unforgetting all that massa thinking they forgetting or not remembering, and Africa sailing right across the Middle Passage of the Atlantic and coming to land right at the crossroads where the Moko Jumbie[25] tingling your spine as it walking high high above the crowds like the dreams of the Africans who freeing up their moving. Papa Bois and Mama Deleau and Jab Molassi[26]—all of them coming and taking root in Trinidad and driving out the European massa who controlling the moving of Totoben and Maisie for so long. And the French pulling back into their pretty pretty houses, and the coloured middle class that wanting to be white but loving Black deep inside pulling back and they leaving the street wide wide open and clear for the powerful moving of Totoben and Maisie who catching the African spirit and dancing and fighting and sporting and fighting some more, because is plenty plenty anger they holding down in those four hundred years when they not moving and is so it bursting out and everybody, Indian, Chinese, European, even the Black and Brown middle classes, frighten too bad and pulling back back and Totoben and Maisie moving as they wanting.

Is the moving that changing things that everybody frighten of—the moving of what the whites calling "savage songs" into calypso, and beka[27] writing in his newspaper about "the disgusting and indecent scenes" and "the African custom of carrying a stuffed figure of a woman on a pole, which was followed by hundreds of negroes yelling out a savage Guinea song."[28] The moving of tamboo bamboo bands, pot covers, dustpan covers, and bottle and spoon into steel pan, into pan into orchestra, so that today every music machine program with the sweet-too-bad sound of pan music.

You must be starting in 1838 if you wanting to understand this thing that Totoben and Maisie doing; 1838, the year of emancipation for all the Totobens and Maisies in the English colonies; 1838—four years after the apprenticeship period that starting in 1834—when Totoben and Maisie finally free and doing what they wanting, eating what they wanting, drinking what they wanting, working where they wanting, walking where they walking, and moving where they wanting. Or so Maisie and Totoben thinking.

So is true the French having Carnival, but a free French man or woman masquing and masquerading in a colony they owning, and Totoben and Maisie, who coming over in the hold of a slave ship, playing marse as free man and woman after three or four hundred years of slavery is two different things. And for a while there Totoben and Maisie controlling the streets and pushing everybody back—back back until they controlling what they never controlling before—their own moving, and so they playing marse in the streets, at the crossroads, fore day morning at Jouvay time. And is Totoben and Maisie time now for putting on white masks and playing like white just like their former massa blacking his face and playing negue jadin. Beka writing in his newspaper: "Every negro, male and female, wore a white flesh coloured mask, their woolly hair carefully concealed by handkerchiefs… whenever a black mask appeared it was sure to be a white man."[29]

Totoben making fun of massa and missis and suddenly "Canboulay! Canboulay! Canboulay!"[30] running from mouth to mouth and excitement spreading like wildfire during slaving time. "Cannes brulées! Cannes brulées! The canes burning!" and turning into "Canboulay," and Monsieur et Madame and Massa and Missis getting Totoben and Maisie from all the plantations round about and whipping and beating them to be fighting the fires and harvesting the cane before the fire destroying everything. Sometimes Maisie and Totoben working all day and all night and putting out the cane fires.

When Totoben and Maisie freeing up and having their moving, they taking revenge and turning the tables and putting black varnish on their face. Beka writing in the newspaper and saying they carrying chains and sticks and they yelling and singing and cracking whips. Totoben and Maisie carrying on just like massa used to and they making fun of slavery. Massa newspaper saying that Totoben and Maisie making "an unremitting uproar, yelling, drumming and blowing…horns" as they remembering when they fighting the cane fires.[31] Totoben and Maisie carrying their lighted flambeaux and their sticks for their stickfighting through the streets shouting "Canboulay! Canboulay! Canboulay" on August 1st, the date massa changing the laws and freeing them. And is so through marse they remembering their slaving time.

The English bekas who running the country trying and controlling Totoben and Maisie playing marse and even trying to stamp it out:

—In 1833 beka saying that Totoben and Maisie not respecting the Sabbath and he arresting two people and holding them in the Cage. Then beka saying that nobody must be wearing masks before February 18th: "Any person found masked in the streets will be immediately arrested and dealt with according to the law."[32]

—In 1838 beka not liking what Totoben and Maisie doing any better and he still talking about the "desecration of the Sabbath." Beka writing:

215

We will not dwell on the disgusting and indecent scenes that were enacted in our streets—we will not say how many we saw in a state so nearly approaching nudity as to outrage decency and shock modesty—we will not particularly describe the African custom of carrying a stuffed figure of a woman on a pole, which was followed by hundreds of negroes yelling out a savage Guinea song (we regret to say that nine-tenths of these people were Creoles)—we will not describe the ferocious fight between the "Damas" and the "Wartloos" which resulted from mummering—but we will say at once that the custom of keeping Carnival by allowing the lower order of society to run about the streets in wretched masquerade belongs to other days, and ought to be abolished in our own.[33]

—In 1843 beka telling Totoben and Maisie that they can only be wearing masks for two days and not three, and he protecting his Sabbath by saying that Carnival only beginning on Sunday night.

—In 1846 beka saying that Totoben and Maisie must not be wearing masks ever again: "We trust this will prove a final…stop to the orgies which are indulged in by the dissolute of the town at this season of the year, under pretence of Masking."[34] But Totoben and Maisie not happy and they rumbling and beka changing his mind and pulling back and saying that people could be going in bands from house to house and putting on masks when they getting close to the houses.

Beka ears not liking the drum and trying to ban it although Totoben and Maisie needing it not only for their Carnival but when they practising their religion: "Since midnight on Sunday, this festival has broken the slumber of our peaceable citizens with its usual noisy revelry and uproarious hilarity."[35]

All the while Totoben and Maisie playing marse on the street, their brothers and sisters who beka calling "coloured" not joining them, but they going from house to house playing music and they not liking the government interfering with Carnival any more than Totoben and Maisie.

—In 1858 beka saying again no more masking and writing about "the noise, tumult and barbarian mirth."[36] Then beka calling on his police who arresting Totoben and Maisie who wearing masks and even people who not wearing masks. Totoben and Maisie fighting back: "[A] band of Negroes 3,000–4,000 strong passing the police station, armed with hatchets, woodmen's axes, cutlasses, bludgeons and knives…had the bold temerity to give a derisive shout of triumphant defiance to the police."[37] Then beka calling out the military to stop Totoben and Maisie moving and driving them off the street.

After 1858 Totoben and Maisie controlling Carnival even more and the middle-class creoles pulling back inside their houses. Beka calling Totoben and Maisie "idle and vagrant" and saying that they "taking advantage of the general laxity to outrage public decency."[38] Beka and the creole middle class calling Totoben and Maisie bad-johns, dunois, makos, matadors, prostitutes and stickmen and say they belonging to the jamette class and how they living in barrack yards and having no use for respectable society.

Totoben and Maisie bringing all the anger they feeling to the street and they fighting with whip and stick; Midnight Robbers talking pretty pretty and taking your money, and sailors throwing powder over you. Jab Molassi paint up in black and frightening everybody and Maisie and Totoben dressing up like cow with horn, playing fisherman and even pretending to be crazy. Totoben, Maisie and their brothers and sisters carrying chains and whips; some of them carrying snakes, jab jabs snapping their whips and Totoben even dressing up like he pregnant.

Maisie, the jamette, opening up her bodice and showing off her breasts and no man telling her what she can be doing and not doing. Totoben dressing up like a woman in lacy lacy nightgown or sometimes he only wearing a blood cloth like he seeing his monthlies and he playing marse in the "Pissenlit" band and wining and singing songs that beka calling obscene.

—Is 1874 and beka calling for a Vagrancy Law and a Reformatory School because he not liking Totoben and Maisie going around in bands and behaving like vagabonds:

Herds of disreputable males and females…organized into bands and societies for the maintenance of vagrancy, immorality and vice… the name and season [of Carnival] is but a cloak…for the shameless celebration of heathenish and vicious rites of some profligate god whose votaries rival in excesses the profligacies and brutalities of Pagan Rome or Heathen India.[39]

—Is 1875 and beka saying that he using the Habitual Criminals Act against Totoben and Maisie who forming themselves in bands and fighting each other: "the bands, which under different names infest the colony, are fruitful sources of immorality and crime."[40]

—Is 1876 and beka police using their batons without mercy on Totoben and Maisie during Carnival.

—In 1877, 1878 and 1879 a beka captain name Baker controlling Totoben and Maisie during Carnival, and in 1880 beka journalists describing them as making a "fearful howling of a parcel of semi-savages emerging God knows where from, exhibiting hellish scenes and the most demoniacal representations of the days of slavery as they were 40 years ago."[41]

—Is l881 the same beka captain name Baker once again trying to get Totoben and Maisie to give up their stick and drum and flambeaux, but Totoben and Maisie fighting back and dropping plenty blows on the police. Beka Baker calling out the army and controlling the moving of Totoben and Maisie, but is the first time Totoben and Maisie tasting their moving in the New World and it sweet sweet, and they hitting back because Carnival and marse is their freeing-up time. They fighting back when the army saying that Sunday is a sacred day and trying to ban marse; they fighting back when the Catholics and other Christians saying how Totoben and Maisie and all their African brothers and sisters pagan and how they desecrating a Christian festival. Totoben and Maisie fighting back when the upper classes saying that Africans not belonging in their upper-class celebration and they using their Kalinda sticks: "Canboulay! Canboulay!" Plenty people feeling the hurt—man, woman and child—and everybody calling this the Canboulay riots and although their brothers and sisters getting hurt, Totoben and Maisie injuring thirty-eight police and the beka captain calling out soldiers for them. And when it all over the beka governor having to go to Totoben and Maisie and telling them that he not wanting to stop their moving, but asking them please to keep the peace.

Beka still not giving up and he outlawing the Canboulay procession and banning Totoben and Maisie from carrying sticks, but they still doing it behind beka back.

—Is 1883 and beka banning the drum!

—Is 1884 and beka saying no noisy instruments! No lighted torches! No sticks! And again the police attacking Maisie and Totoben and their bands but they fighting and killing the police officer who in charge.

—Is 1917 and beka saying no wearing of masks again!

—Is 1934 and beka saying in the Theatre and Dance Hall Ordinance Act that Totoben and Maisie must not be showing any lewdness and still Totoben and Maisie playing their marse.

And so every year that going by the English beka controlling Toto-ben and Maisie a little bit more—no more masquing on Sunday, Carnival beginning on Monday at six in the morning, no more carrying of sticks, but still Maisie and Totoben coming strong in Congo band and Shango band, they coming strong in Cattle and Cow band; they playing marse like Dirty Sailor, Sailor Ashore, Fancy Sailor, King Sailor or Stoker; they coming strong like Wild Indian, Red Indian, Blue Indian and Black Indian; they dressing up like Jab Jabs coming from hell and they playing East Indian Burroquite, Spanish Burroquite and Pajaro; they coming strong playing Sebucan and Maypole that coming from Latin America and England, they even playing Yankee Minstrel and blacking up their face that black already and painting on white lips; they playing Tennessee Cowboy, Clown and Bat and they coming strong in bands that telling about history with names like "Quo Vadis" and "Serpent of the Nile" or bands like "A Day at Helsinki," "The People of Iceland" or "Spanish Vagabonds." Totoben and Maisie coming strong because they knowing that their moving through the streets is a remembering of how their moving always threatening those who wanting and controlling them.

As beka getting more and more control over Carnival, Totoben and Maisie "coloured" and Black brothers and sisters who living in the middle class coming back to the Carnival. Even the whites joining in. Middle-class women who playing marse riding on trucks and not mixing with Totoben and Maisie. And it looking like everybody even some Indians[42] coming together around the moving that is Carnival.

> During the Carnival season, an entire population is gradually released from moral and civic obligations, and the diverse social, economic, and religious groups become closely united in a single mass activity. Heterogeneous as the wandering Carnival bands are, they intermingle vast numbers of people who, by indulging in similar activities with thousands of other people, become conscious of a unity a social cohesion, a oneness with the crowd itself. During this time the Haitian peasant experiences the widest range of partial integration that he is likely to realize during the year.[43]

But is still Totoben and Maisie who driving Carnival and one intellectual writing:

In a true sense, Carnival "belongs" to the black, lower class. It is they who, through most of its history, have been the outstanding partic- ipants. But whilst Carnival is a direct expression of the folk, it also acts like a magnet for the coloured population.[44]

When the English beka banning the drum, Totoben and Maisie moving around that and using bamboo and making the tambu bambu bands[45] and when beka banning tamboo bamboo Totoben and Maisie using biscuit tins and making biscuit tin bands; they using pieces of iron, parts of cars, metal boxes, dustbins and even piss-pots, and all the time they moving toward pan[46] and making their music through their moving.

Totoben and Maisie moving what beka calling their savage songs into calypso and they singing in French patois, and then in English and they rude rude and mimicking everything and everybody who putting them down *sans humanité*.[47] When the English beka stopping Totoben and Maisie from singing their calypsos in public because they saying that they obscene, they moving them into calypso tents.[48]

Totoben and Maisie moving through English and French and singing their songs that full of picong[49] and wit and anger and singing about "rich- man and poorman who say I am a poor man, I got plenty cash and I driving motor car / richman wearing trousereen and poorman wearing garberdine, I got plenty cash and I driving motor car," and how the yankees gone and Sparrow taking over: "Jean and Dinah, Rosita and Clementina / round the corner posing / bet your life is something they selling / and if you catch them broken / you can get it all for nothing / the Yankees gone and Sparrow take over now."[50] And is so the moving of Maisie and Totoben words tie up tight tight with their moving on the street. The crossroads! Where the spirit of word meeting the spirit of music and driving each other and Totoben and Maisie who singing calypso marking it with their struggling just like Totoben and Maisie beating it out in steel.

When World War II breaking out the English beka governor telling Totoben and Maisie that they can't be having their Carnival, but when the war over in 1946 Totoben and Maisie coming back even stronger. Totoben and his friends like Winston "Spree" Simon[51] using gasoline oil drums and they tuning their pain in steel and they turning the steel pans into instru- ments—turning the weapons of war—old oil drums that leaving over from the World War II—into music and they making another art form for Car- nival: "Steel pan came out of pain," the chantwell[52] David Rudder saying:

"The culture was born in life's shadowed places. It came out of the ghetto areas out of the need to express one's self."[53]

Destination Tokyo, Renegades, Invaders, Desperadoes, Casablanca—is names like these that Totoben and his friends from "behind the bridge" who playing the steel pan giving themselves, and just like the names Totoben and Maisie giving themselves when they singing calypso—Exploiter, Roaring Lion, Tiger, Lord Kitchener, Lord Melody, the Mighty Sparrow, Calypso Rose—the names talking about how Totoben and Maisie moving from slave shack to the street, about how Totoben and Maisie ready to fight for their moving:

> I spend so much a money to buy this costume
> now I ready to jump
> you better give me room
> I make so much a plan just to play this marse
> now is time to play
> give me room to pass
> I want to jam down
> roll down
> shake down
> all around town
> dis marse is for you and you and you and you
> so move, move you blocking up the place
> so move move
> I want to shake my waist
> the people want to jam
> so get out of the band
> I say move
> move—[54]

Totoben and Maisie knowing that they needing the music and the drums and the singing to keep moving. The chantwell David Rudder saying:

[O]n Carnival Day we roam the street for the two days because the music is carrying you. You have to get a music that can drive people, keep them moving constantly... [W]hen a man goes behind his marse, whatever that marse is, he comes out and says on that particular day, this is how I feel.[55]

221

For Totoben and Maisie who living in John John and "behind the bridge" where the downpressed and downtrodden living, playing marse is how they expressing themselves, and is in the music and dance and even the fighting you seeing and feeling the violence they living with all year round:

But this Carnival, putting on his costume not at dawn, Aldrick had a feeling of being the last one, the last symbol of rebellion and threat to confront Port of Spain…. Once upon a time the entire Carnival was expressions of rebellion. Once there were stickfighters who assembled each year to keep alive in battles between themselves the practice of a warriorhood born in them; and there were devils, black men who blackened themselves further with black grease to make of their very blackness a menace, a threat. They moved along the streets with horns on their heads and tridents in hand. They threatened to press their blackened selves against the well-dressed spectators unless they were given money. And there were the jab jabs, men in jester costumes, their caps and shoes filled with tinkling bells, cracking long whips in the streets, with which they lashed each other with full force… And these little fellars waiting for the band to get underway so they could glide up to the steeldrums and touch one, or wave to a brother or cousin who was playing one of the pans, or help the men push the stands on which the big steeldrums were mounted…. This is the guts of the people, their blood; this is the self of the people that they screaming out they possess, that they scrimp and save and whore and work and thief to drag out of the hard rockstone and dirt to show the world they is people. He felt: "This is people taller than cathedrals; this is people more beautiful than avenues with trees."

For two full days Aldrick was a dragon in Port of Spain moving through the loud, hot streets, dancing the bad-devil dance, dancing the stickman dance, dancing Sylvia and Inez and Basil and his grandfather and the Hill and the fellars by the Corner, leaning against the wall, waiting for the police to raid them. He was Manzanilla, Calvary Hill, Congo, Dahomey, Ghana. He was Africa, the ancestral Masker, affirming the power of the warrior, prancing and bowing, breathing out fire, lunging against his chains, threatening with his claws, saying to the city: I is a dragon. I have fire in my belly and claws on my hands; watch me! Note me well, for I am ready to burn down your city. I am ready to tear you apart, limb by limb.[56]

And the European beka still controlling marse and trying to stop Toto-ben and Maisie moving, so they passing a regulation that saying Maisie and Totoben must be stopping their marse before twelve midnight on the Tues-day before Ash Wednesday, and to this day the law still on the books. Even when Africans running the country they trying and controlling Totoben and Maisie, so in 1956, Dr. Eric Williams, who everybody calling De Doc, the first Black prime minister of Trinidad and Tobago,[57] sponsoring and supporting Totoben and Maisie as a way of controlling them. And chant-well David Rudder talking a true thing when he saying: "Every government is afraid of a million people on the street. There's no government that's not afraid of a million people in the street."[58]

"[Y]ou better move and move and move." Moving, the metaphor for what the New World promising. Moving toward progress, away from the Old World toward the bettering of life. Except for Totoben and Maisie who the European bekas bringing through time and space to the New World and then trying to stop them moving. Everybody living the promise that is moving in the New World—moving up from low beginnings, moving to a better life or to a new life, but not Totoben and Maisie. Is only Maisie, Totoben and their African brothers and sisters who not moving to the New World for a better life. The bekas who calling themselves Puritans, and those who fleeing the bassa bassa of the Old World, and those who coming after the Africans expecting and bettering their living: the Jews, the Ital-ians, the Greeks, the Poles—the poor that the Statue of Liberty begging the world to be giving to America. All—*tout bagai*[59]—except Totoben and Maisie who not choosing and moving to the New World, but who coming in chains. Everybody who moving to the New World either moving to better themselves, or even if they not bettering themselves in money they finding a safe place from those who persecuting them—everybody except Totoben and Maisie. Maisie and Totoben losing everything when Beka moving them to the New World—they losing their culture, their religion, their language, and their tongue, and all the while beka trying and holding Totoben and Maisie back from the dream that is moving.

The pressures that holding down Totoben and Maisie so strong that Marcus Garvey dreaming and working and talking and wanting and mov-ing Totoben and Maisie and all their brothers and sisters who wanting back back to Africa. Moving again—all the way back—across the Atlantic—to where they being all the time—Africa.

I have a dream! I have a dream! Is so the warrior for justice, Martin

Luther King talking about moving Black people up from where they nothing to being something. I have a dream! I have a dream! For everybody who coming to the New World, the dream that calling them is the dream of moving: moving through space to the new land; moving through time to the future; working hard and moving up; moving out to the suburbs from the cramping city—always moving. But although Totoben and Maisie moving through space and time, beka cutting them off in time and telling them they having no past and that their past not worth anything. Beka also stopping them from moving forward and making progress like everybody else doing and telling each other to do.[60] The American beka in the United States making up the public and national lie that everybody could be moving up to the sky if they wanting and even becoming president. Everybody, that is, except Totoben and Maisie. And beka making rules about where Totoben and Maisie living, where they going to school, where they walking, where they working, where they taking their sick bodies, and where they burying them. And the moving of the spirit in Totoben and Maisie moving through the warrior Malcom who moving his name to Malik al-Shabazz saying that by "any means necessary" he moving his people to a place where they moving without beka controlling them.

Although the American bekas taking those rules off the law books and saying everybody free, he still controlling Totoben and Maisie. Today, the beka police still telling young Totoben where he moving and if he not looking sharp he shooting down Totoben stone cold in the street. Totoben and Maisie still living in ghettos and beka even start saying once again that Totoben and Maisie born stupid and bad and that governments throwing good money behind bad if they creating space for Totoben and Maisie to move and move and move and move… So, for one day, two days—Totoben and Maisie taking back the streets, those same streets that the police patrolling every day—to dance down, wine down, parading and presenting their dreadness, making real the unreal. The spirit of Totoben and Maisie moving through Kwesi Owusu who living in beka country they calling England and he writing:

> An elderly woman shook herself free of her elaborate costume which fell like waxed wings facing the sun…she had woken up with forty different dreams when she thought about making a costume for Carnival. She could only use four of them. She made a sea dragon costume for her little grandson, two turtles for her grand-daughters

and a sea queen for herself. She had thirty-six more dreams left for next year's. But "listen young man," she said, "I is someone who bound to dream again before then."[61]

For one—two days, the doors to the prison that the black skin making for Totoben and Maisie opening up and they escaping into the promise of moving. And so Totoben and Maisie jamming and jocking[62] their waist all the way down University Avenue in Toronto, in Notting Hill, in Port of Spain, in Miami and wherever they making marse they creating something new with the language of their moving.

For a long time is Totoben as man, as stickfighter, fighter, warrior who controlling marse: "I Lawa (*le Roi*) with stick, with fight, with woman, with dance, with song, with drum, with everything." And when Totoben disappearing as stickfighter and chantwell he living on in the calypsonian and the steelbandsman. In Totoben Black nationalism and manness coming together and fighting the racism American servicemen bringing to Trinidad along with their Yankee dollars when they coming to the American base at Chaguaramas during World War II. And Sparrow the calypsonian singing about how the "Yankees gone and Sparrow take over now."

Maisie, who living in the barrack yards and who belonging to the jamette class, is the only woman who playing marse with Totoben when it first starting. And Maisie, the jamette,[63] is sister to other jamettes like Sara Jamaica, Big Body Ada, Darling Dan, Piti Belle Lily, Mossie Millie, Ocean Lizzie, Sybil Steel, Ling Mama, Queen Bee, Myrtle the Turtle, Techselia and Boadicea, and they all fighting man and woman alike with their poui stick,[64] which they calling Man Tamer. As the years going by, Maisie from the middle class joining Maisie from the streets and remembering how to wine and together they taking their wining into the public spaces. Maisie taking over the street and strutting her sexiness up and down Port of Spain, Toronto, Notting Hill, New York, Miami and she not frighten because today is her day and she wining and wining as Blue Boy singing:

> Shake up de bam bam
> roll up de bum bum
> wine wine wine Virginia wine Virginia...
> Virginia say give me room
> I want to wine
> Virginia say I don't care

Is my time
women will slander
men will admire
…
she wine on de pan man
she wine on de pan stan
woi woi woi
shake up de bam bam
roll up de bum bum[65]

And Maisie sisters—Brown, Black, White, Indian and Chinese—joining Maisie as she wining—round her staff, round her bottle, round anything sometimes. But a man. Women wining round their space—their inside space, the space of their becoming, where anything happening—the crossroads! That is their space—their inner space where woman meeting woman meeting man meeting woman:

Virginia dey shame about de Native dance
Virginia is culture we inheriting
Is part of our history
A gift to the body
So how come we discussing immorality
You like playing sailor
So wine for your lover
Wine wine wine
Shake up your bum bum
Roll up your bam bam

And is like Maisie taking over Carnival—taking over the streets with her rampant, raucous, strident and her sweet-too-bad sexuality, wining and wining around and around on something, anything—but a man. Is the one time Maisie showing her sexuality open open and not feeling threatened; is the one time Maisie freeing up and not dealing with men if she not wanting to, and she wining and wining on anything.

Externalization, catharsis, sexual stimulus, and sexual release seem to be the fundamental psychological functions of the seasonal crowd dance. There is every indication that at one time the seasonal dances were associated conceptually with some fertility cult (the planting season and emphasis on the sexual form of the dances) but this significance has been submerged in the function of sexual catharsis. The emphasis on the sexual function is confirmed by the increased birth rates at a reasonable time after Mardi Gras... To release or to externalize energy is the psychological function of practically every dance which is not purely formal... Closely bound up with externalization of energy is the function of escape from emotional conflict through the dance, an escape that is a form of externalization, usually voluntary. In the seasonal dance, primary gratification is derived from the complete externalization of inhibition, an escape sanctioned by country wide license.... [T]he Mardi Gras acts as both a stimulus and release of energy, chiefly sexual. This release process might be called sexual catharsis.[66]

And so long time after leaving Africa, Maisie and Totoben still having "the instinct to dance the ritual dance of procreation" although they unremembering the meaning.[67] Totoben and Maisie knowing that these dances not having to do with having babies, but their bodies remembering the instinct and that it not easy or safe to get rid of it.

The crossroads! That is Trinidad. Where Carib, Arawak and Taino meeting European and dying; where African meeting European and dying *and* living, where Asian meeting European and African and living and dying; the crossroads! Where anything can be happening, where Eshu-Elegbara ruling. Totoben and Maisie wining around the space of the crossroads and creating the callaloo[68] that is Carnival and creating the moving out of Trinidad to away and big country and foreign. Totoben and Maisie moving from the islands, by boat and by plane they moving overseas to foreign, they moving in time and space once again, to be bettering themselves, following their money and their raw material that the banks and companies taking overseas and abroad. They following Barclays Bank, Shell, Lever Brothers and Fry's Cocoa to England; they following Texaco and Amoco to the United States and they following the Bank of Nova Scotia, the Royal Bank of Canada, and Alcan to Canada.

"Move and move and move." Totoben and Maisie moving to the promising and promises of the mother country, big country and away and when England not wanting them anymore they moving to Canada and America and they seeding and sporing these countries with their desiring and doing better, only they finding that while no plantations waiting for them, beka still not wanting Totoben and Maisie moving and they streaming them into low-level jobs. And when Totoben and Maisie hearing a beka name Botha from South Africa saying that they must be learning that there are certain greener pastures that they never owning, they knowing that the other bekas who running England and Canada and the United States thinking the same thing. Totoben thinking of the jobs he not getting and Maisie about the money she not earning; Totoben and Maisie thinking of the moving they not doing, and so they taking their bodies to the streets, to the crossroads of their minds, and they moving, bearing the sounds of their ancestors on University Avenue, in Notting Hill, in New York, in Calgary, in Miami—everywhere.

In England Carnival turning to ole marse when the natives confronting Totoben and Maisie in Notting Hill in 1976:

Then the police Mas arrived, more than 300 men in blue costumes and helmets. They carried no instruments except one percussive item, a baton concealed in their costumes. They started their ritual dance in silence, except for the radios and sirens. The revellers moved back into a tight space in front of Acklam Hall as the blue Mas formed a loop around them. All possible exits were blocked, tension mounted and loud pleas rose above the cacophony of voices. The police charged into the besieged crowd "to arrest pickpockets." It was frightening. Half of the people who initially tried to run fell over, children trampled underfoot, bleeding and crying. Those who tried to help also went down in the stampede…. The inevitable response came. Some of the cornered youth broke through the rain of batons and broke the siege. As soon as they regrouped they launched an offensive which surprised the police by its effectiveness. They knew the terrain intimately. Their only weapons: bricks from nearby building sites, cans and bottles. For four hours these untrained youths waged a guerrilla battle with the police on the streets of Notting Hill, and won. When the police retreated only the sirens of ambulances stirred the still of the night. The streets were empty; the red, gold and green still flapped in the wind from the third floor window.

In the morning all the newspapers were simply and literally fuming with rage…. The initial baton charge (by the police) which provoked the reaction was ignored by almost all the newspapers. Black

casualties were ignored in favour of photographs of bleeding policemen being rushed to hospital.... The young warriors of Notting Hill
have a noble history. They were the descendants of the stickmen of
the famous Arouca riots of 1891 who beat off police constables sent
to break up the drum dance.[69]

Totoben and Maisie in 1976 in Notting Hill keeping faith with Totoben
and Maisie back in Trinidad in 1858, 1881, and 1884 and resisting beka controlling them. In London the English bekas wanting to move Totoben and
Maisie from Notting Hill and putting them in Hyde Park, and in Toronto
they moving Totoben and Maisie first one way then another because as
one of the founders of Caribana, Romaine Pitt, saying: "The police have
never liked Caribana—if it were not for Caribana's economic infusion, the
police would have stopped it. It would make a lot of people happy if it was
moved."[70] And finally in 1991 the Canadian bekas getting their way and
moving it from University Avenue where Totoben and Maisie moving past
the United States Embassy, past the police station, past the courts, past the
hospitals where Totoben and Maisie working in the kitchens and cleaning
the floors, past statues glorifying wars between one beka country and another which having so much meaning for Totoben and Maisie who living
up there in the cold, and they putting it down on the Lakeshore[71] where
is only into lake people can be running if any ruckshun breaking out. The
people who running it saying they making more money from it by moving
it, but it giving beka another way to control Totoben and Maisie even more.
Is 1967 in Canada, Totoben and Maisie turning Carnival into Caribana
for Canada's centennial celebrations and everybody liking it so much, they
doing it every year and bringing plenty money into Toronto. And brip brap
just so what Totoben and Maisie doing no longer African or Black and the
chairman of the Caribana committee saying on the radio, the Canadian
Broadcasting Corporation: "I can't repeat this enough. Caribana is not a
black festival necessarily. It is a *Canadian* festival that reflects black and Caribbean culture."[72] Is where Totoben and Maisie? Still there on University
Avenue wining in the "*Canadian* festival" of Caribana. Totoben and Maisie
laughing and laughing and knowing that is not just so Caribana turning
Canadian and they wondering how the Black beka, Lewis, turning Caribana into "not a black festival." Totoben and Maisie remembering when the
broadcaster beka on the radio not knowing his microphone on and using
the "n"-word when he describing Totoben and Maisie playing marse on

University Avenue. Totoben and Maisie knowing that if Canadian stretching enough and including all the Totobens and Maisies who Black and Caribbean in their wining and their playing marse and their struggling for respect, then and only then Caribana becoming Canadian.

Totoben and Maisie knowing that every year their wining and dancing making millions for businesses in Toronto,[73] yet they still not getting the support they needing from the government or from the businesses who making money and every year they running a debt. People who running Caribana looking at it as a "marketing tool" and Totoben and Maisie laughing fit to kill because they knowing what they doing in Trinidad and in Toronto and Notting Hill and New York is not no "marketing tool." Totoben and Maisie who organizing Caribana trying and trying and looking for ways and making money from Caribana and is like they trying and putting reins on a hurricane, because playing marse not working in the way white bekas making things work.

Totoben and Maisie facing the same problem in Toronto as they facing in Notting Hill: "It is Europe's largest street festival and clearly has the potential to be self-funding if the money generated by Carnival goes back into the Carnival and the Black community. However contracts are given to Cockspur Rum and Kiss FM."[74] Caribana is the biggest festival in Canada, people saying is the biggest festival in North America and yet Totoben and Maisie still scrunting.[75]

The police still seeing Totoben and Maisie moving as a catastrophe and bassa bassa waiting to happen and they putting them behind barricades on the Lakeshore so that if you watching Totoben and Maisie playing marse, you mustn't be jumping up in the bands. And they bringing out the troops because they not understanding that what Totoben and Maisie doing is freeing up and they not looking for trouble unless trouble troubling them. So they watching Totoben and Maisie close close.

> What creates the tension is the understandable angry reaction to the fact that it is so heavily policed and shackled into a small area. The Carnival was literally surrounded by coach loads of police on standby, with as many roadblocks as would be employed in a war or state of emergency. To African Caribbean people, Carnival is much more than a dance in the street; it represents our sense of collective freedom and right to be free. Imagine the humiliation and anger of our community when we are herded around a few square miles, then

told to get out of the area by dusk. There were 36 crimes, 46 arrests and 1 fatal stabbing and there were one million people.[76]

The police not understanding that Totoben and Maisie who standing and watching and Maisie and Totoben who dancing in the band is one and the same; they not understanding that Carnival and marse meaning that you crossing from looking to dancing and back again to looking, from not moving to moving and back again to not moving. For Totoben and Maisie marse is moving and not moving; is man dressing up as woman and woman dressing up as dirty sailor and playing man; is woman loving man yet wining on anything—but a man; is Crazy the calypsonian singing "if you can't get a woman, take a man!" And marse is living *and* dying. And then living again.

When the Canadian bekas putting Totoben and Maisie behind the barricades and telling them they must only be watching, they controlling Totoben and Maisie moving again. When the beka police in Toronto even putting up a sign at the end of the route that saying "STOP MUSIC," Totoben and Maisie recognizing it from way way back in Trinidad where beka trying for over a hundred years and controlling their moving and their playing marse. The beka police in Canada even sending helicopters overhead and watching Totoben and Maisie because with one million Totobens and Maisies anything is possible.

Totoben and Maisie understanding and tasting the power of the crossroads of Eshu-Elegbara and the power of anything happening; they breaking up space into rhythm which is time, and time and space making one; they knowing when they reaching the crossroads where living and dying meeting, they forgetting the jobs they not getting, the money they not making and so they taking to the streets and to the crossroads of their minds bearing the sounds of their ancestors on University, on the Lakeshore where if they running the only place they running to is a lake, but they urging and freeing up, they keeping moving as they wining and dancing their history and is sweat and jostle and push and shove and sway hip wine hip up down and around as the last band coming, only is not a band but a whole set of white men dress up in dirty white overalls with broom and dustpan and they cleaning up and reconquering the street for one more year, doing work that Black men and women like Totoben and Maisie doing, sweeping and washing the street clean clean of the stain of sweatandjostleandpush-and-pulseandbeatand the nightmare of Maisie, Bluesman, Boysie and Totoben and his belly who conquering their own universe on University Avenue with their moving for the blinking of an eye. In time. And space. And just so the war over for one more year—

is sweatandbeatandjostleandpulseandmove andmoveandjostleandpulse-andpush and...

CODA: Never Always

Carnival, Caribana, or Toronto Carnival offers another example of how we, African-descended people, occupy the streets, this time in pleasure, joy and even remembering, as Wynton Marsalis says in a commentary on the African American practice of the second line in New Orleans: we have never done this before and yet we have always done this before.

Caribana has always presented a challenge for the city, the challenge of controlling a large number of people and in this case a large number of Black people. The festival, entirely volunteer-run, has historically been wracked by controversy, some of it generated by the fact that despite bringing in millions of dollars to the city, it was never adequately supported. It was moved out of downtown area to the Lakeshore and finally taken over by the city a few years ago. The 2017 celebration of Caribana/Toronto Carnival, marking fifty years of the festival, appears to have been entirely restricted to the grounds of the CNE, with no parade along the Lakeshore. To my knowledge, 2017 is the first time there has been no street parade of Caribana. The goal has always been to contain Caribana in one way or another; it appears that this has happened with it being restricted to the CNE.

Consider also that Afrofest, the wonderful, family-oriented, African music festival, was peremptorily moved from Queen's Park to Woodbine in 2011. Every summer the grounds of Queen's Park blossomed with the cultural and ethnic diversity of continental Africa as well as that of the Afrospora (African diaspora). Under the trees, listening to the music, watching families with young children picnicking, one could be forgiven for thinking one was in Africa. There was no consultation or discussion with the African Canadian community or stakeholders before the move was made. There is now no Black or African Canadian festival that takes place in the heart of the city.

This has never happened to us before; this has always happened to us before.

NOTES

1   Caribana began as an event to celebrate Canada's centennial in 1967.

2   In his work *ABC of Reading*, Ezra Pound defined languages according to their vary-ing qualities, which he identified as phanopoesis (beautiful to look at), melopoesis (beautiful-sounding), and logopoesis (logical). He identified Chinese, Greek and English as respectively representing these qualities. I have added another category and quality, kinopoesis (dynamic and quick-moving). African demotic languages, such as the various Caribbean vernaculars in English—for example, Jamaican patois—best reflect this latter quality. Ezra Pound, *ABC of Reading* (New York: New Directions, 1960).

3   Margaret Drewal, "Dancing for Ogun in Yorubaland and in Brazil" in *Blackness in Latin America and the Caribbean, Vol. 2*, ed. Norman E. Whitten and Arlene Torres (Bloomington: Indiana University Press, 1998), 259.

4   Derek Walcott, "On Choosing Port of Spain," in *David Frost Introduces Trinidad and Tobago*, ed. Michael Anthony and Andrew Carr. (London: Andre Deutsch, 1975), 22.

5   Gordon Rohlehr, "Pelvis Festival," *Sunday Express* (March 1, 1992).

6   Earl Lovelace, *The Dragon Can't Dance* (New York: Persea Books, Inc., 1998), 125. Future references to *The Dragon Can't Dance* are from this edition.

7   Julia Kristeva, *The Julia Kristeva Reader*, ed. Toril Moi (New York: Columbia University Press, 1986), 36.

8   "Wining" is a popular Afro Caribbean dance movement in which the hips are circled and which is based on African fertility dances.

9   To "play marse" is to take part in the Carnival parade, usually wearing a costume.

10 Under colonial regimes, civil servants from England who lived in the Caribbean were granted extended holidays to return home. The practice was known as "home leave" and was continued after independence, when the civil servants were no lon-ger English but from the former colony itself. The expression "long leave" was used interchangeably with "home leave."

11 This avenue is situated within the business area of the City of Toronto. It is divided down its centre by a median on which there are several statues commemorating Canadian participation in World War I and World War II.

12 Head covering worn by South Asian women in Trinidad.

13 George Lamming, *The Pleasures of Exile* (Ann Arbor: University of Michigan Press, 1992), 97–8.

14 Carnival festivities begin at 6:00 a.m. on the Monday before Ash Wednesday. This is referred to as "jourvert" or "jouvay," from the French *jour ouvert* (open day). Foreday morning refers to this time.

15 A socially and economically depressed area in Port of Spain.

16 The Yoruba of Nigeria regard Eshu-Elegbara as the god of the crossroads as well as a messenger of the gods.

17 Instituted by Spain in 1783, the Cedula of Population stipulated that only Catholic immigrants could enter Trinidad.

18 In the demotic *Native* would be used rather than *Indigenous* or *First Nations*.

19 Toussaint L'Ouverture and Jean-Jacques Dessalines were liberators of Haiti from French rule, making the Haitian Revolution the only successful slave revolt in

history. After the United States, Haiti was the first country in the New World to achieve independence.

20   Ole marse is a type of carnival performed at jourvert or jouvay time in the early morning hours of Carnival Monday before daybreak. At this time all conventions are subverted. At jourvert celebrations, masqueraders are said to be playing "ole marse," arising out of the tradition of wearing old clothes. This is in distinction to "fancy marse" or "pretty marse," which happens later in the day on Monday and Tuesday, when masqueraders wear costumes that have been imaginatively designed and created.

21   Yoruba words meaning destruction, now a part of the Caribbean demotic.

22   The cultures of Guinea, Dahomey, the Yoruba and Ibo of Nigeria as well as the Ashanti of Ghana were the sources of these dances and rituals.

23   For the five years prior to 1838, the year slavery was abolished, slaves were supposed to serve an apprenticeship period in preparation for freedom. During apprenticeship, their lives were little different from when they were slaves.

24   Andrew Pearse, "Carnival in Nineteenth Century Trinidad," *Caribbean Quarterly* 4, Nos. 3 & 4 (1956), 187.

25   Moko Jumbies in colourful costumes played (and still play) marse on stilts.

26   Papa Bois and Mama Deleau were familiar and traditional folk figures derived from the African pantheon of gods who were an integral part of Carnival. Papa Bois's home was the woods and he was considered the protector of animals; Mama Deleau was literally mother of the waters. The Jab Molassi, meaning molasses devil, roamed the streets demanding money and frightening spectators.

27   Caribbean demotic word for white person.

28   Pearse, *Caribbean Quarterly*, 184.

29   Ibid., 185.

30   Ibid., 188.

31   Ibid.

32   Ibid., 183.

33   Ibid., 184.

34   Ibid., 185.

35   Ibid., 184.

36   Ibid., 187.

37   Ibid.

38   Ibid., 187-88.

39   Ibid., 189.

40   Ibid.

41   Ibid., 187.

42   After the abolition of slavery, the colonial governments brought in indentured workers from India to work on the sugar plantations.

43   Catherine Dunham, *Dances of Haiti* (Los Angeles: Center for Afro-American Studies, University of California, 1983), 42.

44   Barbara E. Powrie, "The Changing Attitude of the Coloured Middle Class towards Carnival," *Caribbean Quarterly* 4, Nos. 3 & 4 (1956), 226.

45 Musical bands in which the instruments are pieces of bamboo cut at different lengths which the players strike against the ground. The sound varies depending on the length of the bamboo.

46 "Pan" was formerly known as "steel pan" because steel drums (initially used to ship oil) were initially tuned and used as musical instruments.

47 The *sans humanité* (without humanity) tradition is one in which calypsonians sing in a fearless manner about any subject.

48 Initially tents were erected during the Carnival season so that calypsonians could perform. Even though calypsonians no longer now perform in tents, their performance venues are still called tents.

49 Sharp, satirical wit.

50 In the calypso "Jean and Dinah," the calypsonian the Mighty Sparrow sang of American sailors and soldiers leaving in Trinidad, which resulted in the lowering of rates for prostitutes.

51 Winston "Spree" Simon is credited with the creation of pan.

52 "Chantwell" is the early name for calypsonians.

53 David Rudder, *Kaiso Calypso Music: David Rudder in Conversation with John La Rose* (London: New Beacon Books, 1990), 31.

54 Black Stalin, "Move," Straker Records, GS 2337 A, 1991.

55 Rudder, *Kaiso Calypso Music*, 31.

56 Lovelace, *The Dragon Can't Dance*, 122-24.

57 On August 31, 1962, Dr. Eric Williams led the nation of Trinidad and Tobago into independence.

58 Rudder, *Kaiso Calypso Music*, 31.

59 *Tout bagai* is a French patois phrase meaning everything and everyone.

60 Bonnie Barthold makes this argument in her work *Black Time: Fiction of Africa, the Caribbean, and the United States* (New Haven: Yale University Press, 1981).

61 Kwesi Owusu, *The Struggle for Black Arts in Britain* (Gloucestershire, UK: Comedia Publishing Group, 1986), 20.

62 Movement of the hips backwards and forwards during dancing, simulating the sexual act.

63 *Jamette* is a French patois word derived from the French *diameter* and referred to men and women of the lower classes.

64 Poui—*Tabebuia serratifolia*—a tropical hardwood, is primarily used for furniture. Its hardness recommends it as suitable material for the sticks used in the African Caribbean practice of stickfighting.

65 Blue Boy, "Virginia," 1992.

66 Dunham, *Dances of Haiti*, 42.

67 Gordon Rohlehr, *Sunday Express*.

68 Callaloo is a Trinidadian dish made from a spinach-like plant by the same name in which the many ingredients are blended together to a smooth consistency.

69 Owusu, *The Struggle for Black Arts in Britain*, 3.

70 Romaine Pitt, in interview with writer in Toronto in 1991.

71 An expressway named after the fact that it runs along the shoreline of Lake Ontario

in the City of Toronto.

72 Sam Lewis in interview with the CBC on August 2, 1991, in Toronto.

73 According to research carried out in 1990 by Decima Research, Caribana generated $187 million in that year. As of 1994 the figure is in excess of $200 million.

74 Pauline Henderson, "A Carnival Under Siege," *Spare Rib* (1991), 37.

75 Caribbean demotic word meaning economic hardship.

76 Henderson, "A Carnival Under Siege," 37.

ON MICHAEL COREN:
AMNESIA AND THE EVERYDAY EMBRACE
OF RACISM AND SEXISM

B etween 1995 and 2005, Michael Coren hosted The *Michael Coren Show* on CFRB-1010. His brand was the racist, sexist, homophobic diatribe that would be right at home in the alt-right today. His targets were women, First Nations, people of colour and gays. He was, for instance, particularly incensed by the National Action Committee on the Status of Women and often drew a bead on Sunera Thobani, who became president of NAC in 1993, with some of the most racially offensive statements. He accused her of being racist because at the end of her term she expressed a desire that another woman of colour become president.

In 1995, Coren made a scurrilous broadcast about me, accusing me of many things, including "defecating" on Canada and calling June Callwood a racist.[1] The only accurate statement in his broadcast was that I had come to Canada in 1968.

In the wake of Coren's broadcast about me, I launched a lawsuit against him and CFRB. Through a petition and letters, complaints were also lodged with the CRTC against CFRB by different groups for its anti-feminist, homophobic and racist broadcasting, and we were able to prevent them twice from obtaining the usual seven-year licence they were accustomed to obtaining. Licence renewal for radio stations is a costly process, so our work did have an economic impact. During that time, the Mayor's Committee on Race and Community Relations, chaired by then-Mayor Barbara Hall, called on CFRB and Coren to apologize to me and the Black community for his comments. They did not. Coren was eventually fired by the station in 2005 when he made disparaging remarks about the weight and size of a call-in listener. It is always important to know what the boundaries are for institutions.

Coren, now a reformed homophobe, writes of his Saul-on-the-way-to-Damascus moments. The title of his 2016 book on the subject, *Epiphany: A Christian's Change of Heart and Mind over Same-Sex Marriage*,[2] is self-explanatory. I am more than willing to embrace the idea of humans changing their views and behaviour, however what interests and disturbs me is that Coren has never publicly disavowed his racist, sexist comments. Like the good Christian that he is, he has confessed his sins regarding his homophobia; why hasn't he done the same regarding the racist and sexist views he has expressed over the years? Even more disturbing and significant is that none of the media, neither the left liberal papers like the *Toronto Star* and *NOW*, nor the more conservative, such as the *Globe and Mail*, has ever challenged Coren about his earlier comments. It is, indeed, astonishing how the media have embraced his more recent commentary, thereby creating the image of the progressive, liberal commentator. Why hasn't he been challenged on those earlier views? He has acknowledged how mistaken he was in being homophobic—why not in his attitudes toward women and people of colour? Are we to conclude that Coren's present pro-gay stance stands in for his views on women and people of colour? The elephant in the room is his silence on these issues.

Concerned with the media's response to Coren and with *NOW's* publication of an article Coren wrote about his first Pride parade, "Recent Gay Ally Michael Coren Goes to His First Pride,"[3] I wrote to *NOW* in July of 2016:

> Who cares that Michael Coren attended Pride? And why is a supposedly progressive newspaper like *NOW* featuring this utter nonsense that passes as news? Will we see him next at Caribana wining[4] on a Black masquerader? I think not—he hasn't yet had his epiphany regarding Black people, has he? We are all waiting.
>
> M. NourbeSe Philip[5]

Although *NOW* did publish my letter, they removed the second sentence, to which I responded as follows:

> It is deeply concerning that you removed my statement about *NOW* providing the sort of coverage it did of Michael Coren's appearance

at the last Pride parade: "And why is a supposedly progressive newspaper like *NOW* featuring this utter nonsense that passes as news?" This coverage comprised a photograph of Michael Coren as well as an article by him. My comment about *NOW*'s coverage of Coren's attendance was and is as important as my comment about the questionable relevance of Coren parading his new-found acceptance of gays. Your newspaper presents as a progressive newspaper, yet it has never challenged Coren on his racist views. He has not, to my knowledge, ever eschewed his earlier racist comments and positions as he has his earlier homophobic views. Why hasn't *NOW* challenged him on that? None of the mainstream news media have challenged him either. This is not simply an oversight: in failing to challenge Coren on those views, *NOW*, like other news outlets, is actively colluding with Coren in his silence about his former racism that he so egregiously expressed. Is it that *NOW*, like Coren, thinks that homophobic views are more worthy of attention than racist views; that he can recant his homophobia and he will be returned to the fold of respectability, but that no one will challenge him on his racism? And yet *NOW* is all too ready to hold itself out as a supporter of BLMTO and its positions vis-à-vis Pride. The buzzword I believe is *intersectionality*—in other words, it's all of a piece. *NOW* cannot and should not be allowed to embrace Michael Coren as a former homophobe and not be challenged on its silence about his well-documented anti-Black, anti-First Nations, anti-Asian, anti-feminist views. Your removal of my question shows that *NOW* doesn't understand the significance of its role in this performance of passive racism.

M. NourbeSe Philip[6]

When a self-avowed right-wing personality who disavows his publicly articulated negative views on gay people and gay marriage publishes a work on this sea change and the media fail to ask whether or how his virulently negative views on women and people of colour have changed, it is tantamount to a failure on the part of the media in a democratic society. In failing to challenge Coren, the media actively collude with him in his dismissive attitude toward the groups he has attacked. This is illustrative of how so-called democratic societies like Canada tolerate a certain level of racist and sexist attitudes toward certain groups, all claims to being against racism and sexism to the contrary.

Western democracies have always allowed a certain amount of racism to exist in their societies. Until the election of Trump in 2016, there appeared to be a certain unspoken understanding that forebade open and explicit expressions of racist, sexist comments. This approach radically changed with the installation of a new administration in the U.S. in 2017; racist commentary and acts are now on the upsurge. South of the border, we have seen that the most outrageous comments about sexually preying on women are no barrier to being elected to the highest position in the land. Coren's pedigree becomes even more relevant in the current climate. It is a pedigree that includes his gender and his race, qualities that allow him to shape-shift—yesterday, hate-spewing loudmouth; today, urbane liberal commentator—and yet remain entirely acceptable to the mainstream media. This is a local example of a much larger issue—how whiteness and maleness function in the world; they are always innocent, always blameless. History is replete with examples.

NOTES

1   I believe he was referring to the confrontation between June Callwood and me outside Roy Thomson Hall, which is discussed in "Disturbing the Peace."

2   Michael Coren, *Epiphany: A Christian's Change of Heart and Mind over Same-Sex Marriage* (Toronto: Signal, 2016).

3   Michael Coren, "Recent Gay Ally Michael Coren Goes to His First Pride," *NOW* (July 5, 2016), <https://nowtoronto.com/news/michael-coren-goes-to-pride/>.

4   A Trinidad vernacular word meaning a sexualized form of dancing.

5   Part of this letter was published in *NOW* in their "Readers Love and Hate" section. NourbeSe Philip, "Michael Coren's Masquerade," *NOW* (July 14, 2016), <https://nowtoronto.com/news/letters-to-the-editor/readers-love-and-hate-this-dyke-with-black-lives-matter/>.

6   This letter was not published by *NOW.*

DIS PLACE—THE SPACE BETWEEN

April 22, 1986

Dear C.

I write as an African Caribbean woman. This consciousness permeates my work—I am referring here to my poetry. True, "Earth and Sound" has no overt reference to my being female, or to feminist issues—which is what I think you're saying—but feminist issues did not impinge on my thinking these issues through, and it would be false to put them in to satisfy current fashion.

Yours truly
M.

P.S. This is not to say that those issues aren't there—for instance, I recollect that my relationship to my environment was very much affected by the severe curtailment of being a female child in Trinidad. I'm sure you know what I mean— home-school-home and on and on. Boys, men had a lot more freedom—this is bound to affect how we respond to place.

CASE STUDY

Facts

In 1985, a Black, female poet completed an essay—"Earth and Sound: The Place of Poetry"[1]—in which she examined the concept and idea of "place" and how the poet attached herself to a place so that she began to write *from* rather than *about* a place. These issues were significant since the poet was in exile from her place. The essay ranged over issues of colonialism, racism, and language, and considered in some detail the work of two writers, Les Murray and Aimé Césaire, as examples of writers who had found their "place" and wrote from it. The poet did not deal with the issues of gender or feminism as they relate to place or the public space.

Issues
Why did the poet write herself—the female body—out of place, the public space of the text? Why did she impose the sentence of silence on herself?

Ratio Decidendi[2]
What follows tells how and why the sentence of silence was imposed.

THE BODY

which is to talk about the space that lies between the legs of the female and the effect of this space on the outer space—"place."

In patriarchal societies (the only societies we have known), the female body always presents a subversive threat. By far *the* most efficient management tool of women is the possibility of the uninvited and forceful invasion of the space between the legs—rape.[3] Which is a constant. A threat to *the* space—the inner space between the legs. Even if never carried out, this threat continually and persistently inflects how the female reads the external language of place, or public space—the outer space. One woman raped is sufficient to vocalize and reify the threat of the outer space, and the need to protect this inner space means that the female always reads the outer space from a dichotomous position—safe/ unsafe, prohibited/unprohibited. How the female poet interacts with the land, the countryside, or the urban-scape—with the outer space in all its variety, or place in this most physical of senses—is entirely affected by gender. She must read place—the outer space—in a gendered language. Is the choice, therefore, either to accept the restriction in physical behaviour and available space that the threat of rape brings—limit one's activities to the daytime, and to specific places? Or what? The female poet's understanding of place in its most physical sense will be different from, and necessarily a more restricted one, than that of the male poet's.

SPACE INNER AND OUTER

All women have imprinted in them the basic politics of male territoriality.
—A. Fell[4]

Whether we conceive of the space between the legs as one space, the cunt;[5] two spaces, the cunt *and* womb; or one continuous space extending from cunt to womb, control of and over this space or spaces is a significant marker of the outer space. The problematic is whether the threat of the outer space originates there, or whether it is the generative potential of the inner space—its baby-making potential—which threatens the outer space, which in turn seeks to control the inner space.

Space and place—the public space—must not only be read and interpreted from the point of view of the space between the legs, but also from the perspective of how safe the space between the legs is or will be.[6]

The Body. And that most precious of resources—the space. Between. The legs. The Black woman comes to the New World with only the body. And the space between. The European buys her not only for her strength, but also to service the Black man sexually—to keep him calm. And to produce new chattels—units of production—for the plantation machine. The Black woman. And the space between her legs. Is intended to help repopulate the outer space:

> *Female slaves will be provided who, through marriage with the male slaves, will make the latter less eager for revolt, and the number of runaways will be reduced to a minimum.*[7]

The space between the Black woman's legs becomes. *The place.* Site of oppression—vital to the cultivation and continuation of the outer space in a designated form—the plantation machine. Harness the use value of the inner space to the use value of the outer space so that the inner space becomes open to all and sundry. Becomes, in fact, a public space. A thoroughfare. The "black magic" of the white man's pleasure, the "bag o' sugar down dey" of the Black man's release. *And* the space through which new slaves would issue forth.

"She nuttin but a thoroughfare!" is how the Bajans (Barbadians) describing a woman who have a lot of men.

243

For the Black woman, place and space come together in the New World as never before or since. To create. S/Place. The immutable and irrevocable linking of the inner place or space. Between the legs. With the outer space—"place" of the New World plantation machine. The Caribbean s/place living its post-modernist realities long before the advent of the theory. If theory it be.

S/Place. Where the inner space is defined into passivity by and harnessed to the needs and functions of the outer space—the place of oppression. Run it down[8] even further into Caribbean demotic English: s/place mutates into "dis place" (dis/place?). *"Dis place"*: the outer space—the plantation, the New World. *"Dis place"*: the result of the linking of the inner space between the legs with the outer place resulting in "dis placement." *"Dis place"*—the space between. The legs. For the Black woman "dis placed" to and in the New World, the inner space between the legs would also mutate into *"dis place"*—fulcrum of the New World plantation.

A GENEALOGY OF JAMETTES[9]

Jamette: from *diamêtre*, the diameter, dividing the world between the space and place of respectability and that of the underworld, the lower classes. Jamette, always female, and belonging to that latter world and class. Jamette! A loose woman, a woman of loose morals, whose habitat is the street. Jamette! A woman possessing both the space between her legs and the space around her, knowing her place. On the streets of Port of Spain.

We could be starting our genealogy with Nanny of the Maroons.[10] Or we could be going even further back. To Nzinga of Ngola (Angola).[11] Women warriors taking their inner space into the outer space of battle and war, where men violate the inner space of women.

Rum shop, cockfight, steel pan yard, street corner—only jamettes hanging about these places. Men *and* women who above the diameter/diametre would be calling these women out of their names, describing them over the years as wajanks, jackabats, spoats, and hos (whores).[12] We call them jamettes. For the present. Is what they doing in these places? Only servicing men? Signifying another reality? About the balance between the inner and outer space?

BUT JAMETTES GET RAPED TOO!

THE STREETS

The street, the only region of valid experience.
—André Breton[13]

CAST OF CHARACTERS

Boadicea—(Jamette, stickfighter leader of the **Don't Give a Damns**)
Alice Sugar—(Jamette, stickfighter, leader of the **Mousselines**)
Man Tamer—(a poui[14] stick)
Piti Belle Lily—(Jamette)
Mossie Millie—(Jamette)
Ocean Lizzie—(Jamette)
Sybil Steel—(Jamette)
Big Body Ada—(Jamette)
Darling Dan—(Jamette)
Ling Mama—(Jamette)
Queen Bee—(Jamette)
Myrtle the Turtle—(Jamette)
Zinga—(Jamette)

Preliminary Notes

Boadicea, the Jamette queen, just set up her reign of the city streets by fighting and beating Cutway Rimbeau, king of stickfighters, for showing too much interest in another woman, Piti Belle Lily. Cutway Rimbeau knowing when he beat so he giving Boadicea his stick, Man Tamer. Earlier, Boadicea also beat up Alice Sugar in a fight over Cutway Rimbeau.

Time: 1865
Act I, Scene I

Everything happening at a crossroads in Port of Spain in a lower-class area. One narrow street running from upstage centre to downstage centre, where it meeting up with another narrow street running from downstage right to downstage left. All kind of garbage littering the streets. The houses small small and run down and is fade the paint fade, although you could see somebody building them good. The little windows with their jalousies looking onto the street *which don't have no pavements, and doors opening right onto the road. As the curtain rising you not hearing any sounds, but little by little you hearing cries and shouts. Then suddenly from downstage left a group of stalwart, handsome women bursting onto the stage; two women leading them carrying a red banner with black words—**WE DON'T GIVE A DAMN!** The women carrying long, heavy-looking sticks, and the way the wood gleaming in the light you could tell the women polish them up. Some women also carrying stones and rocks, and all of them wearing red head wraps tie up in some real fancy shapes. The women swaggering around the stage now, their long, prettyful skirts trailing in the street and sending up little clouds of dust. They laughing big big and loud and some of them walking with their arms around each other. At a given cue the women start chanting and beating on empty tin cans some carrying with them:*

> We don't
> we don't
> we don't give a damn
> we don't give a blast
> we don't give a shit
> we won't give an inch
> not for you or you or you
> we don't give
> we don't give a damn
> we have we poui stick
> we have we iron
> we have we machete
> and when we done
> is only mousse leave from mousselines

*As soon as they done singing, another group of women bursting onto the stage from downstage right, taking the spotlight and pushing the **Don't Give a Damns** upstage to the left. These women dressing all in white—fresh wash and starch white muslin dresses and white head wraps which giving them their name, the **Mousselines**. They big, just like the **Don't Give a Damns,** and they striding around the stage like they owning it. With the white cloth against their black skin, they pretty too bad. Like the **Don't Give a Damns**, the **Mousselines** carrying sticks and stones; some even carrying broken bottles too. The spotlight moving from group to group: here, two or three **Mousselines** standing talking and laughing; there, a bigger group making rude gestures at the **Don't***

246

Give a Damns who now on the margins of the stage, muttering under their breath and cutting their eyes at the women in white. The white muslin head wraps of the **Mousselines** *gather up at the centre of the stage, and surrounding them is the red of the* **Don't Give a Damns** *and it all set off against the black background. It startling for so. Suddenly two more women in white entering from downstage right with a banner still wrap up and as they moving centre stage they pushing the others back. They unfurling the banner in the spotlight and spelling the word* **MOUSSELINES**. *The women in white start singing:*

> Watch we hard watch we good
> keep your eyes pon we
> each one a we have we wood
> that good to beat and crack head
> bottle and stone we know
> we sleep pon rock
> bottle is we bed
> so watch we hard
> watch we good
> we have we piece a wood
> we is the Mousselines
> this town is we own
> the Don't Give a Damns
> had better begin to give

They singing loud loud and aggressive and making obscene gestures to the **Don't Give a Damns**, *who muttering louder and louder now. Soon a fierce and brutal fight breaking out between the two groups of women. Sound of stick against flesh, stick against stick, or stone against bone or flesh, is all that filling the theatre. Quiet quiet flesh getting cut, but the red staining the stage. Suddenly a shrill whistle piercing the air and someone shouting:*

"Police!"

The stage black black now. When it come up light again, the two groups of women standing together watching the town's law enforcers—all men—coming down the narrow street that running from upstage centre to downstage centre. The women looking untidy and dishevelled, some missing their head wraps, others having their skirts tear up; some bleeding and a few sitting or lying at the side of the road, too hurt to move. Is clear they forgetting their differences facing this new threat. The men, mainly white and brown, all suit up in blue serge uniforms, and careful careful they moving down the narrow street hem in by the houses belonging to these very women. All the men knowing these women; they meeting them before in similar situations and they frighten of them, especially if they not having other officers backing them up. This is why the men coming down the street slow slow, holding their batons which they know not matching the women's sticks. As the men approaching, the women pulling closer together and making as if to charge. The men back back down the narrow roadway. The women now carrying their furled banners like weapons. This toing and froing happening three times. In silence. Suddenly the jamette Boadicea turning her back to the men lifting up her skirt and baring her behind. All the women doing the same and laughing loud and raucous. The men backing off now even further and looking real shocked and angry.

"You're a disgrace to womanhood! All you jamettes—a disgrace, you should be locked up." *An officer shouting out.*

"Lock we up nuh, lock we up!" *Is Boadicea who first challenging them like this, then Alice Sugar and the other women picking up the cry:*

"Lock we up, lock we up! We waiting, come and lock we up!"

As the women chanting these words, they moving up the street again toward the men. Boadicea tearing off her dress and now she standing naked like the day she born in front of her troops and the police officers. The women shouting out their approval and everybody tearing off their dresses. Some of the men turning away, their faces disgusted and angry at all that nakedness in front of them. The men pulling back even further. Over her head, Boadicea waving what was once her dress, but is now a flag.

Now Boadicea turning her back on the police and talking to the women:

"Is fraid we fraid dese men?"

"No!" *the women roaring back at her.*

"Who dese men protecting?"

"Not we, not one o we!"

"Who de street belong to, dem or we?"

"The streets is we own!"

Boadicea turning now to face the men: "You see we here in all we naked-ness—you see any of we shame of it? Not one, not one a we shame of we nakedness or frighten of you."

Boadicea advancing slowly on the men as she talking, and the women following her.

248

"De space between we legs is we own to do with as we please, and we not frighten of these streets. Dese streets is we own—we have a right to be here and we beating any man who telling we different—just ask Cut-way Rimbeau!" *Is clear the men recognizing the name. The women moving faster now and suddenly they charging the men who turning tail and running. The women laughing loud loud like real jamettes. Suddenly the stage black black.*

Act II, Scene II
Same crossroads as in Act I, Scene I

The light spotting a man sitting on a corner, playing a guitar singing:

> Boadicea the jamette who we all know
> Is a real disgrace to we Cariso
> I really can't understand
> Why she didn't take the training of the Englishman
> Roaming all about the vicinity
> Cat and dog passing they mouth on she
> Is better she die or lock up in jail
> She disgrace every woman in Port of Spain[15]

THE MISSING TEXT

When a text goes missing in the computer, it is not completely lost—another language is necessary to translate the language of "missing" text so that it becomes readable once again.

Is it silence that shapes the words of the "missing" text, or do the words shape the silence? How to read the silence? Much like those children's books where pictures of animals and people are hidden within the larger picture, I hunt the pieces of my silence within the larger text of silence—words. When the missing text is silence, what is the language with which you read the silence? What is the grammar of silence? Start with the word. The poem. The text. To deal in silence one must learn a new language.

On behalf of past generations
the body mediates
fleshing out the shadows of ghosts
soft songs lurk
sometimes so soft—a silence
wails
and the trumpet of words
brings down the Jerichoed walls

of silence

Composition is everything. —Miles Davis, trumpeter.

It is.

Each poem has its own silence. Technique but the discerning of that silence. And composition—*how* you shape the words around the silence. To understand one's own silence is, therefore, to understand one's words. To understand one's silence, one must go to the place of silence. In the body. In the words. Dis place—the s/place between the legs!

Jean, Dinah, Rosita and Clementina[16] were four prostitutes. They all lived in a calypso by Sparrow, the world's greatest calypso man. Jean, Dinah, Rosita and Clementina, their space a corner, a street corner, where they posing and selling what all men wanted and still do—a piece of their space, the space between their legs. Jean, Dinah, Rosita and Clementina—

bet your life is something they selling
and if you catch them broken
you can get it all for nothing
the Yankees gone and Sparrow take over now.[17]

Because of the Yankees, Jean, Dinah, Rosita and Clementina charging a higher price for their space, the place that was theirs and theirs alone. Sparrow man, calypso man, putting them round the corner posing, and believing he could get it all for nothing. Because he controlling the outer space, which controlling their inner space. Jean, Dinah, Rosita and Clementina—their space, their place, dis place between the legs—public

women, women in public on the street corner, round the corner selling…
your life   mine and theirs.

EARTH AND SOUND: PLACE OF POETRY

The space and place of silence—the silence around "Earth and Sound";
my own silence locked in my own words—silencing me. The sentence of
silence! Césaire, Murray, Walcott, Pound—how they stride around my
silence filled with their words—wonderful words. And like past generations, I lurk with Piti Belle Lili and Boadicea—abbreviated traditions—the
jamette, the only choice for those with no choice. Earth and sound—the
place of poetry in the culture of silence: the silence of Black, the silence of
woman, the silence of silence.

> silence is
> silence is
> silence is
> the sound, the very sound   between the words,
> in the interstices of time divided by the word
> between
> outer and inner
> space /silence
> is
> the boundary

Why didn't "I"—the female body—surface in the text, or was it there all
along? In the silence? "Missing" becomes a metaphor for the silence around
the text that omits the woman's s/place. Words crowd her out into silence.
Women have, in fact, left their mark on the many silences that surround
language—we must, therefore, learn to read those silences.

If we talk of silence and assign to it a validity equal to the word, is it then
right to talk of a "missing text," since the text of silence is already embedded
in the word? Silence, as in the silence around "Earth and Sound," sometimes says more than the word does. Earth. Sound. And Silence. To read
the silence around the text, one must become a jamette poet—possessing
the space between the legs—the inner space—uncompromisingly—as the
outer space.

AS IF

For was there not also the wisdom which had shaped my body up through the years from a single cell?

—Marion Milner[18]

The question of possession: true ownership/belonging: is one that will always exercise creole societies: non-native: and especially slave Caliban, most dispossessed of all.

—E. K. Brathwaite[19]

1.
He walks gets into his boat
as if
he has always done that
his boat   his space   his place

2.
high heels
push
pushing body up
away from
earth
thin bodies taking
up
less & less
space

3.
   foetus in place
pushing
pushes body to occupy
      more
space
dis
tended belly taking
up

more & more
   space

4.
oh, for a race of women
mashing the ground
as if!
they owned it
not like he does

5.
to move
   leaping from occupying space to
occupying the idea
   the thought
to make it your own
taking up
   more & more…

6.
the force of baby
  forces
you to
take   more
& more &
more…
   space

7.
breasts thighs belly buttocks
flesh swell
ripen into the full
of time filled with
carefully choreographed expansions
of plenitude and ful/
fillment

8.
crazy wild distension of belly belly
and more belly
that will
not
can
not stop
yet nothing wild here—
everything following
deep codes
yet we take
(up)
space
differently

9.
oh, for a race of women!

10.
he walks
as if
he owns the earth
steps into his boat   his car
his plane
his fighter jet
his idea
his war
as extensions of his
very self
he occupies
possesses them
    car
    house
    children
    women
    ideas
no memory of murder
in his walk

no memory of death
and we who
carrying
and carrying
life
who taking up
space
honestly
carry fear
of our move
      ments
 expanded dis
      tensions choreo
graphed
        through the centuries and
one hundred years
because we did
    not
    choreo
graph the pain
     the poem

this dance
this song
this lament
we did not
       this idea
he possesses

BUT THE BODY

A history of bodies —Michel Foucault[20]

   silence is
   silence is
   silence is
   body and

```
text
text and
body    filaments of silence holding them together
Text  Body  Silence
Earth Sound Silence
EarthSilenceSoundBodyText
```

Unlike all other arrivals before or since, when the African comes to the New World, she comes with nothing. But the body. Her body. *The* body—repository and source of everything needed to survive in any but the barest sense. Body memory bodymemory. The African body. Its resources: strength, resistance to disease. The African body. Including the space between the legs, the *raison d'être* of her importation to the New World.

The African body. At cross purposes with the African body—
>   the African body: spirit
>   the African body: intelligence
>   the African body: memory
>   the African body: creativity

>   : its resources

Time and again these resources impelling her to flee, run from, subvert, the institution of slavery.

Is we bodies saving we—forcing we to live in them we coming to understand that surviving needing the body. African. Pulling we down: Source of enslavement / road to transcendence: holding we up. The Body African. Is Mind.

What I learned from the slave is that I can control my body. Music movement—this was outside the reach of the oppressor…this we could control.
>   —Rex Nettleford[21]

And so the maroons taking their bodies completely outside the reach and ambit of the white European—but only in those places and spaces where the land allowing it. Mountains!—you having to have them and "I will lift mine eyes to the hills from whence cometh my salvation." Maroonage—the coming together of the exploited physical s/place—"place" and "space"—and the exploited s/place—"place" and "space"—of the body. Maroonage—the coming together. Creating something new—an inner space and place—s/place—of African self-sufficiency which the European, emissary of the outer space, and what Brathwaite calling "missile cultures"[22] continually trying to penetrate.

Foucault (the white male European) speaks. On sexuality:

> ...deployments of power are directly connected to the body—to bodies, functions, physiological processes, sensations, and pleasures; far from the body having to be effaced, what is needed is to make it visible through an analysis in which the biological and the historical are not consecutive to one another, as in the evolutionism of the first sociologists, but are bound together in an increasingly complex fashion in accordance with the development of the modern technologies of power that take life as their objective.[23]

THE BODY FEMALE and black

= a history of sexuality = A history of bodies
—to harness female reproductive power to the machine of the plantation. The inestimable value of the space between the legs—the black (w)hole that could replenish plantations and keep men calm and non-rebellious. *The Handmaid's Tale*, but a vision of the future past in white face.
—to distort the body's impulses and learnt wisdoms
careful choreography of diastole and systole
choreography of birth and death
he walks   gets into his boat   his plane
has no memory of murder   no memory of death

the Body   African   the silence at the heart of the word is

body—the irreducible—the body african
black ivory
piecesofblackgold

piezas
meubles
chattels
things

oh for a race of women
                    African
mashing the ground
dis
tended bellies
careful choreographed expansions of plenty
tude
full
fill men(t)
and fear

the body female and black = a history of sexuality where biology and history forever tie up in the black space and place of s/place birthing "modern technologies of power that take life as their objective." And take life.

In the New World the African woman creating life and seeing the men—the white men—taking away her children and selling them. The man who walking, getting into his boat, his plane, his ship—taking the product of her body and the body's wisdoms—her children—like he taking the crops she tending. Body and place. Fertilized. Cultivated. Harvested. In the same way. Between parent. And child. Mother. And child. Father. And child. Rupture. Umbilical cords to centuries of learning and culture severed. The Body African   Place   The inner space between the legs linked irrevocably to the outer space of the plantation.
AfricanBodyPlace
                    of warfare
                    resistance:
Some African women nursing for long periods of time postponing sexual relations which postponing pregnancy which postponing children which postponing... Silence
Some African women nursing—Infanticide![24]

Re-producing
A-borting
    life
—a warping and twisting of the filaments of silence between African
and body—body & text
body becoming text which she learning to read in a newlanguage
andshecomingtounderstandhowtosurvivetextbecomingbodybod
iesdeadbodiesmurderedbodiesimportedbredmutilatedbodiessold
bodiesboughttheEuropeantrafficinbodiesthattellingsomuchabout
themandwhichhelpingfueltheindustrializationofthemetropolises
bodiescreatingwealththecapitalfeedingtheindustrialrevolutions
manytimesoverandoverandoverandoverthebodies...

        Between the legs   the space
        /within the womb   the space
        colonized like place and space

                            around her

       thesilenceof
       thespacebetween
          the legs

       thesilenceof
       thespacewithin
                thewomb
       broken into words of master
                lord
                 massa
       and silence

       silence is
       silence is
                the space
       between
          the legs
       is silence
                the womb
       broken into
       words

master

lord

massa

silence is…

The Body African henceforth inscribed with the text of events of the New World, body becoming text. In turn the Body African—dis place—"place" and s/place of exploitation inscribes itself permanently on the European text. *Not* on the margins. But within the very body of the text where the silence exists.

OUR ROYAL WILL AND PLEASURE

Columbus, emissary of the outer space and the Old World, penetrates and enters the inner space of the Caribbean. Violently. From this time on, the Caribbean will be described "in terms of," shaped to fit. C(o)untoured to the needs and demands of the outer space.

Jean, Dinah, Rosita and Clementina, Piti Belle Lily, Boadicea and all the other jamettes decide—if the space of silence—the silence of the space between the legs   has to be fractured by massa and his word they would at least decide who would fracture it and they would charge for it.

This is some progress. Perhaps.

Royal Prohibitions
It Is Our Royal Will And Pleasure
To protect the space that lies between the legs of the female otherwise known as *dis place* and in effort of these ends, *dis place*

    —must not be sold

    —must not be given away

    —must be sold

    —must be given away

    —must always be given to men

    —must not be given to men

    —must be taken

    —must be sewn closed

    —must be mutilated

—must be hidden
—must be a thoroughfare
—must not be a thoroughfare
—must never be given away by the one who possesses it.

Indulgence in any action described above by the female, *on the iniative of the female*, serves to subvert the hegemony of those who control the outer space.

It Is Our Royal Will And Pleasure
The Black male be all times prohibited from entering the space lying between the legs of the white female—the white space.

It Is Our Royal Will And Pleasure
The space lying between the legs of the Black female is hereby declared a thoroughfare. A black hole.

white space/black hole

How you interact with the outer space is determined by protection of the inner space. And by whom.

Who is the you?

It Is Our Loving Will And Pleasure

> don't let nobody
> the mothers teach
> fear
>   but no
> body touch
> you
> there

"Don't let nobody touch you there." Our mothers are right when they making this blanket prohibition, because if they not controlling entry to that space, *dis place*, by markers like the right man, the right colour, the right class, and in the right circumstances, you—the woman behind the space—bound to be permanently affected. The mothers knowing the outer space controlling the inner space which in turn inflecting and affecting the interpretation of the outer space. The mothers, therefore, intervening—*Their Loving Will and Pleasure*—and ensuring the best. For their daughters. "Don't let nobody touch you there!" So the mothers teaching fear. Naming the space Between. The legs—the young girl's legs. The MUSN'T DO.

But consider. The Black mother under slavery—*her* loving will and pleasure—wanting to protect—"don't let nobody touch you there!"—herself—the daughters. Knowing. Everybody touching her—There! The Black mother naming what the men have. The MUST DO.

"It was a safe place for a girl," my friend tells me, describing her childhood on a Manitoban farm, and yet on moving to the city, she found that her mother has passed on all the lessons of fear:

> don't let
> no!
> body touch
> don't let
> you there!
> nobody touch you
> there

Further Prohibitions Regarding Dis Place
—those who take these prohibitions to their logical end and prohibit entry to men—those who decide to explore each other's spaces must be dis/placed;
—so too must those who treat the space between the legs as having no monetary value, including loose women, nymphomaniacs and jamettes;
—as well, those selling the space between the legs will also be dis/placed.

We Hereby Decree Under Our Hand And Seal
That the outer space must *always* determine how safe the inner space is; that the way in which women know the space around them must always be determined by how safe or unsafe they perceive their inner space to be.

It Is Our Royal Will And Pleasure

If any number of persons shall find out the Pallenque of the said Negroes, they shall have and enjoy to their uses all the Women and Children and all the plunder they can find there for their reward.[25]

"Chile you know what dem say about Nanny of the Maroon—that she used to be catching de bullets dat dem baccra[26] firing pon she people right inside she crotch. Beat dat!"

Consider! dis place—the inner space repelling and resisting the aggressive penetrations from the outer space.

SILENCE AND THE SPACE BETWEEN

silence shapes
　　　　　　that space
between
　　　inner and outer

the space between
　　　　　　　the legs
c(o)unt/ours
　　of silence

the outer space of text
borders on the
　　　inner space
my body

To balance the equation of inner and outer space we must factor in silence. The text—the silence at the heart of. My text—I writing my own silence... and if you cannot ensure that your words will be taken in the way you want them to be—if you are certain that your words will be misunderstood, that, in fact, those who listening not interested in what you having to say, and saying, and wanting to silence you, then holding on to your silence is more than a state of non-submission. It is resisting.

Silence c(o)unt/ours the inner space!

textbody—
body as text
body inscribed

                    on text
                    on body
to interrupt
    disrupt
    erupt
the text of the new world
is a text of
a history of
                inter/ruptions
                      of bodies
a body of interruptions
bodies of interred
                eruptions

how to interrupt
                disrupt
erupt
    the body
of the text
           to allow
the silence
           in erupt

the space between: dis place—defined within the context of fear or control of
penetration which c(o)unt/ouring has silenced the inner space
dis place between
                    the legs
what does it say—this inner space—how read
its silence beyond
fear
                  of the outer space

Does the inner space exist whole in any language? Other than "threat" and "fear"? What is the language of the inner space? Beyond the boundaries of control and fear. Is its language silence? A silence other than the imposed silence. To read the text that lies "missing" in the silence of the inner space, we needing a new language—the language of jamettes, possessing their inner and outer space. The be-coming and coming-to-be of a jamette poet. The outer space c(o)untouring and shaping the inner space; its language of silencing exerting pressure of threat and fear causing the inner space to collapse in upon itself like a black (w)hole absorbing everything around it.

> How to make the black hole (w)hole?
> What its shape
> where begin and end
> the (w)hole
> of my silence
> this black (w)hole collapsing
> in
> upon
> itself

:You sound like—fishwife! virago! jamette! The mothers warn.

> *How does the inner space*
> *sound*
> *what the sound of*
> *the space*
> *between*
> * the legs*
> *once found*
> *how does the inner space*
> *sound*
> *loud*
> *like a jamette!*
> *turning in*
> *out—*
> *that inner sound*
> *found*

loud
like a jamette!

Words wombed in silence wish to speak in sentences paragraphs
With no closures.

THE BODY RE TURNS

dis/place   dis place   dis place
affecting how we take up space—outer space: fearfully
no memory of murder in his walk
agoraphobia: a dread or horror of open spaces. Protection of dis
place—the inner space—means all women manifest a degree of
agoraphobia
the paradox: carrying the potential for life within   the inner space
we become afraid of the outer space, lurk with Boadicea in the
silencing—the space between—inner and outer

Question
What is it about the outer space of my own text ("Earth and Sound") that
silenced my inner space—dis place?

Answer
If dis place—the Caribbean—is the threatening outer space—*dis place* of
oppression, to which they harnessing *dis place* between the legs of the Black
woman (which also c(o)untouring that inner space by silencing), it following that I outing out[27] *dis place*—inner s/place—from the text, metaphor for the outer space—the space of man. Bordered. Controlled. And
patrolled. By men. *And* their words.

If "the street, the only region of valid experience" and the street was and
is prohibited to women, what is their valid field of experience? The inner
space—s/place—*dis place*? And can the street be the only valid field of experience if what constitutes its experience prohibits, often obliterates through
its threat to "dis place," the presence of women.

At fourteen my son takes up space in ways I never could, and he lets me
know this—that he is safe on the streets in a way I, more than twice his age,
can never be.

We peeling back layers of silencing and finding what "dis place" is really about. Silence. A different text lying there, a spirit world, an imaginative universe. Marion Milner writes about "an insideness, a kind of womb space where there's both a protectedness, a cocoon, but also something initiating change, an unfolding from some inherent potentiality, a possibility to be realized."[28] Jessica Benjamin says, "the significance of the spatial metaphor for a woman is likely to be in just this discovery of her *own, inner* desire, without the fear of impingement, intrusion or violation."[29]

Diary Entry (1988)

I can point to the exact place on my anatomy, the left abdominal area, which I sacrificed for those poems—kinopoesis of African languages. Tongue, lips, physiology of speech, dismemberment—the body erupted forcibly in She Tries*—careful choreography—these images of the body are rooted in that experience—the foundation of language is the body. (my body) I am finding this out after the fact—seeking out the silences.*

March 6, 1989

Dear A.M. (a male musician/poet)

I liked your linking of the body and place—they belong together. In a recent work of mine the body has erupted very powerfully and I believe I will be adding some of the knowledge gained in that work to the enclosed essay, "Earth and Sound."

Have you explored at all how gender determines and affects our relationship to place? When I think of Trinidad and Tobago, which is where I am from—at least more recently, being African by heritage—I am aware of how circumscribed I was as a female growing up. There were certain places that "decent" women and girls just didn't go to—even within one's immediate environment. Those places are shot through with fear and danger—the ultimate fear of rape. I believe many women must have similar feelings about places they have come from—places where they have grown up. This is a theme I want to explore further.

I saw a film some time ago—around the same time I heard your interview on the radio—about a South African cleric, Beyers Naudé, an Afrikaaner. In that film, a white South African says, "We love this land, this land is ours." I asked myself how it was possible for someone to say that they loved a land, yet hated the people of the land—the people who belonged to that land. You can see why your comments about the body being integrally related to place resonated so vividly for me. Of course there is a danger in this concept, which Nazi Germany typifies so clearly—the danger being, of course, the development of that bond between a land and a people—a *volk*—to the extreme and justifying many outrages in the name of that bond. What is even more disturbing is that the fascist Afrikaaner is taking that very positon, and in so doing, desiring to obliterate the very people of the land.

What confronts me daily as a poet and writer is that original loss of place for the African brought to the New World—place lost not willingly, not in anticipation of a new life like the immigrant, or of a better standard of living, not in the assured belief that they would find their El Dorado, but place as in language, religion, culture and kin—lost irrevocably. What I try to do in my writing is to repair some of those fractures. I can't ever recover or recapture the former "Paradise," if there ever was one, but through memory, in which the body plays such a vital role, I can give voice to those who passed on and over silently.

I have on occasion written that when the African came to the New World, she came with only the body—unlike so many immigrants, she didn't come with the material and physical trappings of "home." The body would be the repository of everything she could or would need to survive—physically, spiritually and psychically. The body became text and text became body.

I have enclosed postage for return of the essay.

Yours truly,

Silence. I ought to have known. Better. If you know your words will be ignored or not taken seriously, isn't it better to remain silent?

Meditations—

and fingertips commune with tongue and mouth
seek to know again what was once friend

now is hostile in its dumbness
seek to enter secret ways now probed
lips spread
see how virgin I am
and tongue tastes the murder of your blood
is all that would satisfy
now—to drink the blood of my master
and conqueror
to confirm the "I" in savage
and freedom in one small drop

body must remember song and drum
and story and tale and
how it was
how it stay
and how it wasn't
it must remember touch
of mother
father, brother and
sister
it must
must remember or seize its ineffable right
and die
body must remember the reign of life
and death
that body is not thing
and thing is not body
must remember how we knew and what
we knew
was knowing that knew and
knew not
finite end
and as body re-members to bleed
swell with seed and
child
so body must remember to remember the
forgotten
the not-known yet known

that each begins and
ends in cell
that between cell and cell is
but a microcosm

a universe drawn tight by memory

THE BODY RETURNS...BEYOND THE BOUNDARY[30]

All she have is two fine leg and a gully.[31]

Caribbean men using cricket, the game of place and space, beating their former masters at their own game and putting their mark on the outer space. "Two fine leg and a gully"—cricket—shaping the image of the Caribbean in the outer space of the world, where women not even playing the game let alone going "beyond the boundary." "Two fine leg and a gully." To move beyond the boundary of fear—of penetration—unwanted and unwanting—c(o)untouring the inner space—to find the source and sound of our silencing, we must become cartographers of silence, mapping not only the known edges—the boundaries of our inner space—we must be moving beyond the boundary. To take soundings of the deep, where the voice is not one but "the many-voiced one of one voice / ours."[32] Polyvocal and many-tongued.

"You better know your place"—the question at the centre of "Earth and Sound." What *is* this place? The body linking the place between—*Dis Place*—to the beyond of boundary—*dis place*.

AIN'T I A WOMAN[33]

If the Black woman's inner space doing the same work as the white woman's inner space—making babies—ain't she a woman? But OUR ROYAL WILL AND PLEASURE saying the inner space of the Black woman nothing but a baby-making factory. Or, they saying she shouldn't be having no more children. Either way they trying to make her less of what they saying a woman is. And even if the Black woman working like a man in the outer space, they still not giving her the rights and freedoms he having.

But still an' all, ain't I a woman?

Sojourner Truth asks "ain't I a woman?" What is the question? If she works like any man, but is still a woman—what is it that makes her a woman? The inner space? *Dis place*? Filled with "inherent potentiality." And the loudness. Of the jamette. Possessing the street. The polyvocality—the many-voiced one of one voice—that is the sound of *dis place*...

"Oh for a race of Women..."

But women are raced. And so too their space. Inner and outer.[34]

CARNIVAL/BACCHANAL/WINING[35]

A race!—of women mashing the ground—dancing and wining their all, any and everything and is Carnival time again and the jamettes coming back and pulling all those middle-class and upper-class women onto the streets; the only war now is between the Carnival bands and is so the women coming, flowing down the streets with the skimp and scant of their costumes, carrying their staffs—their *lingas*[36] and they wining and wining round and round *dis place*—African and Indian alike—*tout bagai*[37] wining and wining—the *yoni*[38] round and around the *linga* of their Carnival staffs and they dancing through the streets—*oh, for a race of women!*—shaking their booty, doin their thing, their very own thing, jazzin it up, winin up and down the streets, parading their sexuality for two days—taking back the streets making them their own, as they spreading their joying up and down the streets of Port of Spain...

It is the only time of the year that women—old, young, thin, fat, women women—can exhibit their sexuality without undue censure or fear under the benign gaze of OUR ROYAL WILL AND PLEASURE.

Oh, for a race of women...

Act III, Scene IV
The curtain rises to reveal once again the same two streets.

A figure crawling on her hands and knees from upstage centre down the street advancing toward the audience and showing herself to be Boadicea, the jamette queen. Two women with market baskets standing at the intersection of the streets on the left side. As Boadicea approaching the women turning their backs and moving away from her toward the audience. They are middle-class women on their way from the market—their baskets full-up with mango, paw paw, breadfruit, yams, and other fruits and vegetables.

First woman: "But just look at her! She's nothing but a nastiness—she's got sores all over her body—and she smells too—"

Second woman: "You never said a truer word, my dear. All she does is crawl around these streets begging." *The women ignoring Boadicea, and linking arms they strolling along the street downstage right all the while talking:*

First woman: "Yes mi dear, I hear the children does really tease her—they say she's the Devil's disciple!" *The woman dropping her voice on these last few words, and both of them turning their heads surreptitiously to look at Boadicea who now following them.*

Second woman: "I think she blind too, you know—is God's own punishment for her looseness—you remember how she tear off her dress one day on the street?" *Both women shaking their heads and walking off the stage with Boadicea still following them. The stage goes dark.*

Act III, Scene VI

The curtain rises on a courtroom; upstage centre is the judge's bench behind which sits an old bewigged, bespectacled white man. His glasses sit low on his nose. He looks a caricature of a judge. At right and left are two counsel tables at which sit two lawyers. The lawyer on the right is a white male in a barrister's robe and white wig; the lawyer on the left is a Black woman also dressed in a barrister's robe and wig. The white wig against her black skin is startling. At the centre sits Boadicea. There are sounds of shouts and cries of women's voices.

Lady Barrister: "Your Lordship," *she rises,* "I beg of you to let these women in—they are my client's friends. I assure you they will be quiet."

Gentleman Barrister: "Your Lordship," *he gets to his feet,* "this is entirely unacceptable—we are merely dealing with a motion to confine this, this…

Lady Barrister: "Woman, sir?"

Gentleman Barrister: "I can find my own words—I would ask my friend not to put words in my mouth. There is no need for this spectacle, this display of wantonness. These are street women who will no doubt steal whatever they can lay their hands on."

Lady Barrister: "Is my learned friend afraid that when they're done clearing the courts of its benches, these women might also take him away? I can assure my learned friend that he is entirely safe from these women—their tastes tend to run to the more muscular—"

Judge: "Gentlemen!" *The judge strikes his gavel on his bench.* "Enough of this unseemly bickering, we will proceed." *The gentleman barrister remains standing; the lady barrister sits.*

Gentleman Barrister: "Your Lordship, we must make an example of this…" *he pauses, then rushes on,* "this abomination of womanhood. She is a stain on this fair city of hers—I mean ours. If we lock her up, then women like her will know that they cannot wander around the streets at will making trouble. It is rumoured, your Lordship, that she even deals in the black arts, what they call obeah![39] I urge you to exercise your responsibility, nay your duty, and lock her away!"

Lady Barrister: "My plea is a simple one, Your Lordship—this woman, and she does have a name," *she turns to the man who has just seated himself,* "Boadicea—has done nothing!" *At the sound of her name, Boadicea looks up for the first time.* "She has harmed no one and she's long past the stage where she can do any harm to anyone. Isn't she a woman, my Lord, and aren't there special laws to protect women? All this talk of the devil and the black arts is but hearsay and intended to prejudice your Lordship against her. The streets have been her home, and those women out there want to look after her." *As the lady barrister talks, the noise offstage becomes louder and louder and suddenly the door upstage left bursts open and several jamettes rush into the courtroom. They are all armed with sticks and rocks. The judge cowers below his bench.*

Gentleman Barrister: "Enough! Get out! Get out!"

Jamettes: "Is you to get out!" *A buxom woman lifts him and carries him to the door and throws him out. The lady barrister sits at her table, a small smile playing at the corners of her mouth.*

Piti Belle Lili: "Come, Bo, is Piti Belle Lili, come girl, we going look after you—we not letting none of these damn faysty men—white or otherwise coloured—push we or you around. Dis place is not for you or for we. We have we own place—come let we go."

Jamette: "Woh! dese men lucky oui—dey damn lucky we don't break dey head open and mash up de place." *The women lift Boadicea and chant the anthems of the* **Don't Give a Damns** *and the* **Mousselines***; they carry Boadicea offstage through the same door they just threw the gentleman barrister.*

The stage darkens.

CODA: Place Out of Place

Women expend enormous energy assessing and verifying the safety of their external environments. Even in these so-called Western havens of democracy. The degree of risk women are forced to assume as they negotiate the outer space astonishes me still. The country of my birth, Trinidad and Tobago, comes to mind—there the system of transportation is a mix of government-run buses which are limited mainly to intercity travel; maxi taxis plying a particular highway corridor between the capital city, Port of Spain, and the many towns to the east of it; and what are referred to as PH taxis, which are supposed to be licensed as private taxis and carry passengers into places the maxis and buses don't go. The licensing system, such as it is, is honoured more in its absence. There is no police enforcement of PH taxis; this means that anyone can decide to run one, putting women at risk of being abducted and murdered, as has happened on too many occasions. Suffice it to say that there are many other contexts in which women are at risk, particularly from former partners, resulting in the prime minister suggesting that women should take better care in their choice of men. That men should be urged to abstain from violence against women is not mentioned.

Canada—Toronto—appears a much less violent place, but colonialism is always violent, although it can always hide its face in the folds of time. Consider the French Congolese writer Alain Mabanckou commenting in his 2013 memoir about the renaming of his lycée to the Lycée Victor-Augagneur. He writes that Victor Augagneur press-ganged "all able-bodied men living along the construction route of the Congo-Ocean railway line," resulting in over 20,00 people losing their lives.[40] The violence in colonial spaces like Trinidad and Tobago and Canada is but a continuation of the original primary violence of colonialism.

Consider how unsafe Canada is for First Nations women; the Native Women's Association puts the missing and murdered at over 4,000.[41] Consider the irony that I, an un-belonged person in *dis here lan*, find Canada a relatively safe space to move around in, compared to my country of birth and compared to the experiences of FN women. These two realities are integrally linked. Their psychic expulsion as women from their own lands parallels my own psychic expulsion from my country of birth. In similar ways, as women we are condemned to police ourselves, restrict our movements and consider that which should nurture us, our environment, as actively hostile to us.

Consider, finally, the hydra-headed nature of colonialism—

NOTES

1   M. NourbeSe Philip, "Earth and Sound: The Place of Poetry," in *The Word Behind Bars and the Paradox of Exile*, ed. Kofi Anyidoho (Evanston: Northwestern University Press, 1997), 169-82.

2   *Ratio decidendi*—literally the "reason for the decision"—is the expression commonly used in the reporting of legal cases to identify the kernel of the legal reasoning, as opposed to *obiter dicta*.

3   Anthony Giddens writes that in "pre-modern development of Europe rape flourished mainly on the margins, at the margins, at the frontiers, in colonies, in states of nature amongst marauding invading armies." Anthony Giddens, *The Transformation of Intimacy: Sexuality, Love and Eroticism in Modern Times* (Palo Alto: Stanford University Press, 1992), 122. Allegations of mass rape of Bosnian Muslim women in 1992 by Serbian forces as a way of spreading terror and asserting control suggests that these practices defy a simple linkage to "pre-modern" times. In a *Ms.* editorial, March/April 1993, on the issue of the rape of Bosnian women, Robin Morgan asks: "If rape in war is a weapon, then what is it in peace time?"

4   Alison Fell, "One Night a Stranger…," *New Statesman and Society* (Oct. 25, 1991). Fell, in the same piece, answers Robin Morgan's questions by describing how women in cities are "under siege, controlled by the fear (of men)." In her novel *Virgin Territory*, Sara Maitland echoes this in her description of one of her characters, a nun: "But Sister Kitty had been raped, the weapon held over women's heads always and everywhere." Sara Maitland, *Virgin Territory* (London: Joseph, 1984), 66.

5   I use this word advisedly rather than *vagina* to draw attention to how language separates us from our bodies. When writing or speaking of the female genitals, our choice is a stark one: between the anatomical Latin word, *vagina*, replete with medical overtones, and the horrific (for many of us) and more vulgar expression, cunt.

6   Gayatri Spivak sets up a theoretically useful opposition between the clitoris and what she describes as the "uterine social organization (the arrangement of the world in terms of the production of future generations where the uterus is the chief agent and means of production…)." Society, therefore, perceives the clitoris as a marker of excess and a threat to this order. It is arguable that even society's overweening interest in the womb is but a sublimation of its fear of this power—a fear manifest most clearly in the abortion struggles. In fact, both the clitoris and uterus are feared and are constructed in this way. Gayatri Chakravorty Spivak, *In Other Worlds: Essays in Cultural Politics* (London: Methuen, 1987), 153.

7   Letter, April 1514, from Ferdinand, King of Spain, to Miguel Pasamonte, treasurer for Hispaniola. In Eric Williams, *Documents of West Indian History, 1492–1655* (Port of Spain: PNM Publishing Co. Ltd., 1963), 155.

8   "Run down" is a Jamaican Caribbean expression for a dish cooked with coconut milk, the success of which depends on the milk turning to oil during the cooking process. The dish is also known as "oil down" or "come down" in other islands.

9   The jamette class in Trinidad, according to Bridget Brereton, was comprised of "singers, drummers, dancers, stickmen, prostitutes, pimps, and badjohns in general." Jamette women often worked as domestics in middle-class homes, but middle-class society regarded them as transgressive. Jamette gangs or bands often met and fought for supremacy. Bridget Brereton, *Race Relations in Colonial Trinidad, 1879-1900* (New York: Cambridge University Press, 1979), 166.

10   Maroons were Africans in the New World who, having escaped slavery, fled to inaccessible areas where they set up self-contained and self-sustaining communities, most notably in the islands of Jamaica and Dominica, as well as Surinam. During the years of active colonization, Maroons engaged in warfare with the Europeans to keep their independence. Nanny, a well-known leader of the Maroons in Jamaica, led several battles against the British.

11   Queen Nzinga or Zhinga, leader of the Ndongo people in what is now Angola, was a formidable opponent of Portuguese colonization in the early seventeenth century.

12   These are all words which have been used to describe women who frequented the streets, and who middle-class society perceived as immoral and improper.

13   André Breton, *Nadja* (New York: Grove Press, 1994), 113.

14   "Poui"—*Tabebuia serratifolia*—a tropical hardwood, is primarily used for furniture. Its hardness recommends it as suitable material for the sticks used in the African Caribbean practice of stickfighting.

15   Andrew Pearse, "Mitto Sampson on Calypso Legends of the 19th Century, *Caribbean Quarterly* 4, Nos. 3 & 4 (1956).

16   "Jean an' Dinah," a calypso by calypsonian Francisco Slinger singing under the sobriquet, the Mighty Sparrow.

17   Mighty Sparrow, "Jean an' Dinah," *Sparrows, Greatest Hits*, RCA, LPB 1067, 1960.

18   Marion Milner, *Eternity's Sunrise* (London: Virago, 1987).

19   Edward Kamau Brathwaite, "Caliban, Ariel and Unprospero in the Conflict of Creolization: A study of the Slave Revolt in Jamaica in 1831–32," *Annals New York Academy of Sciences* 292, No. 1 (1977), 41.

20   Michel Foucault, *A History of Sexuality, Volume 1: An Introduction*, trans. Robert Hurley (New York: Random House, 1990), 152.

21   Rex Nettleford, *Globe and Mail* (July 9, 1988). Rex Nettleford is a former Rhodes scholar and a professor at the University of the West Indies; he is also director of the National Dance Company of Jamaica. In the years since this essay was written, Rex Nettleford passed away; he died on Feb. 2, 2010.

22   Brathwaite, "Caliban, Ariel and Unprospero," 141.

23   Foucault, *History of Sexuality*, 152.

24   Many African traditional practices prohibited sexual intercourse during nursing, which would thereby postpone any further pregnancies. Lucille Mair, "Recollections of a Journey into a Rebel Past" in *Caribbean Women Writers: Essays from the First International Conference*, ed. Selwyn R. Cudjoe (Wellesley, MA: Calaloux, 1990), 51–60.

25   "Resolutions from the Council of War." Article of War by Governor, Sir Thomas Modyford and Council, August 15, 1665, occasioned by "the Rebellion of the Carmahaly Negroes and other Outlying Negroes."

26   Caribbean demotic word for white people.

27   "To out out"—Caribbean demotic for erasing.

28   Milner, *Eternity's Sunrise*.

29   Jessica Benjamin, *The Bonds of Love: Feminism, Psychoanalysis and the Problems of Domination* (New York: Pantheon, 1988), 128. Benjamin critiques Eric Erikson's concept "inner space" as the receptive and passive half of a phallic dual unity. She

recognizes the inner space not only as a passivity, but "as a metaphor of equal importance to 'phallic activity and its representations'" (128).

30   The late C. L. R. James in the definitive work on cricket, explored the West Indian psyche and character, and the relationship between the imperial power, England, and its colonies through the game of cricket. C. L. R. James, *Beyond a Boundary* (New York: Pantheon, 1984).

31   Both "fine leg" and "gully" are cricketing terms referring to fielding positions.

32   M. Nourbese Philip, "And Over Every Land and Sea," *She Tries Her Tongue; Her Silence Softly Breaks* (Charlottetown, PEI: Ragweed, 1988), 36. (by Wesleyan University Press, Middletown, CT, 2015).

33   Sojourner Truth, "Ain't I a Woman," speech delivered at the Women's Convention, Akron, Ohio, May 29, 1851.

34   Those who police and patrol the outer space treat Black and white people very differently so that space becomes raced. The most obvious example of this is the police harassment of Black men in the Western world, as they go about their daily lives. Black men's enjoyment of the benefits that come with territoriality is mediated by policing practices. Space becomes, therefore, not only gendered but raced.

35   "Wining," is a popular Afro Caribbean dance movement in which the hips are circled, is based on African fertility dances.

36   "Linga," or "siva-linga," commonly refers to the phallus, although linga also refers to the "all-pervading space in which the whole universe is in the process of formation and dissolution." Ajit Mookerjee and Madhu Khanna, *The Tantric Way: Art, Science, Ritual* (London: Thames and Hudson, 1977), 33.

37   French patois word meaning everybody.

38   Yoni symbolizes the Hindu female principle. It is represented visually by a circle or, in an active state, by a triangle.

39   An African form of spiritual divination that is practised in the Caribbean.

40   Alain Mabanckou, *Lights of Pointe-Noire* (London: Serpent's Tale, 2015), 173.

41   "Questions over Number of Missing Indigenous Women in Canada," *BBC News* (Feb. 17, 2016), <http://www.bbc.com/news/world-us-canada-35590442>.

RIDING THE BUS
WITH ROSA IN MOROCCO

The air in the Medina is cool, crisp and fresh. The first call to prayer has already happened; there is burgeoning activity as proprietors begin to ready their stores and stalls for the business of the coming day. Men push carts with produce down cobbled streets too narrow for cars, and it is for this reason I am following the driver of the minibus which has come to the *riad* to collect me for a trip to the desert.

Gaunt and elegant, cats stalk past me arrogantly, tails erect in the brisk morning air. I am carrying my two bags, one with a change of clothing and toiletries, the other with writing gear—notebooks, a book and my computer. The driver's lack of willingness to help me with my bags feeds my nervousness, and for some unaccountable reason, my trepidation increases as I take in his somewhat dishevelled appearance—I can see the top of his underpants where his shirt has become caught in the elastic. I'm being petty, I tell myself as I hurry after him—it's early in the morning, after all, what do I expect?

Ten minutes later, we arrive at a street stop where larger buses are parked, the area a hub of activity with a steady stream of minibuses like the one I arrive in pulling up to let off passengers. Primarily through gestures, I'm directed to get onto one of these larger buses—it's more spacious and well-appointed, with air conditioning and ceiling windows which can be opened. As I'm facing a journey of some fourteen hours over two days, these amenities matter a great deal. At 7:30 a.m. I'm the third person on the bus but second to arrive, since the other two are a couple. I say hello to them—they don't answer. I sit behind them in the window seat in the last-but-one row. Through the window I observe the early-morning rituals of passersby buying coffee and pastries and think of the desert—the Sahara.

Deserts, especially the Sahara, have fascinated me for the longest while: perhaps it's the idea of the existence of life amidst so much aridity and desiccation, or the coexistence of desert and oasis, two states held in tension by an inherent opposition, which mutually heightens their individual essences; the desert becoming more desert because of the idea of the oasis, and vice versa. Perhaps it's the idea of the Sahara being a ruin of what was once a verdant, green land, which continues to harbour life, albeit in very different conditions. Whatever the reason, for the last several years a constant companion on my bedside table has been the book *Deserts*,[1] whose title is self-explanatory and which attempts to explain the ecosystems of the major deserts of the world. Every so often before falling asleep, I'll open it, thumb through the various sections, and invariably find myself turning to the section on the Sahara.

Zagora, gateway to the Sahara, is my destination, and I am excited, quietly so, and nervous. I won't be seeing those sculpted red or yellow pillows of sand, whose images I've feasted on the last few years before falling asleep—I need four days and three nights to do that, not the two-day/one-night trip I'm taking. My time might not allow me to satisfy those longings, but it is still the Sahara, I tell myself.

It's the tone of voice that first grabs my attention—a mixture of superiority, condescension and officiousness that exists in all the languages of empire, its owner a mature-looking white man with sandy hair, who stands outside the bus: *Are you sure this is the right bus?* he demands of the driver. *I'm doing a three-night/four-day trip*, he announces. Assured by the bus driver that it is, the man gets on, letting us all know that he'll be joining another trip on the following day. I dub him Rational White Man and make a mental note to avoid him. At all costs.

Passengers continue to board, and among them is a young couple, one of whom sits next to me, the other across the aisle in a single seat. We say hello to each other—they both speak English, she with a posh English accent that must have cost a lot of money. I would later find out that they were Latin American, he from Argentina and she from Peru. There'll be sixteen of us when the bus is full; I decide that once we're settled, I'll suggest to them that we switch so that they can sit together; that way I'll be able to stretch my legs out and still have a window seat on the other side.

When did it happen? Did I see him approaching? I think I remember a man walking down the aisle—I don't exactly know—memory is such a faithless companion, a fragile witness. Even if I had noticed him, I would have had no reason to think that I was his target, but suddenly he is standing before me: *You*, he points at me, *move!* He speaks to me as if I were an animal, a thing not worthy of any mode of address other than a brutal command. Why is he speaking to me this way?—my thoughts awhirl as he gestures for me to move, pointing to Rational White Man who is in the front row of the bus with the sole remaining seat next to him. He wants me to move and sit next to him!

Why? I challenge him—a single question standing in for so many others: why are you speaking to me like that?—why do you want me to move?—why should I move? Why?—to the myriad ways humans attempt and succeed in degrading each other. And like that tone that I recognized when I heard Rational White Man, it echoes in every language of empire. Why? One word addressed to the logic of empire that has shattered and pulverized the world's cultures and traditions. A single word that is a portal to the persistent human attempt to find meaning to all the phenomena that constitute life and which is a fundamental marker of being human. In response to my question, he gestures to the young couple sitting next to me, suggesting that they should sit together. Is there a law, I wonder, that requires couples to sit together? I'm at a loss for words—I don't speak Arabic, so I can't argue with him, and my spoken French is in no way robust enough to challenge him, not to mention I'm feeling as if I'm under attack. They, the young couple, say nothing, do not demur at his actions. Determined not to sit next to Rational White Man, I turn to them and suggest they switch with me.

The man who has spoken to me as if I were an animal is content, happy even. He turns and leaves. I resent his tone; the manner in which he spoke to me bothers me deeply, but I take a deep breath, shrug internally and settle myself in the seat I had intended to sit in all along. At least I am not sitting next to Rational White Man.

The bus driver starts the engine—we, some fifteen passengers, all strangers to each other, are about to set off for the desert when, as if summoned by the sound of the engine, two women show up outside the bus. Consternation grips the group of men milling around on the sidewalk—they all appear to be somehow involved in the trip—and ripples out. There is only one empty seat, next to Rational White Man, and two extra passengers.

Through the window on the right, I now observe men running around, talking on cellphones, arguing with each other. One has a clipboard—he appears to have some supervisory function, which has no calming effect on the confusion. I sense rather than observe anything directly, as if what

I'm apprehending is happening below the radar; is it the glance thrown my way by one of the men that I notice through the corner of my eye? Was it the man who had come onto the bus and spoken to me as if I were an animal? Were there others? And, what was it I actually noticed? I cannot say. I don't know—but all at once I do know—in every fibre of my body—and knowing it, I wait, all my senses poised—on alert like a snake coiled in anticipation of attack.

The two women who were the last to arrive stand outside the bus, chatting and laughing: they are white, youngish-looking with light hair. Their utter confidence and relaxed attitude are remarkable—they seem not at all concerned that there is a problem. They are happy—Happy White Girls—Happy, Happy White Girls.

Suddenly, what I was waiting for, what I knew would happen, is happening—one of the men who had been standing outside the bus is now standing before me—is it the same man who had spoken to me earlier, as if I were an animal? I don't know, but whoever he is, he is demanding I get off the bus. He doesn't speak English, but his face and his gestures make it plain that he wants me to come with him, to get off the bus and go to another bus. How do I know that that is what he is demanding? He may have said, *Come,* I don't remember. He may have pointed to another bus parked along the roadway. What I do know is that these people have no interest in my well-being or what happens to me, based on how they had spoken to me earlier, and that once I get off that bus, I might never make it to the desert. I know that because, like me, Rational White Man is travelling alone—we are the only two single travellers on the bus—but they have chosen to approach me, not him, to ask me to leave the bus. Unlike every other traveller on that bus, Rational White Man is going for three nights and four days and is intending to pick up another trip the following day, as he had loudly announced on his arrival. Logically, if they were wanting to move someone, he would be the one to move.

But then, racism has always treated in the irrational. I know that because they could have chosen to place Happy, Happy White Girls on another bus—they were the last to arrive, after all; I know that because the man who had first come on the bus and demanded that I move had spoken to me as if I were lower than an animal; I know they want a full bus, and in their eyes, I am disposable.

Finally, I know that because I'm the only Black person on board. A foreigner. And a woman.

Intersectionality, we call it.

I refuse—

I am not getting off this bus, I tell him, refusing to do what he wants. He is taken aback; glaring at me, he turns and leaves the bus. My refusal creates even more consternation. Was that when I hear him ask Rational White Man, *What about you?* Perhaps it was later, but at some point the man with the clipboard does ask Rational White Man if he would leave and go onto another bus he's pointing at through the windscreen. Sitting behind the driver, Rational White Man has a clear view of the bus: he asks where the bus is going, pointing out that there is no one on the bus—he is reluctant to leave until he knows more.

If you leave like that, we can't settle the matter, Rational White Man calls out to the man with the clipboard who walks away in exasperation. He's in full, superior mode now as he reasons with the emotional Native: *They're trying to work out whether they have to reimburse one or two tickets,* he says through the open door of the bus to the Happy, Happy White Girls with whom he has been conversing and who laugh and talk outside the bus, appearing fully confident that they will be seated. I watch them, intrigued and fascinated by their relaxed demeanour: I am witnessing the power of whiteness, how it insulates and cushions against worry and negative outcomes.

Out the window, the bickering and talking continue, and before I know it, there is another man standing in the aisle in front of me, demanding to know if I speak English. I reply that I do, as if that was going to change my answer. Did he think that language was the issue, that I had misunderstood what they intended? *Come,* he says, *you must come with me,* and I desperately want to leave this bus—to walk far, far away from this situation that pains me deeply, that humiliates and angers me. Even as I feel this longing to rise to my feet and leave, I know that that is what they want—these men, these brown men who historically have felt the brute force of racism at the hands of their erstwhile rulers, the French, but who themselves are as crudely racist and sexist as their former masters.

The Arab slave trade pre-existed the transatlantic trade in Africans and continued long after the trade in humans to the West had come to an end. Black people descended from enslaved Africans can be found as far afield as Iran[2] and Turkey. The trans-Saharan trade was the conduit through which sub-Saharan Africans were brought to Morocco. Today, Morocco, being the closest point to Europe, has become a magnet for the exodus of people trying to cross. Those who don't make it across remain in Morocco, generating a resurgence of anti-Black racism, which has deep roots going back to the Hamitic myth.[3]

I hold my hands chest-high, palms facing outward as if my body, arms and hands were all of a piece in my resistance. *I was the second person on this bus*, I say, *and I'm telling you, I'm not getting off.* He retreats.

I am frightened—I'm alone in a foreign country in which I don't speak either of the languages; I am refusing to do as I am being told by men in a culture that is patriarchal in ways different from what I know; I am also hurt and at the same time ferociously angry, and my mind continues to spin. There is also sharp and lucid clarity to what I am prepared for: I know I am not getting off that bus; I know it in a place deep within me—a place I cannot map, although I know it exists, has a history, a geography and even a set of rules all its own; it is a place of Blackness[4] in the spiritual rather than the political or racial sense. A place of mystery and potentiality. In that place I know that they, whoever "they" are, would have to drag me off that bus—it was the only way I was going to leave. They, those men, whoever they were, would have to get their gendarmes or police; they would have to lay their hands on me, on this Black, female body and pull me off that bus.

My refusals appear to create a frenzy: strangers have joined the crowd outside and everyone is still talking and arguing heatedly—Rational White Man and Happy, Happy White Girls are still talking. Was it my imagination?—but were the men getting bigger? The one who now stands over me, the third—fourth, if you count the first one who spoke to me as if I were an animal—does seem bigger, has jowls with an afternoon shadow that shake as he speaks; in another context I would have thought him avuncular. How many more would come? And, no one on the bus says anything.

You—you have to come with me! I raise my voice and tell him exactly what I've told the other two, that I am not getting off the bus. He continues to press me, then turns and leaves in the face of my recalcitrance. I feel as if I'm in the trenches, surrounded by the enemy and fighting simply to remain where I am. When the next one comes, I tell myself, because it seems as if they will keep on coming, I'm going to raise the issue of race; I'm going to tell them that the only reason they're harassing me to leave the bus is because I'm Black. But I am also overwhelmed by the desire to get to my feet, take my bags, tell them to kiss my Black ass and leave, but I know that

that is what they want. That I should leave and allow Happy, Happy White Girls to get on and Rational White Man to keep his seat.

Why hadn't I raised the issue of them targeting me because I was Black from the beginning? Was it language?—an absence of. Was I afraid of being seen to be playing the race card? But that card has been being played ever since the European brought the first African to the Americas and the Caribbean. Indeed, the whole deck—of race cards at that—has been stacked against us since then. Whatever the reason, I had hesitated.

Out the window I see a bus pull past on the left; one of many men milling about puts his head through the door, points to the newly arrived bus and tells Rational White Man that his bus has arrived. He stands, takes his knapsack and prepares to leave, but not before looking directly at me. I could have missed it, so brief was the moment—the beat between diastole and systole, inhale and exhale; a moment fraught with an expectation of something that resists and belies definition. Was it hope, a leap of longing that he was on the brink of breaking with history, with his preordained role as Rational White Man? In that blink of a moment, everything hangs in the balance. In that moment he could have slipped out of his skin—the one history had clothed him in—shed his Kiplingesque White Man's Burden and met me, supporting my refusal to accept what a long history had conspired to bestow on me: that of the eminently disposable—female and Black. Instead, he looks at me, *As for you,* he says, shaking his head. He is angry and pissed off, determined to embrace his history and his role—*As for you, what can I say?* What, indeed, could he have said—he who has already said so much, indeed, too much? In siding with me as I, for one startlingly improbable moment, believed he would, he could have built an event the equivalent of the Big Bang, as "overwhelming…as the finger of God touching the finger of Adam in Michaelangelo's *The Creation of Adam.*"[5] He said nothing but those seven words and left the bus in the wake of my small act of resistance against something so much larger.

And, what if one, maybe two, persons on that bus had stood with me, refusing to hide in the privilege of their skin? Not one voice was raised in support, all these well-educated, white, Western tourists who knew what was happening was wrong. "The appalling silence and indifference of good people" in the face of injustice meted out to others is how Martin Luther King Jr. describes what I had just experienced.[6] As long as they were not being targeted, it would be business as usual and in that warm, almost balmy, morning air of Marrakech, I am chilled to the bone. As if a cold, cold wind had blown through me, causing everything—including my heart—to curl, shrivel and shrink. As he passes by my window on the sidewalk outside, Rational White Man continues to shake his head, not realizing that he and I had just made history: he, Rational White Man, had had to get off the bus, and I, the Black woman rejected by history, his history, had rejected my historical role of being the one to be thrown off the bus, off the boat.

Happy, Happy White Girls are now ensconced behind the bus driver, still chatting and laughing—"God's in his [white supremacist] heaven and all's right with the world." We are now ready to leave—two days and one night in the Sahara. A trip I had been looking forward to now creates stomach-churning feelings.

One of the Happy, Happy White Girls has her shoes off and her feet perched on the rail behind the driver. She is twiddling her toes. Disingenuously she asks the driver: *Can I put my feet here? You can do anything you want* is his reply. I think of the body and its many languages—Happy, Happy White Girl with her twiddling toes, entirely indifferent to what had just happened on that bus, and me with my hands raised in a strenuous attempt to stave off further attacks. I think of how the white body can do "anything it wants," while the Black body must push constantly against restriction and constriction.

My thoughts are dark, ugly and not worthy of being documented here, the "best" of them being encapsulated in the image of Morocco sliding off the map of Africa into the Mediterranean and me being ecstatically happy. I wanted revenge, personal and collective, on all Moroccans—how easy it is to live in those places where the only salve for wound, for *la blessure*, is hatred of the Other, no matter how justified it is. In my internal frenzy I even wonder whether it is possible to contact the King and talk to him about what had happened, so angry and helpless do I feel. I will broadcast it on Facebook and TripAdvisor, I tell myself. Now there is only me, the window, the landscape rushing by and a bus full of people who were witness to what had happened and had said and done nothing. Except Rational White Man who, in the face of my refusing to know my place, the one set aside for those like me by him and his kind, apparently lost his capacity for speech— *What can I say?* His apparent incapacity for speech saying so much. He who historically has had so much to say about everything and everyone was now speechless. Me gazing out the window, the landscape rushing by and, like so many before, trying to make do in a space of confinement.

What was I to do now, trapped with people who, through their silence, had been part of an attempt to force me to leave the bus? *Blesser*—to wound: the word surfaces suddenly; I am *blessé, l'accent aigu* over the last "e" of the past participle. Wounded, but I am female, so I need another "e"—does this mean I am wounded twice? So close, yet so far from being blessed, the English word it sounds like but has no etymological relation to. My heart—*mon coeur*—is hurt, my heart was where I was wounded— in French, English and in every language in the world. As well as in those that never existed and will never exist. My heart hurts, feels bruised, as if someone has rubbed it raw with sandpaper; it is *blessé*, not blessed, and I know it can only have one *é* with *l'accent aigu*, because my heart, *mon coeur*, is not feminine, it is masculine—mon, mon, mon—man. Man heart. I must develop and grow a man heart which cannot be *blessé*. And what was it that had *"blesséd"* me? And my heart. *Un acte de racisme.* I text a newly made Moroccan friend, my French as fractured as I feel: "*J'ai eu blessée dans mon Codie par une acte de racisme trés terrible.* I just wanted to share *avec quelqu'n. I will write more,*" not even seeing the autocorrect that results in *coeur* becoming "Codie," a name of Gaelic origin meaning helpful, or that I was using *eu,* the past participle of *avoir* instead of *être.* I hit Send, my message of pain pinging its way in broken and fragmented French to some-one I barely know. I never did write more. I couldn't. I reread that message now in some embarrassment—linguistic evidence of my brokenness in yet another tongue.

In 1781, the captain of a British slave ship, *Zong,* crossing the Atlantic from Sao Tome, off the coast of West Africa, to Jamaica, makes the fateful decision to throw overboard some 150 enslaved Africans to save the ship's owners further monetary loss. My book-length poem *Zong!* is a lamenta-tion and mourning song for those disposable Africans, sacrificed in order to collect insurance monies. For the last five years I have, through perfor-mance, been memorializing that event that took place on board the *Zong* and exploring the healing resources of performing the work. That massacre on board the *Zong* and my work around it is what has brought me to Morocco—to explore *Gnawa* music as an example of the healing practices developed by enslaved Africans brought there centuries earlier. The ironies do not escape me—that the very same combination of brute racism and the profit motive that resulted in the Africans being thrown overboard from the *Zong* are present some 235 years later on this bus in Marrakech. Then the issue was collecting insurance monies. Today it's the cost of a bus seat.

Time and history complicate because in 2016 it is Moroccan Arabs, not Europeans, who are the perpetrators. Geographically, Moroccans are Africans, albeit of Arab heritage and they, too, have been subjected to racism perpetrated by the European over centuries of colonialism. They have, however, slotted themselves into the hierarchy of race, preferring to see themselves as part of the Arab world rather than Africa, and themselves project anti-Black, anti-African (as in sub-Saharan African) racism. It was not unusual, for instance, to hear people refer to Africa as being south of the Sahara—in other words, Morocco was not in Africa. That which has remained hidden in the country's psyche, the African presence in Morocco, now reveals itself in deeply held racist feelings.

I think of the Arab slave trade and of how contemporary politics dampens the critique of Arab nations who were deeply implicated in trading Africans, which results in current practices of racism. I think also of the Black apologists for that trade in the West, who argue that it wasn't as extensive as the transatlantic trade.

My mind turns to an article I am reading on Egypt and the Arab Spring by Talal Asad in which he discusses the necessity for Muslims to carry out right actions:[7] I wonder how the men who tried to force me off the bus would consider what they had done within that religious and spiritual requirement. Would that be considered a right action?

The cost of racism is myriad and often hidden, particularly for the victims. We, on that bus that was now speeding toward Zagora, had all paid the same price for the trip to the desert—in money, that is; my trip, however, turned out to be far more costly than theirs. Every day, courts are charged with putting a dollar figure on pain, suffering and trauma, on the physical and emotional residues of aggressive acts done by so many against too many. What would I say to a judge, how would I tally my anguish, because that is what it was, if I had to? Is there a dollar figure? How do we tally the costs to Africans and their descendants of being taken from their homelands, of being stripped of their languages and cultures. Of losing a wife, a husband, a child—of losing meaning. This movement toward justice is summed up by the word *reparations* whose reach is not, will never be, wide enough to gather us all up and help us to heal.

My hand shakes as I write on the pages of my journal, and not just because of the bus's reverberations; my hand shakes as I trace these clumsy markings that attempt to script my pain, the wound, *la blessure*; my hand shakes because it and my body don't know what else to do but shake and write, write and shake. This would be the second time in my life that writing would save me.

Not very long into the trip, the unmistakable voice of Bob Marley comes over the sound system, which has been playing music ever since we left Marrakech and fills the bus. A brilliant, lyrical, reggae adaptation of the words of the Emperor Haile Selassie, which he addressed to the United Nations General Assembly in October 1963, "War" has become an anthem of the Black world: "Until the philosophy which holds one race superior / and another / inferior / is finally / and permanently / discredited / and abandoned— / everywhere is war / me say war...."[8] Selassie's message is clear—until racism is eradicated, there will be war. My rage at hearing the song is intense and corrosive: how dare they, I think, even as I know my response to be somewhat absurd. If I could, I would have ripped out the innards of whatever machine was playing that music. No one on that bus, I felt, had earned the right to play that song whose creator had come from a particular history of which I was a part.

Rastafarianism, which Marley practised, remains one of the powerful examples of Africans managing, understanding and healing what has happened to them as victims of the transatlantic slave trade. Marley's rendition of "War," as his Rastafarianism, was a part of the struggle of Afro Caribbean peoples against colonialism. Selassie's speech was also significant in addressing colonialism, and the scourge of racism toward Africa and Africans: "until...the colour of a man's skin / is of no more significance than the colour of his eyes— / me say war,"[9] Marley sings, echoing Selassie's warning that the "African continent will not know peace" until racism ends.[10] There are powerful international and Afrosporic currents running through this particular song, and to have "War" played as background, entertainment music, after what had just happened on that bus, was as unbearable as it was deeply ironic.

What had happened on the bus had been a war of sorts, hadn't it? A war against Blackness and against women. I suspect that if I were a Black man, they would also have approached me before they approached Rational White Man, but I also know that my being female played a part in their aggressive behaviour toward me.

No sooner had "War" finished playing than the words of "No Woman No Cry," also by Marley, took its place.[11] I will not let anyone see me crying, but the tears well up all the same: this was the song I had my young character, Zulma, sing in *Harriet's Daughter*, my young adult novel, to comfort herself in Toronto, having recently left her beloved Gran in Tobago.[12] This is a song that speaks of love between Black people, in this case a Black man and woman, in Trench Town, a materially poor area of Kingston, Jamaica, revealing the astonishing ability of Black folk in the Afrospora to make beauty wherever they are. This is a song of comfort that further broke my heart on that bus to the Sahara desert. Once the song is done, I know my feelings of rage and sadness to be just that, feelings—understandable in light of what happened. We live in an age of rampant commodification of culture—that which has sustained us will be bought and sold, as has happened with *Gnawa* music, the Blues, jazz and so on. This is merely an observation, not a judgment.

The ride is a bumpy one—in many places the road surfaces are being repaired—so I have very little control over shaping the letters, but I continue writing. When we make our first stop, I and the white Peruvian woman with the posh English accent, who now sits across the aisle from me, are the last to get off: she is putting on a top to cover her arms; I am composing myself.

I'm so sorry about them talking to you like that, she says. I turn my face to the window and weep, my shoulders shaking. I weep because although I see her as deeply implicated in what had happened—she hadn't demurred when the first man had demanded I move so that she and her boyfriend could sit together—her comment is a confirmation that something had happened. I weep because someone acknowledges witnessing what had happened. She observes that I am crying and asks if I want a hug, and I am ashamed to admit, even to myself, that yes, I did want a hug from someone—from *quelqu'un*, from anyone, even this silly, young woman who had said nothing when three men tried to get me to leave the bus. Now she was offering me a hug! The satisfaction of having someone acknowledge what has happened is, however, short-lived, because she then attempts to excuse all that has happened by saying that she comes from a developing country, Peru, and that that is how they spoke to people. I turn on her, vehemently tell her that I, too, come from a developing country, Trinidad and Tobago, where I had never witnessed this kind of behaviour; what had happened, I said, had been a clear example of racism. She's taken aback. *Oh, do you think so?* she asks innocently. Like a true Caribbean woman, I suck my teeth loudly and turn away.

I am on the bus alone, the others haven't got back on yet after one of the many stops. I begin to practise the gesture I made earlier on of putting my hands up, palms facing out in front of my chest, when I told one of the men that I was not leaving. What was I doing when I did that? Why had I done it? As I reenact and rehearse the gesture I try to feel a connection between the centre of my palms and my heart. Not my man heart, my woman heart, my human heart, that hurt so much at times I felt I would throw up.

Before I leave Morocco, I would buy a small silver amulet with a spiral on the palm, the *khamsa* or *hamsa*, known as the Hand of Fatimah. Its roots appear deep, possibly going back to Egypt as well as Mesopotamia and Carthage (Phoenicia). In Berber culture it is an image used to ward off evil energies. That symbolism resonates with me and what happened on the bus to Zagora.

It is only later on, much later on, that I would think of Rosa Parks and her refusal to give up her seat on that fateful bus. I cannot presume to equate what she was fighting for with this—what shall I call it: event, occurrence, act of aggression?—but she comes to mind as I wonder what it was I called on to make me hold my ground, refusing to leave that bus. Being very clear within myself that I was willing and ready to be manhandled to get me off that bus. I also think of Nanny of the Maroons, who led maroon troops against the British in Jamaica, and of Yaa Asantewaa, the Ashanti queen who led an Ashanti rebellion against the British. Women, Black women, in public spaces usually reserved for men, or whites. I seek to locate myself in some tradition because I am Othered and alone and wonder whether they, too, recognized that place of Blackness within them that was the bedrock of their resistance.

The journey to Zagora would take some seven hours. After four hours of writing, I felt something shift within me: the anger and rage had dissipated and while I felt that I never wanted to visit Morocco again—a childish, though understandable, response perhaps—I knew I couldn't and shouldn't judge an entire country through the context of a single incident. I remembered Aisha who ran a *riad* in Tiznit, and who had got up at 5:30 a.m. to drive me to the bus stop. She didn't have to. There was also my newly made friend to whom I had earlier texted my pain, who had invited me to have lunch with his parents and grandmother and showed me around some ruins south of Tiznit all afternoon. I also recall a few occasions on which darker-skinned Moroccans, shop proprietors, all male, attempted to establish a racial bond with me. Was this attempt at bonding through an unspoken acknowledgement of what our skin signifies—somewhat akin to the mutual nod Black folk in North America exchange as they cross paths—commercially driven, as so much in Morocco was? Perhaps, but it still touched my heart to remember.

There had, however, been enough small acts of racism for me to know that what had happened on that bus was not an exception. In the meantime I would discipline myself to be courteous to the other passengers—we had to eat together and would share a tent that night. Others are courteous back to me, and now that they were not being called on to be their sister's keeper, some even smile. Happy, Happy White Girls never speak to me. I would see Rational White Man at several stops along the way to the desert and back, since the different buses all stopped at the same watering holes. He and Happy, Happy White Girls continue their new-found camaraderie, chatting and laughing whenever they meet. I think of how whiteness always has a space made for it in the world and how being Black is so often made illegitimate.

At our destination I fall in love with the ungainly, patient camels, the way they fold their front legs, as if in prayer, to allow you to climb on, then suddenly in one smooth yet abrupt unfolding you're up, high up, above the ground. I think of the camel trains that would have crossed the Sahara with sub-Saharan Africans in tow, leaving a trail of bones. I think of that and believe that in remembering those unnamed Africans, they have not died in vain. Someone remembers them.

The trip would have an unfortunate end for a couple of the other travellers—an older Dutch man, travelling with his daughter, fell off his camel and broke his hip with the possibility that he would lose his leg. It was sobering. Perched on my camel, waiting for over an hour for an ambulance to come, I could only feel compassion for him. It could have been me.

It was me.

NOTES

1   Marco C. Stoppato and Alfredo Bini, *Deserts*, trans. Linda M. Eklund (Toronto: Firefly Books, Ltd., 2002).

2   In southern Iran, for instance, there exists a healing practice called the *Zar*, which is African in origin.

3   Chouki El Hamel, *Black Morocco: A History of Slavery, Race, and Islam* (New York: Cambridge University Press, 2013), 62–4.

4   I have capitalized Blackness in an effort to suggest a quality that is more than the sum of its parts.

5   Wassily Kandinsky, quoted in Carl Jung, ed., *Man and His Symbols* (New York: Dell Publishing, 1964), 307.

6   Martin Luther King, Jr., "Remaining Awake through a Great Revolution" (speech delivered at the National Cathedral, Washington, D.C., on March 31 1968), <https://kinginstitute.stanford.edu/king-papers/publications/ knock-midnight-inspiration-great-sermons-reverend-martin-luther-king-jr-10>.

7   Talal Asad, "Thinking About Tradition, Religion, and Politics in Egypt Today," *Critical Inquiry* 42, No. 1 (Autumn 2015): 166–214.

8   Bob Marley & The Wailers, "War," *Rastaman Vibration*, Island Records, ILPS 9383, 1976.

9   Ibid.

10   Emperor Haile Selassie, "Address to the United Nations" (speech delivered to the United Nations General Assembly, 18th Session, Oct. 4, 1963), <https://en.wiki-source.org/wiki/Haile_Selassie's_address_to_the_United_Nations,_1963>.

11   Bob Marley & The Wailers, "No Woman No Cry," *Natty Dread*, Island Records, ILPS 9281, 1974.

12   M. NourbeSe Philip, *Harriet's Daughter* (Toronto: The Women's Press, 1990).

RUMINATIONS

LETTER TO HAITI

Haiti, I weep for you. I hide my tears because I'm on a flight from Kelowna, B.C., to Toronto, and who knows, with all the heightened security I fear they may think something's amiss. That I'm weeping as a prelude to joining my Ancestors. So paranoid have we become. But I weep for you, Haiti, for your people, for the shit—the unmitigated shit—that life seems to throw your way. Again and again. And, to adapt the words of one of your warrior daughters, Maya Angelou, "still you rise," to greet another green, tropic day that holds hope ransom, as you tear your people limb by painful limb from a hell that eschews fire and opts instead for the hardface, stoneface indifference of concrete that, Medusa-like, seems to have frozen all of your magnificent history into slabs of cement. Now fragmented, they litter your landscape as if some giant, angry-at-us mortals, had decided to stamp on your already precarious country. There was a time when our Caribbean houses kept faith with wood, whether one-room homes—some call them chattel houses—or larger, more graceful estate houses. Time was when the thatched ajoupa bequeathed us by Taino, Arawak and Carib would have swayed to the groans of the earth as she eased her suffering, opening herself along her wounded fault lines to the ever-blue skies, the constant love of the sun, to release all her pent-up grief for us, birthing we don't yet know what. Time was when hands steeped in skills of building homes brought from a homeland a slap, kick and a howl away, across a roiling ocean, would have gently patted mud over wattle, weaving branches to create cool interiors, shaping shelters from the earth that would not, could not, betray the safety in home to crush, obliterate, to fall down around your ears. Like the third little pig in the nursery rhyme, Haiti, you built your home of brick—it was supposed to protect you.

Each and every time I hear or read the words that describe you as being a poor nation, the poorest of the poorest—I weep. Poor you most certainly are in all things material, but your riches are immeasurable, woven through your history, your culture and your people. Yours was the first and only successful slave revolt in the Western world and resulted in the second independent nation after the United States in the so-called New World. In taking the name the Taino had given the "Land of Mountains," Ayiti, you returned the country to its First Nations roots. How many know that the U.S.A. embargoed you for sixty years because you fired a shot across the bow of history by liberating your people under the brilliant leadership of Toussaint L'Overture? How many know that you became a pariah in the world for taking a moral stance in favour of justice and freedom and against racial exploitation and oppression? Then, you were at another epicentre, along one of the many fault lines of history, the reverberations of which seismic, political shift would be felt around the world. Indeed, are still being felt, I would argue. No one rushed to help you then, Haiti. Instead, what we had were France, Spain, Holland, Britain and the United States (albeit secretly)—shall we call them the coalition of the ready, willing and able, or simply the usual suspects?—preparing to invade you to reimpose the yoke of slavery. How many know that your liberation determined the eventual downfall of Napoleon? So decimated were Napoleon's troops under his brother-in-law, General Leclerc, by fighting in Haiti and by yellow fever, they could not provide the necessary support for Napoleon's subsequent campaigns in Europe—against Spain, Russia and Prussia, to be exact. In November 1803, France, under Napoleon, capitulated. In January 1804, General Jean-Jacques Dessalines declared you an independent nation. How many know that France, that bastion of revolution and freedom, by the Ordinance of 1825, exacted the sum of 150 million francs as compensation from you for loss of "property"—read formerly enslaved Africans? How many know or even care to know that you did, indeed, pay your extortioner through a series of loans that bankrupted you? The equivalent of that sum is $21 billion in today's money. And how many know that the U.S.A. invaded you in 1915 and occupied you until 1934? Hearing that the U.S. military now controls the airport in Haiti makes me shudder. Makes me want to hold my head and bawl.

Despite the historical and contemporary demonization of *vaudou*,[1] you have enshrined the religion of your Ancestors in your constitution, making it an official religion alongside Christianity. Only South Africa among a continent of African nations has dared to do this—most flee this reminder of who they are. No other Caribbean island nation has followed suit.

Most of all, Haiti, you are rich in your people—their dignity, their love of homeland and willingness to struggle for freedom. What more fitting example of this is the recognition of the language of the people, Haitian creole, as an official language? With the exception of the three formerly Dutch colonies, Aruba, Bonaire and Curacao, no other Caribbean island nation has officially recognized the language of the people, for the people and by the people—the vernacular, the demotic—Kamau Brathwaite's nation language—as worthy of recognition. Ah, but most of all, Haiti, I weep for the "dream deferred" that Langston Hughes so eloquently wrote about. What has happened to the many deferred dreams of your people? Where have they gone? How many know that at the start of your fledgling nation in 1804, democratic principles were central to your constitution? First, you abolished slavery, then moved to enshrine one of the most frighteningly revolutionary and emancipatory ideals in your constitution—racial equality—even granting citizenship to Polish soldiers who had fought alongside Haitians against the French. In 1804, that would have been the equivalent of an earthquake measuring at least 8.0 on a Richter scale of oppression. You were at the heart of the awakening of modernity—albeit a deferred modernity. More than anything else, you presented, in the words of the Canadian poet Jordan Scott, a profound "threat to cohesion." The cohesion of imperial power founded on brute racism.

I weep for you, Haiti, and for I 'n I, because when I bear virtual witness to your despair and your suffering, when I see the mountains of rubble and concrete, the broken roads, the tangle of electrical wires, and hear the voices droning on and on about the lack of infrastructure, I think of my own internal infrastructure—spiritual, psychic, intellectual and political—and realize that your history has played no small part in its structure and design. I recognize you writ large through CLR James's *The Black Jacobins*[2] that I first read as a young Caribbean woman trying to find her place in a world and a history that had hardly begun to be told. Your history, your struggle, your survival, epitomized through the successful Haitian Revolution, as told by James, became a part of my own struggle to understand my place and the place of my people in this world—on all those tiny pieces of coral or volcanic rock scattered in the ever blue Caribbean Sea. Through *The Black Jacobins* we, each and every one of us who read that work, grew in stature internally as Caribbean people, children of the volcano all, to quote the brilliant Martiniquan poet and founder of negritude, Aimé Césaire; became larger psychically, and more intellectually secure in our role as agents of change. In our own history. The Haitian Revolution became woven into our psychic and political DNA, a scaffolding to support our personal structures of personhood; an *aide mémoire* to our silenced history, a map for our journey to greater self-awareness. Toussaint's name lived in our minds and on our tongues as young Caribbean thinkers, the first generation to have access to widespread, tertiary-level education. The colonizer's language may separate us, but only superficially, for C. L. R. James, who brought your struggle home to us and helped us to understand ourselves through the lens of history, is as much a son of yours as Boukman, Toussaint, Dessalines or Christophe. Indeed, your daughters and sons know no borders. For African American poet and writer Ntozake Shange, "TOUSSAINT waz a blkman…who refused to be a slave…TOUSSAINT L'OUVERTURE waz the beginnin uv reality" for her.[3] A dazzling, polyvocal, linguistically innovative tour de force, *For Coloured Girls Who Have Considered Suicide When the Rainbow Is Enuf,* although located in the U.S., grounded itself in a historical reality that began with Toussaint. Samuel Huntington (he of *Clash of Civilizations*) had the impertinence to describe you as "'the neighbour nobody wants'" and as being "truly a kinless country," and in so doing reveals how little ignorance respects knowledge.[4] Little does he know how far, how wide and how deep your kin are spread.

I gaze at a map of Port au Prince in a newspaper identifying high-profile sites of destruction: it is as if someone decided you had to start again, and wiped the slate clean: the Ministry of Justice—gone; the Presidential Palace—gone; administrative offices—gone; the penitentiary—gone; the hospitals—gone; churches—gone; the cathedral—gone. Hundreds of thousands of people—gone. All gone—just like that. In the clichéd wink of an eye—God's perhaps? Or the devil's snap of fingers. Leaving nothing but bright mornings filled with mourning, despair, grief and pictures of little Black girls with locks made blonde by concrete dust, who look out at the world through glasses, bearing the weight of history and a building on their little legs. Oh God, oh God, why hast thou forsaken us? This is the language—the language of the Bible—that bursts forth, as if the apocalyptic nature of the disaster itself demands a language of Biblical proportions. Because flesh hurts, and love and grief know no bounds when your loves are entombed before your very eyes, sometimes leaving no one to mourn, no one to cry out, Why? Why? Why? And, worse than that, no one to answer why.

There was a time when for 500 years the world, with very few exceptions, was indifferent to the suffering of African peoples. They entered the maw of a history drenched in brutality, as history most often is, through the doorway of the slave ship and, by way of what we so euphemistically call the Middle Passage, were washed up on these Caribbean islands like so much flotsam and jetsam the Atlantic was rejecting. To enter the machine of the plantation. Who shed a tear, beyond those left in Africa, for those entombed in slave ships? Who shed a tear for those whose bones litter the sands below the Atlantic? Who shed a tear for the living death of the slave plantation? As recently as 2005 we were witness to the indifference that greets the suffering of Black folk in the aftermath of Hurricane Katrina. By their own government. Under George Bush. This time seems different: the world is responding, although many of those responding have been complicit in beggaring you. Always an agricultural nation, you once grew your own rice, then cheap, subsidized rice from the U.S.A. flooded the nation and your self-sufficiency in rice was lost, so that during the 2008 food crisis (which continues), when the price and availability of staple foods like rice shot up, you were particularly vulnerable. According to Peter Hallward, writing in the *Guardian* in January 2010, during its occupation of your territory, the U.S. "violently and deliberately" resisted "every serious political attempt to allow Haiti's people to move (in the words of Jean-Bertrand Aristide) 'from absolute misery to a dignified poverty.'" And make no mistake about it, had it not been for the support of the Soviet Union, Cuba would have been beggared in the same way by the embargo the U.S. imposed after the Cuban Revolution.

The world has found you now, Haiti, but where was it when France was extorting blood money from you, ably assisted by the U.S., who arranged loans to help you repay France—loans designed to break you economically? Where was it? The world. It is against the principles of international law that a victorious country should pay a country it defeated for its freedom, yet the nations of the world have been silent on this travesty. One of the claims Aristide made during his tenure was for reparations from France for these immoral and illegal payments. Where was the support for these claims from the world? Where was the world when the U.S. occupied you? Busily fighting to save Europe from the calamity that Hitler portended, shoring up the principles of freedom in resounding Churchillian phrases, where the fuck was the world? As the flag bearer of democracy crushed a small but proud island nation, and today, even today, as hungry, frantic

Haitians take to the seas in desperation, seeking refuge anywhere, even in water as their ancestors did, even today, the U.S. Coast Guard turns them back. Where was the world when the U.S. rounded up your boat people to return them, unlike the Cubans, to their home country? Where was the world, Haiti? And will it still love you when you occupy your rightful place? For occupy it you will. Our very survival—the survival of every one of your children—depends on it.

Today I saw a little boy birthed from a concrete womb a mere letter away from a living tomb, his rescuers pulling him from the rubble as if he were being born again—for the second time in his so very short life. They snatch his frail-limbed body, whitened with concrete dust and, cradling him in their arms, run with him. And I think, so it was when you defied the long, the very long, historical odds against you, and out of the living tomb of slavery created a womb to birth yourself. Blood and all. Today, they say it's your culture that prevents you from moving forward—that *vaudon* creates a fatalism that is out of step with the ideals of progress endemic to the West. And I wonder why that fatalism didn't keep you wedded to a slave culture.

But what good is history when your child done dead and gone? Or your mother bury under concrete, or your daddy, grandmère or grandpère nowhere? You cyant eat revolution, you cyant drink freedom. And, as the saying goes, a hungry man is an angry man. It is not surprising, but still I am surprised at the rapidity with which the trope of violence has raised its head: not even a week has gone by before the *Toronto Star* has a front-page picture of a naked, bound man being beaten. The following day the headline screams about violence marring the relief efforts. The following day still a front-page picture appears of a knife-wielding man appearing to attack someone for food. It's the stereotype with which the media and those that "run tings" have bombarded us. Beggars or criminals. Or sometimes both, as the *Star* makes out. Even as they purport to help, they construct prisons of stereotypes for us. How quickly the world has forgotten the unspeakable violence that slavery meted out to African peoples for at least 500 years. Indeed, Leclerc wrote of his intent to "wage a war of extermination" to reintroduce slavery in your barely formed nation. You have never been forgiven for successfully resisting his violent attempt to subjugate you. To decontextualize the violence in Haiti, as the *Star* has done in those three issues, under the guise of needing to show Canadians the "true horror of this disaster," appears to be nothing more than a crass and racially exploitative attempt to sell more newspapers.

I will not romanticize your history; cannot pretend that the dreams and hopes of that seminal revolution have not been curdled over the years. Toussaint may have abolished slavery, reorganized the administrative and justice systems, built roads, schools and bridges, but Papa Doc and the Tonton Macoutes did exist. So did his son, Baby Doc. Class and race divisions in Haiti are alive and pernicious, but when I hear Bill Clinton talk about the need for Haiti to shake off her history, I wonder what history he is referring to. The history of Toussaint, or the history of Papa Doc, or both? And when I hear of George Bush urging people to send money, not clothing, I laugh. I remember him urging his populace after 9/11 to go out and shop. And look where that got them. And I think of Obama appointing these two men to the Clinton Bush Haiti Fund and I laugh again. Because if I didn't, I would sure be crying.

Fired in history's unrelenting sun, we Caribbean peoples who hunger after justice, who long for peace, who have lived cheek by jowl with, and sometimes in the belly of, the beast, have always punched above our weight through history—I need only mention Fidel Castro, Frantz Fanon, C. L. R. James, Aimé Césaire, Sylvia Wynter, E. Kamau Brathwaite, Derek Walcott, George Lamming and Claudia Jones, to name but a few; we grasp the import of our role in history, and no small credit for that must go to Toussaint L'Overture and all the history that swirls around him. We understand, being subjected to them for far too long, the effects of great power machinations; they continue to reverberate in our tiny island nations as well as in the psyches of the people. The colonizer may have withdrawn, but he has left his mark.

The African American dancer and anthropologist Katherine Dunham, another of your daughters, had a long and deep relationship with you, even becoming an initiate of the *vaudou* religion. In *Island Possessed*[5] she describes her relationship with the Haitian people and her involvement in the culture; she talks of buying the plantation that once belonged to the selfsame General Leclerc and of her need to cleanse it of the remnants of the sordid, brutal history of empire she could feel on the property. With the help of her Haitian godmother she does, indeed, shift the negative energies she first felt there. The sheer enormity—the apocalyptic nature of this tragedy—makes me wonder if there is something larger at work here with you, Haiti, once again being at the epicentre of some violently physical, yet spiritual, temblor, echoing that earlier one two centuries ago. Is this simply, and not so simply, the human longing and search for meaning on my part? Is it this urge to find meaning in our lives and experiences, particularly catastrophic ones, that drives the likes of Pat Robertson, a so-called man of God, to describe your plight as punishment for making a pact with devil—a comment so egregiously lacking in compassion as to take the breath away? If nothing else, he has made the choice very clear: if fighting to free oneself puts you on the side of the devil, and being on the side of God puts you in a place where, like him, you cannot express a scintilla of compassion for another's suffering, then my sympathy will be with the devil. Always.

It is early days yet, I tell myself, to attempt to find meaning in this violent catastrophe whose scale and scope often appear to exceed language, even as my mind feverishly tries to find meaning. Trying to link your history as an unblinking beacon for the Black struggle for civil and human rights, for the quest for freedom, for justice and for dignity on the part of African peoples, to this present maelstrom, as if we didn't have maelstroms aplenty already. Indeed, in this time of acute suffering it feels premature, if not sacrilegious, to rush to meaning. So I resist that for the present, understanding and accepting that any meaning to be found lies, perhaps, in the sheer absence of meaning—shit just simply happens, it seems. But I do recall another of your English-speaking sons, the novelist George Lamming, who feels the heft of your history, making reference years ago in *The Pleasures of Exile*[6] to the Haitian Ceremony of the Souls which brings together the people and their ancestors—the living and the dead. What links them is a shared interest in their future—in the one case, continued life; in the other, eternity. There is a sense in which James's *The Black Jacobins* drew us all in the Caribbean into an extended performance of the Ceremony of the Souls: we, the living descendants of the enslaved, being in active relationship with the memory of Toussaint and his supporters. Today your dead lie all around you, and despite the lack of dignity of their final resting place, you honour them in your deep dignity, notwithstanding the pictures in the *Star*, and in your resilience. And once again, through your undeserved suffering, but then suffering of the innocent is never deserved, you become a symbol for me, for us all—your children in spirit—a symbol of the will to survive in the face of apparently insuperable odds. It is what makes us human and simultaneously calls on our humanity. In that respect, we are all Haitian.

Many years ago, David Rudder, one of Trinidad and Tobago's most beloved performers, sang a soca ballad titled "Haiti," its refrain a simple lament: "Haiti, I'm sorry." It begins: "Toussaint was a mighty man / and to make matters worse he was Black / back back in the time when a Black man's place was in the back." The ballad recounts your history and how badly served you have been by history; how we, and in particular Caribbean peoples, have misunderstood you, turning our faces from you. It pains me that more of our island nations have not, over the years, offered refuge to your people—how many heads of state from the anglophone Caribbean attended the 200th anniversary of your revolution in 2004? One, I believe. Haiti, I too am sorry, but I do not weep for you, for that would be to pity you; I weep with you, Haiti, with compassion, wanting to share your suffering, which lies at the root of the word *compassion*. Today I am Haitian and forever in your grief and your undeniable survival, because survive you will. You must. For all our sakes. All I have are my broken words. And my tears. And my more tears. My so many more tears. With you, Haiti.

Viva Toussaint!

M. NourbeSe Philip

NOTES

1   Vaudou or coudou or the more commonly used voodoo all refer to a Haitian spiritual practice with roots in the West African practice of vodun.

2   C.L.R. James, *The Black Jacobins: Toussaint L'Ouverture and the San Domingo Revolution* (New York: Vintage Books, 1989).

3   Ntozake Shange, *For Colored Girls Who Have Considered Suicide When the Rainbow Is Enuf* (New York: Scribner, 2010), 40.

4   Samuel Huntington, *The Clash of Civilizations and the Remaking of the World Order* (New York: Simon and Schuster, 1996), 137.

5   Katherine Dunham, *Island Possessed* (Garden City, NJ: Doubleday, 1969).

6   George Lamming, *The Pleasures of Exile* (Ann Arbor: University of Michigan Press, 1992).

LETTER TO A YOUNG ACTIVIST

On July 31, 2015, I read an op-ed article, "The Suffocating Experience of Being Black in Canada," by Anthony Morgan in the Toronto Star. *The article suggested that, in contrast to Black Lives Matter, the actions of the previous generation of the Black community had not sufficiently impacted the mainstream in Toronto and that they had settled for "tolerating degrees of anti-black racism." I wrote to Anthony, a young African Canadian lawyer, listing examples of the Black community's impact on the mainstream coming out of a number of activist engagements.*

~The activism against the *Into the Heart of Africa* exhibit in 1989, the fallout from which is still being dealt with by the ROM today. The demonstrations against the museum led to the ROM bringing an injunction against the demonstrators. The then–Toronto Board of Education actually prohibited classes from attending this exhibit based on presentations made by community members, including myself. Further, as a result of the opposition to the exhibit in Toronto, four curatorial institutions in the U.S. cancelled the exhibit.

~The activism against the 1993 Garth Drabinsky/Livent production of *Show Boat* at the then-named North York Centre for the Performing Arts. Opposition by the Black community in the form of weekly demonstrations began when construction of the centre began and continued for at least a year, until opening night. The producers actually invited noted African American scholar Henry Louis Gates Jr. to come to Toronto to give a public lecture on why the show was not racist. The conflict was covered extensively by the mainstream media.

~The activism by Black educators who worked to ensure that the Heritage

Language programs instituted by the then–Toronto Board of Education in the '70s included African Heritage classes and programs—the very programs the author wrote that he participated in as a student.

~The struggle by the Black community in the '80s, spearheaded by Charles Roach (lawyer), Dudley Laws, and Sherona Hall (all deceased) and Lennox Farrell, to establish a civilian complaints review system for the Metropolitan Toronto Police. The Special Investigations Unit is the legacy of this struggle.

~The Black Education Project, begun in the '70s, which provided educational and cultural support for families and young people four decades ago, to ensure a culturally relevant education for Black children.

~The Transition Year Program, now a department at the University of Toronto, co-founded and spearheaded by Black educator and activist Keren Brathwaite to enable African Canadians who had not attended university to have an opportunity to obtain a university degree.

~The more recent establishment of the Afrocentric primary school, in the face of great opposition and accusations that it was a form of segregation.

I could go on, but these are just a few of the activities that the Black community of the "previous generation" has engaged in, a community which has never settled for "tolerating degrees of anti-black racism." All of these accomplishments have made Toronto a more equitable and better city for everyone. Anti-Black racism continues because the system remains powerful and resistant to making changes to ensure the demise of white supremacy.

M. NourbeSe Philip

Other examples of African Canadians pushing back against racism and having an impact on the mainstream, which I didn't include at the time, are:

~In 1991, in response to Dudley Laws of the Black Action Defence Committee describing the Metropolitan Toronto Police as the "most brutal and murderous in North America," the Metropolitan Police Association launched a lawsuit against him for defamation. The claim was eventually dropped in 1994.

~In October 1994, a firestorm erupted when Arnold Minors, a member of the Toronto Police Services Board, stated that many in the African Canadian communities did not cooperate with the police in investigations because they saw the police as an "occupation army" in their communities. He was forced to step down.

~In 1989 then–police staff inspector Julian Fantino called for police to collect race-based statistics; according to him, Blacks committed crimes way out of proportion to their numbers in the then–City of North York. The response from the Black community was swift, vocal and, particularly in light of shootings of Black men by the police, angry. A week later, Metro Police Commission banned the collection of race-based statistics. Ironically, some members of the Black community now see some value in collecting race-based statistics, believing that it will show if Black Canadians are being targeted disproportionately.

The young activist lawyer graciously accepted my letter:

Your note marks an important moment for me. It made me stop taking what I knew about Black Toronto history for granted and pushed me to go even deeper into our histories of Black resistance in Toronto to guide and inform my own work and thinking through how I support resistance to anti-Blackness today. I also feel really privileged and grateful that the piece brought us in contact with each other and that I have the honour of being friends with you as a result of the article.

Anthony Morgan and I are now friends, and in my seeking his permission to mention him, we further shared our thoughts:

March 14, 2017 — from NourbeSe

We do ourselves a disservice as a people if we think we are always reinventing the wheel. We are each and every one of us standing on the shoulders of those who tilled the soil, made it ready for the next generation.

The young students in South Africa had to rise up and take to the streets in the face of their parents being more restrained during the anti-apartheid struggle. I don't think it can ever be argued that their parents' generation did nothing. I recall seeing a young woman on TV at a demo last year or the year before in the U.S.—her T-shirt read: "This is not our Momma's Civil Rights movement," or something to that effect. When I think of all the young people who left their studies and got on buses and risked their lives to go south to register voters, I am astonished at the amnesia. No, it's not the same, can't be the same, shouldn't be the same, etc.—the way the younger generation is going to conduct the struggle—but remembering is one of the most powerful acts of resistance there is.

Response from Anthony — March 14, 2017

The main thing I've learned about Black Canadian history (recent and not) is that we're taught to forget. This is especially true of African Canadian histories of resistance. Indeed, it is a disservice to ourselves, our communities and our collective future when we forget. It allows systems to take advantage of us. These systems of power can do this because they have the institutional memory of how they previously managed our ideas for change in a manner that rendered them ineffective. So, at times, we (today's young Black advocates and activists) think we're coming up with innovations, when in actuality, the state and major institutions have already seen and heard our suggestions come from those who came before us. This allows the state to almost immediately recognize and seize our recommended reforms as another opportunity to appear to be changing while simultaneously neutralizing our resistance. It reminds me of what you wrote about in *Frontiers* about systems changing to remain the same. When we don't know or allow ourselves to be grounded and guided by our Black histories of resistance and struggle, we support anti-Black power structures in doing just this: changing to remain the same.

Kind regards,

Anthony

BANANA REPUBLICS OF POETRY

Whole and undivided, the banana leaf begins life as a long, green flag, its pliable centre spine dividing the intense expanse of flutter. Within a couple of days, at the most, it will be a fringed flutter in the wind as the leaf splits, then splits again and again along its horizontal ribs. What was once whole, single and unitary is now many.

The torn, fluttering tatters of the banana leaf reawaken a memory I never knew I had. Having grown up in the Caribbean, I must have witnessed this shredding many, many times, yet as if and, indeed, for the first time, I notice this process of whole become multiple. And, as if there are specific receptors at the cellular level within my eyes that awaken at this particular image—the torn fluttering of the banana leaf—there is a small explosion of recognition—behind the eyes. A knowing again of that which I didn't know I knew.

Each torn strand sparks a memory—a burst of potentiality—as if my eyes were not simply receiving the images passively, but reaching out to the split, the torn and the broken happily fluttering in the wind. Medieval theories of optics and vision suggest that the act of perception alters us; that seeing is a much more active relationship than we think of it today. But these were not the thoughts that occupied my mind as I gazed at the now-fringed flag of possibilities.

Nor was it simply a matter of my recognizing a familiar image—I had never seen this particular image which I had always seen before. It was simultaneously never and ever; a forget and a remember; a then and a now. And, in my gazing at the moving fronds, some now brown, there seemed to arise a relationship between me and the image. Is this what the medieval thinkers meant by ocular desire? Perhaps also a Lordean example of the everyday exotic?

Bananas are not indigenous to the Caribbean. Neither am I. We could say that they and I share the experience of diaspora—agricultural and human respectively, linked and interconnected by cycles of violence. We, the banana plant and I, appear also to share an experience of shredding, being literally torn by the wind in the one case and, in the other, being torn and fragmented, metaphorically at least, by the winds of History. Could the banana leaf fluttering in its glorious brokenness become a metaphor for the tattered flags, not of nation states, but of states of being where the shredded, torn and broken can be held together? As metaphor for poetry going forward, if there is such a thing, and backward; inhabiting contradictions, unravelling old systems of control and domination, untelling facts that present as truth which lies. Is it too easy a metaphor?

Perhaps the history of how we, *genus Musa* and I, both remapped ourselves in the Caribbean, the New Old World, is to be found in the fluttering fronds and spaces in between. That is, in the very act of shredding. In the case of the banana leaf, the tearing has the beneficial effect of cooling the leaf; in my own case there has been tearing of another sort, and one that is not as benign as the case of the banana leaf.

My hippocampal maps, etched by the neuronal firing of place cells, no doubt reveal many levels of memory pathways over time, as in the unmemory of witnessing the tearing of the banana leaf. And while neurons in the brain know about time but not space, surely to know about time is also to know something about space, since space is but time shredded into moments, is it not? So, what of the space between my eyes and the fluttering, shredded leaves, the space of ocular desire? A space also colonized by the shredded memory of a particular history.

In South and Southeast Asia, banana leaves were once used as writing surfaces, the horizontal ribs providing ready-made lines. I want to think of the banana leaf in its regeneration through splitting and tearing as itself writing something new and rich with possibilities of the torn and the shredded, the broken and the wounded. Perhaps we can reclaim the term *banana republic* and give new meaning to the expression as referring to spaces where poetry proliferates through splitting, tearing, and dividing. And dividing once again. Into banana republics of poetry.

I was invited to look at an image, which was sent to me via the Internet, and write a response to it in eight minutes. "Dream Analysis" was the result of looking at a portrait of a somewhat dishevelled white woman wearing a hat, the vague outlines of a landscape behind her, staring directly at the viewer.

DREAM ANALYSIS

What must it be like to live life without a frame: am I awake or asleep when I have this thought? We talk of people being large-framed, so perhaps there is some relationship between the skeleton and the frame, although one is on the inside and the other on the outside—an exoskeleton of sorts.

Perhaps I am fooled by how still she sits—looking out—or perhaps it is in—at the viewer. But here is a gaze to launch a thousand questions. A gaze to support the medieval belief that seeing is a far more active act than we moderns credit it with being. Here is a gaze that needs no frame but rather frames you, the dreamer, the viewer. A gaze that brings to mind, on the outer reaches of memory, the recollection of my mother's eyes—her most effective disciplinary tool—that she would turn on us misbehaving children. A gaze that frames the moment and freezes, Medusa-like.

Why is she in my dreams at all, and what does she wish to say to me? If, according to one mode of dream analysis, I, the dreamer, am every object and figure in a dream, how am I her? And here? This person with a nondescript hat perched atop long, lank brown hair, her face turned ever so slightly, the better to impale you with the gaze—the eyes so wide, as if you could see the whites all round, not just at the sides—the ayes have it and all that. Is that it? Do I need to be more aye and less nay—neigh, neigh neigh! The neighbourhood is going to the dogs! Behind her the merest suggestion of a landscape.

She floats alone—a frameless face—a pair of nameless eyes, the better to see past the past, present and future. Am I the gazed-upon or the gazer? Or both? Am I the frameless, nameless one or the frame to this act of—...? Once you see, can you forget or must you remember that to see is to witness, to witness is to be conscious, and to be conscious is to be, which still today is not sufficient.

If we are nothing but the "stuff that dreams are made on," is that "stuff" the frame, the skeleton, the stuffing of dreams, and more particularly this dream with a gaze that can lance the boil of history; a gaze that not simply receives the outer phenomena of life, but arises of a morning, clothes itself in whatever is necessary to the day and rides—nay, sashays—aye!—out to meet the all and sundry of life. A gaze that, should you meet it, might leave you wounded, dead or so alive to the idea of life lived on the brink of, the edge of, the frame of nowhere. On the road to somewhere none of us know.

THE MORNING AFTER

Email to an American friend living in Canada, composed in the immediate aftermath of the U.S. election in the still-dark, early-morning hours.

**&!#&%##!!!^^!!@##!!
I should use emoticons if I could, but I think you get the drift.

You recall my saying at lunch yesterday that I felt the need to write something about the upcoming vote, that I felt as if we were on the brink, the cusp, of something. I did—in the wee hours of the morning of November 8th—in bed, so notes really. After having watched the *SNL* election special consolidating the metamorphosis of the election process into the politics of spectacle.

Written at the spectre of a Trump victory—November 8
I think of the gutter—summing up the tone of the election, gutter politics. My mind turns to how historically this has been projected onto Blacks as being the bearers of impropriety, yet so much at the heart of Western society has been scandalous and improper, if not downright obscene. Yet so little sticks. The polls all say that Hillary Clinton will win, but the polls have been wrong before—witness Brexit—and even if she does win, Trump has won the hearts and minds of the American public that is the raw underbelly of a bloated, imperialist state. He has given new meaning to the expression: Anybody can become President of the United States—anybody as in serial harasser and predator of women; as in known racist supported by the KKK;[1] as in a shady dealer, snake oil salesman; as in confirmed liar. Anybody! But a competent, experienced, intelligent woman. (Was amused to hear Trevor Noah say the same thing a few hours ago on his show.)

America's greatness has been based on exploitation of the world's people and their resources, beginning with its own Indigenous populations, continuing on over into the enslavement of Africans, and over into the Monroe Doctrine that held the Southern Hemisphere in its vice grip and over and over and over. The American dream has been our nightmare.

On my walk earlier today, or yesterday rather, I listened as Michael Moore on *Democracy Now!* talked about a movie he had recently made, *Michael Moore in TrumpLand,* addressing Trump supporters' who intended to use their vote to get back at those whom they feel have ignored them. Moore talked about the short-lived satisfaction they'll get from voting in anger, and I recall the alternative school my children attended, and how a group of us parents attempted to increase the diversity of the student body. Rather than let that happen, the white parents opposed to those changes opted to close the school instead. I recall how the Portuguese, at the end of their colonial regimes in Mozambique and Angola, destroyed as much as they could in those countries, rather than leave an infrastructure for the incoming regimes. The people whom they had exploited for centuries should have nothing of what they had helped to produce. For some reason, as I listened to Moore's impassioned plea to the people, reminding them of Brexit and the fallout, my mind turned to those events—one very personal, the education of my children, the other large and very much removed, the end of Portuguese colonialism—because in a flash I have the sense that those who see Trump as their saviour would rather destroy the country as they know it than have it remain in the hands of those whom they believe they must take it back from. The rage—what is a Black man doing in *our* White House?—and the commitment to a belief in the rightness of white supremacy that provides them a privilege are so total and totalizing that they would rather see the U.S. destroyed than let "them" have it.

Can we thank Trump for showing us the murky, abysmal depths that a politics of salvation in the media-saturated digital age can engender? Can we thank him for illustrating the Teflon quality of whiteness and revealing the extent to which different sets of rules exist for men and for women; for Black and for white people? Could, for instance, a Black man have the c.v. of deplorable activities that Trump has and be a serious contender for president? Can we thank Trump for the insights he provided into the make-America-great-again way of life, at the core of which is hatred of the Other? Can we thank him for showing us the depth of the resentment?

In these small, lonely hours of a morning before the day after, I ask myself—what will it look like?

—will we survive?

—how much harder will it be for African Americans, Muslims, Indigenous people, women, LGBTQ2 communities, the disabled—indeed, for everyone who is not white, male and straight?

Perhaps, I should thank him for showing us the gap between the bottom and those who adhere to some semblance of civility.

Written after the vote in the small, beginning hours of the aftermath— November 10

There is much to admire in the U.S., which, at the end of the day and much like every other society, is a human and therefore flawed attempt to allow that humanity to flourish within a set of rules. Too often these rules are imposed from above, but, especially in the case of the U.S., they are challenged over and over again, by Black people, women, gays, trans people, the poor, and many, many others, as people scrabble and lurch toward a place where the individual in all her difference and sameness can exist and flourish with dignity. Like it or not, the struggles, successes and failures in the U.S. affect struggles in other parts of the world. Donald Trump at the helm of the most powerful state in the world just made the distance between the longed-for ideals and a brute reality that much wider. And I want to weep.

Three days later

I am astounded at how all those who have been scapegoated by Trump are expected to forget the hurtful words and move on. Predatory sexual behaviour toward women must be forgotten; misogyny viewed as a thing of the past; barefaced lying chalked up to campaign shenanigans; racist views and words overlooked.

I am astounded at how quickly the markets have rebounded. Even Brexit created a longer period of financial turmoil in the U.K.

I am further astounded by how easily the explanatory script for Trump's election is the ignoring of the plight of those who now inhabit the rust belts of the U.S.—the white working class who have been dispossessed by the workings of capital, of which Trump is a major player. I sympathize and have compassion, but where is the understanding and compassion for the historically dispossessed, like African Americans and Indigenous people, marginalized and forgotten (except as objects of fear and threat) far longer than their white brothers and sisters of the rust belt? There has been no saviour for them. Not even Obama.

I want to turn my face away from the horror of it all. I do not live in the U.S., so why should it matter? Do I really have any authority to speak, not being a U.S. citizen? I do, because the U.S. as an exemplar casts a long shadow: here in Canada, for instance, we have politicians who have commended Trump on his win and wish to emulate him; in France and other European countries, Trump's script is welcome to many right-wing politicians. What are we to do? My mind turns to Simone Weil, philosopher and passionate advocate for the poor and the broken, who was of the opinion that hunger presupposed the existence of bread. Similarly, I believe, the keen hunger for justice and equality among so many of us presupposes their existence and, in the words of the a capella singing group Sweet Honey in the Rock—"we who believe in justice cannot rest," knowing that as Martin Luther King Jr. said, "the arc of the moral universe [may be] long but it bends toward justice." Always.

M. NourbeSe Philip

NOTES

1   Some seven months have passed since writing this email, and Donald Trump, in the wake of the Charlottesville debacle, has refused to condemn or distance himself from white supremacists or neo-Nazis.

THE AFTERMATH

Email from Los Angeles to an American friend

Am in L.A. and last night went to a reading at Skylight Books. About 150 people jammed in and reading their own and others' work—Rich, Whitman, Galeano—in response to Trump's election. Very moving. Your comments bring to mind a comment about how quickly things will become normal, particularly the seduction of life in a powerfully capitalist culture that promises to deliver everything.

There is a crisis of legitimacy...and I think that what we, people, are mourning is that the entire game has been changed by Trump doing what he did. There was, I believe, a messy kind of rule book that everyone was (not) playing by. Romney had to be caught on tape saying his racist nonsense, yes? What Trump did was come right out and say it, which pulled out all those who resent no longer being on top, although those at the bottom—Blacks and First Nations—are still there, Black celebrities notwithstanding. Yet we are called on to feel that it was because it was white people who were "forgotten" the election was lost. There are populations that have been historically forgotten, and no one, not even Obama, rescued them. So, the rules say he has won, but we all know he has torn up the rules, imperfect as they are and always will be. I think that is what we all know in our bones—in the marrow of our bones. I think that is partly what the mourning is about. It is about the fact that Americans had struggled and brought themselves to a place where the rhetoric had changed—and we poets know the power of rhetoric—the ideals had been put in place through horrendous struggles—Civil War, the Civil Rights Movement, feminist waves, gay and trans rights. These are hard, hard ideals to hold in place because our default is tribal in the negative sense. (I think we should reclaim the word *tribal* in another sense—as in the shaggy, baggy tribe of those who love those ideals and are willing to fight for them.) We will murder the Other.

We will rape his women and kill his children. We will do it in a flash. We mourn the fact that we have edged closer to seeing our wild, hoary, nasty, brutish selves reflected back at us. I felt and thought it, then heard it said by someone on Bill Maher, that this was equivalent to 9/11, except that the threat there was external for Americans. Now it is internal. It is also the logical coming to fruition of a system that has fed itself to bloating on celebrity and excess in an age when too many can get anything, anytime, and too many have nothing all the time but are surrounded by the unlimited—unhinged perhaps?—seduction of the capitalist, American dream.

Is it a good thing that these suppurating wounds have come to the surface? I don't know. I hear the fear and feel it too when I think of the earth—I saw the super moon rise last night on a hilltop in LA—it left me humbled. Scores of us waited—most with cameras and cellphones but all waiting for something—holding faith with an old, old practice—engaging with the natural world around us. When it came up, it was marvellous to behold—this red-gold disc that was like the sun, and we all took in breaths and sighed out loud—a couple of us clapped quietly. Waiting—we seldom wait for nature any longer, but I could feel a different sense of time as we did this. A crowd—privileged, white, with one or two exceptions—and I wondered if the people in Watts watched the supermoon rise, a question laden with so many issues, and if they didn't, as I suspect, why not? I think I know the answers, as do you. We wait—generally impatiently, at least I do—but last night it was with expectancy, as the moon seemed to be taking its own sweet time to poke up above the hills. And I think of our conversation about repetition—I thought about how that very moon shone on my ancestors. On yours too. The last time it was this close to the earth, I was one year old. It would have shone on those on board the slave ship *Zong*, on their Old World and on those who survived the journey to the (un)New World. The next time it will be this close again, I will in all likelihood not be here. And last night it shone on Trump and his nest of crooked cronies without any opinion about his plans (such as they may be) for Americans and for the rest of the world. That Biblical statement comes to mind about the sun shining and the rain falling on the just and the unjust alike. I think I'm grappling with this idea of repetition—make America great again—and the repeating tropes of empire and exploitation, the repetition of issues around racism, and the repeating tropes of those of us who push back, and the repetitive cycles of the natural world, like the supermoon. Don't know where that is taking me…. I mourn the possible extinction of all this. I did bow to the moon—I felt the need to get down on my knees in awe at the generosity that this golden disc seemed to spread. This is loosely written and not edited—just ruminations....

Evil exists and sometimes we are (un)fortunate enough to witness it. I think we are seeing it flex, Obama and all those people notwithstanding who say he, whose name I sometimes cannot bring myself to say, should be given a chance, he is not a racist, etc., etc. That is reason enough to mourn.

My faith in us, flawed as we are,
NourbeSe

NASRIN AND NOURBESE

In January 2017, Nasrin Himada and I sat down to talk about the upcoming publication of Bla_K, *the past publication of* Frontiers *and my thoughts on the intervening twenty-five years. Our conversation ranged over a number of areas and issues, many of which have been addressed in "Jammin' Still," the introductory essay of* Bla_K. *What follows is an excerpted collage of our exchange, interspersed with and elucidated by my commentary.*

MNP: When I first met you, you said "Interview with an Empire" was very important to you, in terms of your own practice and thought and, indeed, it was your deep interest in the essay that catalyzed this publication of *Bla_K*. I deeply appreciate that, particularly given that I have felt like a disappeared writer in Canada for the last twenty-five years. My work is much better known in the U.S.

NH: And that's how I even found out about your work in the first place, through the U.S.

MNP: Well, there you go. It's a deeply troubling place to be, because emotionally it's as if you're a memory of yourself.

Regarding the reprint of some of the essays from *Frontiers*—it is troubling that after twenty-five years these issues remain. So much and so little has changed. There has been an African American president in the White House, but has that changed anything fundamentally regarding race? Yes, there was a classy Black couple as president and first lady, but I don't believe Black folk, particularly those at the bottom, have noticed any significant changes. This may be cynical—I prefer to think it's realistic—but what I have observed is that systems change to remain the same. The challenge is how to find ways out of the system.

We talked of how the present system of student loans ties young people into the economic system so that the proclivities that are a natural concomitant of the young—for change and innovation—are stymied when a young graduate is faced with a $40,000 loan repayment. We moved on to Black Lives Matter Toronto (BLMTO) and Idle No More.

MNP: You raised the issues of BLMTO and Idle No More. I think BLMTO is a movement of its time, and its importance is undeniable. My concern has to do more with the fact that it is essentially a U.S. import, unlike Idle No More, which began in Saskatchewan and has expanded from there to all of Canada. Being a U.S. movement in its origin has not affected BLMTO's efficacy, but my concerns are larger—because of the hegemonic nature of the U.S. and the influence of events that happen there, Blackness has often been collapsed with Blackness as filtered through the lens of the U.S. I am concerned, have always been concerned, about the totalizing aspect of the U.S. Indeed, it is a significant marker of a colonial society—that events in the metropolis affect the satellite. What I'm arguing here is that Canada is in a doubly colonial relationship—vis-à-vis its original colonizer, the United Kingdom, and the United States. George C. Grant's *Lament for a Nation* explores these issues, although he is writing very much within the context of the colonial state. His opinion is that Canada had ceased to exist as a sovereign nation.

Now let me critique myself here, because one of the most important movements in international organizing among Black people against colonialism was the Pan-African movement, and Marcus Garvey himself was all about internationalism. Stephen Biko, the South African revolutionary, adapted the Black power ideas of the U.S. to the South African context. There has always been a kinetic quality to the circulation of Black ideas of liberation. I don't know enough about BLMTO, only what I see in the media—the white media—and those reports often portray BLMTO in an ahistorical context and as the only game in town. In other words, there appears to be an erasure of the struggles that took place in earlier times, some of which I write about in *Frontiers* and *Bla_K*. This, to my mind, fits with the deep impulse in capitalist societies to erase memory, particularly the memory of groups that have been oppressed. It's important that we resist that. That is what I mean when I talk about the kinetic quality of memory that can impel us to action. I am, however, at the end of the day appreciative of BLM bringing to the fore, once again, issues that the Black community in Toronto has been dealing with for at least for the last thirty years (even before the publication of *Frontiers*)—the unwarranted killing of Black people by the police.

We can say that racism is racism is racism and it doesn't matter where it's happening. But racism is filtered differently through different spaces. For instance, one of the things that has always concerned me about racism in Canada is how polite it is and how difficult that makes challenging it. Witness the very Canadian response to my critique of racism in Canada—you disappear the person. I've heard myself sometimes saying that being in the U.S., where there appears no debate about whether or not racism exists, might be easier. (As of November 8, 2016, I have changed my thoughts on this.) Whereas here in Canada, we're always good people, we're kind people; people fled here from the States and so on. The fact that BLMTO is an extension out of the U.S., as opposed to Idle No More, in no way makes it illegitimate—indeed to extend my arguments about the pernicious politeness of white racism in Canada, I welcome their in-your-face approach. Further, given the demographics of Canada, where Black Canadians are a very small minority, hooking our wagon to the U.S. when it comes to approaches to racism has some validity. My final concern is that for non-Blacks for whom Black life and concerns are at best on the periphery, because BLMTO garners so much attention, it becomes synonymous with the anti-racism struggle, which is long and deep in this city and province and country. Indeed, the media's coverage of BLMTO sucks the energy from the equally good work of other groups. Many organizations have been working against anti-Black racism and are still doing it, but they don't get the same attention. Whenever the issue of racism comes up, the response today is, *Oh, we have to include BLMTO*, which I don't necessarily disagree with, but there are other community groups who have been doing anti-racism work for decades.

NH: Such as the communities who were involved in the ROM protests.[1]

MNP: Very much so, and that example illustrates that good community work takes years. Think about it—twenty-seven years! Think of Oliver Tambo, the South African freedom fighter who was sent overseas by the ANC and worked tirelessly for forty years building a movement.

Before we moved on to the discussion about be/longing, we touched on the issue of reconciliation:

MNP: *Reconciliation* is the buzzword now, and I confess to having concerns about it, especially when it is government rubric, because until I see hard, tangible changes—like Grassy Narrows, like the veto Trudeau promised to First Nations people concerning oil extraction and pipelines that cross their territory, like the promise by Trudeau to put more money into building First Nations schools—I remain skeptical about government commitment. Forty years after the government became aware of Grassy Narrows, Kathleen Wynne is still talking about how we have to do further studies.[2]

NH: Your putting the slash in be/longing opened it up for me.

MNP: The slash is important because it says so much. A lot of our struggle resides in the language, I believe. Jewish people talk about the *Shoah* in reference to the Jewish holocaust. There's a word in Swahili, *Maafa*, which means a great, terrible, tragic occurrence or event. Some people, myself included at times, use *Maafa* in referring to the transatlantic slave trade. I recently started talking about "the Great Scattering," because for me it captures one aspect of what happened to us, the scattering of Africans, within Africa to the Maghreb, as a consequence of the Arab slave trade, and across various lands and oceans, the Indian Ocean, the Pacific and Atlantic Oceans. It has been a great and terrible scattering.

But when I think about us, the descendants of the *Maafa*, it's not just the loss of the homeland and family, it is also the loss of language and culture, and the way into the latter is through the former. What makes us human and sustains us is culture, and we need language for that. The Scottish missionary David Livingstone understood this, arguing that the best way to introduce Christianity to Africans was first to destroy their culture, then introduce commerce and then religion. And one of the most effective ways of doing this is to start with destruction of the language. The Kenyan writer Ngugi wa Thiong'o, who wrote *Decolonizing the Mind*, stopped writing in English and began to write in his native Gikuyu and has observed that Africans cannot have a renaissance until they begin to work in their Indigenous languages. How do we speak of what happened to us? In what language? Where can, or where do, we belong in any language?

I've found Simone Weil helpful in understanding how some of this scattering came about. In her book *The Need for Roots*, she talks about how the European, after uprooting himself within Europe, spreads around the world uprooting all the other peoples of the world.

NH: I never thought about it that way, but that's what colonialism does, it uproots people from their land.

MNP: And their own cultures. The Europeans set out to uproot the rest of the world from their cultures. And so I see all of us caught in that net or trap. And so, for me therefore, there's this issue of trying to find a language to rest in, which leads me to the fragment because there's nowhere else to go. But then there's also this physical aspect of where do I call home? Is it possible to be be/long anywhere?

NH: In a place that's a settler colonial place?

MNP: I don't want to use the word *settler*. Because they are not settlers, they are unsettlers. A mother settles her baby, and maybe it's coming from *settle*, as in to pacify, and that's what the Europeans did, they attempted to pacify people violently. I suppose you can pacify violently. Language affects us physically. They are unsettlers. Because they have unsettled everything around us.

In the Caribbean, where the Indigenous people were for the most part wiped out, I believe we still have this issue, how do we belong? Particularly as those societies remain colonial societies despite independence. So for me it has everything to do with how we set about making ourselves a resting place which, in turn, begins with a process of undoing the process of colonialism. I turn to the Martiniquan writer and poet Edward Glissant, who talks about Relationship and how crucial that is to creating different spaces. I am reminded of *Zong!* and how that work is all about words being in relationship to each other. Words creating spaces to allow other words to breathe. Colonialism was not about this kind of Relationship. It was rather about power—power over.

One possibility of developing a culture of Relationship would be for us African-descended peoples and First Nations to recognize each other on both sides of that slash that stands in for the dark water, for us to see ourselves in the Other, and to see that we are really two sides of the same coin. And that maybe we have something to share with each other. I don't know if you're aware, but the first Africans were brought to the Americas on the advice of Bartolomé de las Casas, the sixteenth-century Dominican priest of Spanish origin, because he wanted relief against the decimation of the Indigenous people in Latin America. The rest, as they say, is history. This is what I mean about the importance of understanding the shared roots of our exploitation. Both peoples have a great deal to overcome and what concerns me is that when African-descended peoples of the *Maafa* or Great Scattering are subsumed under the word *settler*, our particular, peculiar and tragic history is erased. I don't think that white unsettler Canadians who now entertain liberal guilt about the depredations of colonialism against First Nations people are either able or willing to entertain that. I also realize that First Nations people may not be particularly interested in making such a distinction, and I entirely understand that. It does not mean that what I know to be the truth is any less the truth—that we did not come to this part of the world as unsettlers. We came as property. In the holds of ships brought by the very people who unsettled this land and its peoples. I have to remember what forces brought me here. We lost everything except what we could remember. To be seen in the same way as the European settler is to do a second violence to us, the descendants of the *Maafa*.

This does not mean that we do not ally with First Nations people; indeed, it strengthens the reasons why we should support them in their struggles. And I believe that until they receive what is rightfully theirs, none of us is free and we are all participating in their oppression by virtue of living in the colonial state of Canada. We all have blood on our hands. But I will not take on the liberal guilt of the white European unsettler. It's a complicated position but a truthful one for me. After all, Canada does have a history of recognizing or acknowledging the existence of different groups, such as the French, the Acadians, the Metis, and so on. I am not necessarily claiming official recognition—although why not?—but we are two years into the UN International Decade for People of African Descent. This is intended to be a period of time in which there should be greater recognition for African-descended peoples, greater social and economic development as well as more access to social justice. This UN-declared decade, however, has been recognized more in absentia than anything else. None of the three levels of government under Harper, Wynne, and Rob Ford, during whose respective terms it was declared, acknowledged it. Which reveals a glaring issue in our communities in Canada—we have no central organization which can speak with one voice on issues such as this. And that is a loss.

NH: When you speak that way, I can't help but think about my own positionality; my family didn't have a choice to come to Canada but they also did. They did have the privilege to apply for permanent residency, to land here, but if we go far back enough, in the sense of their uprootedness, then they really didn't.

MNP: And that uprootedness has a name and an address. There was a time when Britain had its finger in every country around the world. The sun never set on the British Empire was what they prided themselves on. And what is happening today is actually the blowback, the ripple effect. Same with the U.S.

But to come back to the issue of African people here, I think that one of the things that concerns me greatly is anti-Black racism, which I think is universal and not only found among white people but among all non-Black people.

And my argument is not for special treatment; my argument is to be particular about my own memory. For me to be willing to lump myself in with the white unsettler is to erase my memory of how I came here. There has to be a willingness to avoid binary thinking in these issues.

I have heard relatively recent immigrants passing comments on First Nations people—that they don't pay taxes and that they should get over what happened and so on. This is outrageous. First Nations people are right to have an attitude toward newcomers who come into this land and take a position on them and their memories. It cannot happen; it must not happen.

NH: And that makes total sense in exactly how you've described memory. It's in how you activate a sense of self-determination in a collective way.

MNP: I have too much respect for Indigenous cultures to believe that they would be indifferent to the stranger like myself, who has washed up here somehow through the same set of events that has destabilized them and has moved us from our homeland. I am confident that there could be some sort of understanding and compassion for that kind of stranger, and how that would look is up to both parties to work out.

NH: In "Interview with an Empire," you continue with this issue concerning memory but specifically in relation to language. You write, "The challenge for me is to write from that place of loss. Of nothing if you will, to make poetry out of silence." As a poet and writer, how would you describe your relationship to language? How do you see that emerge in a way by speaking to/back to Empire in the interview? In it you write, "To erase the body is to erase the memory, and while this particular Black body is here in this white space called Canada, there is memory." I am wondering if you can speak more about this relation between body memory and writing, particularly in how it shows up in your work, in your practice as a writer. I can't help but think of *Zong!* here as well.

MNP: The most important work that I've done over the last twenty-five years is *Zong!* It has been described as a conceptual work—in the same way that *She Tries* was described as a postmodern work—but it has roots deep in the ancient, oral art form *oriki*, of the Yoruba of Nigeria. Again, it was my engagement with language, which I talked about above, that helped me to understand how the fragment can resonate and have great power. For those of us who often have nothing but fragments of our original cultures, this was revelatory. And life-sustaining. All was not necessarily lost. The work has also moved and moved me to performance, bringing a dimension that is integral to the practice of African cultures.

Every year in November on the anniversary of the *Zong* massacre, we have a collective reading of the entire book. One of the remarkable observations is that although the content is tragic, at the end of the reading/performance there is a feeling of coming to rest, of peace, even. This confirms my belief in the capacity of art of heal. I also realize that I am not interested in speaking back to Empire in a work like *Zong!* or its performance. Which is not to say that we shouldn't be critical about the depredations of Empire—God knows it has unleashed on us all a scorched earth policy. But *Zong!* is its own *raison d'être*—although it comes out of the European archive, it is not a reaction or response to Empire. It simply is. As lamentation, mourning song, extended wake. Indeed, the title for last year's event was "*Zong!*: A/Wake 5 Years," playing on the idea of the wake for the dead, but also being awake to all that has happened—as in remembering. *Zong!* reminds me that we can find our lost selves in the most unexpected of places.

We talked of memory and of how "evoking memory and the practice of remembering work against, or challenge, the ways in which erasure takes form or address the effects of erasure, which can be severe and violent" (Nasrin).

MNP: One aspect of First Nations culture I'm deeply appreciative of is their honouring of their elders, who are the memory keepers. I recognize that—we had something of that in the Caribbean, and it still exists in Africa, but is not found to any great degree among our community here. That is a tragedy, and we stand to learn, or should I say relearn, a great deal in that respect, among others, from the First Nations.

NH: To return to decolonization—what does "be/longing" mean when it comes to decolonization? What does it mean, say, in the context of Canada 150? I feel so upset about this because so many colleagues who I know and respect are applying for this grant that is just reasserting the colonial power of the state as host, celebrating the birth of a nation-state, that then allows for their organizations to potentially thrive and grow.

MNP: The 150 celebrations are a celebration of the colonial state. I'm aware that there are a range of responses being taken by different First Nations groups. One group out west has dealt with the issue by calling themselves 150+ to suggest the fact that the history of Canada, or Turtle Island, is much older than 150 years. I also know that some First Nations groups are opposed to the celebrations. I myself applied for one of these grants, so my comments could be seen to be self-serving and should be judged in light of that. Arts funding in Canada is nowhere where it should be for artists in general. Further, there are no special programs that target Black artists, who still have some challenges getting grants. What concerns me is that what the state has done is drop the artist in the middle of this issue by dangling in front of artists, who are chronically underfunded, an extra opportunity to apply for grants under the guise of 150 celebrations, rather than have this money be available year-round. It seems to me that artists are then between a rock and a hard place—applying for money under a program that is questionable and not applying for grants for their projects. I don't know if your artist friends viewed the grants in a critical way, but one way of subverting the intent would be to use the grants to mount critiques of the colonial state. But let's push this further—the colonial state that is Canada exists and dispenses funds for artists year-round. Whenever you obtain a grant, one of the conditions is that you mention the relevant council in any promotional material, which is a constant reminder of the colonial state. This same state pays for artists to travel overseas representing Canada, the exemplar of diversity and multiculturalism. I suggest that these are ways in which we all, those of us who receive grants, promote, willingly or not, the colonial state that is Canada. We are all contaminated, as I said before. Every grant we receive, whether or not it is a celebration, reinscribes the colonial state. Perhaps what artists should have done, or should do, is demand similar funds be made available year-round, coming out of this. I think what we need to do is always find ways around what the state intends.

In conclusion: I do not know whether I will be alive in twenty-five years' time, but if I were, I would very much like to think that much of what I've written in Bla_K *would no longer be relevant or perhaps would be less relevant. That would be the best reward for the hard work and effort that has gone into producing this work.*

Once again, my deepest appreciation to you, Nasrin.

NOTES

1   To read more about the ROM protests, see "Social Barbarism and the Spoils of Modernism" and "Museum Could Have Avoided Culture Clash," which are included in this collection.

2   To read more about Grassy Narrows, see "Jammin' Still" in this volume.

M. NourbeSe Philip is a poet, essayist, novelist, playwright, and for-mer lawyer who lives in Toronto. She is a Fellow of the Guggenheim and Rockefeller (Bellagio) Foundations, and the MacDowell Colony. She is the recipient of many awards, including the Casa de las Américas Prize (Cuba). Among her best-known works are: *She Tries Her Tongue, Her Silence Softly Breaks, Looking for Livingstone: An Odyssey of Silence*, and *Zong!*, a genre-breaking poem that engages with ideas of the law, history, and mem-ory as they relate to the transatlantic slave trade.

COLOPHON

Manufactured as the second edition of *Bla_K: Essays and Interviews* in the winter of 2018 by Book*hug.

Distributed in Canada by the Literary Press Group: lpg.ca
Distributed in the U.S. by Small Press Distribution: spdbooks.org
Shop online at bookthug.ca

BOOK
PRODUCTION
WAR ECONOMY
STANDARD

Essais are edited for the press by Julie Joosten

Type + design: Carleton Wilson, Kate Hargreaves & Jay Millar
Proofread by Ruth Zuchter & Stuart Ross